Emma D. Sheehy

Children Discover
Music and Dance

A Guide for Parents and Teachers

A HOLT-DRYDEN BOOK

HENRY HOLT AND COMPANY, INC., NEW YORK

PREFACE

> From the beginning of his education, the child
> should experience the joy of discovery.
> —ALFRED NORTH WHITEHEAD

Children *discover* music and dance. In the following pages
I have tried to explore with the reader some of the many
ways in which children make their discoveries. Little can be
discovered in a vacuum. It is the environment, at home, at
school, at play, which stimulates and fosters discovery. Place
a child or a group of children in surroundings that are full
of "invitations to learn," provide them with encouraging and
sympathetic attitudes from adults, and amazing things can
happen—especially to the sensory perceptions which are central to the discovery of music and dance.

This book is written out of experience: the experiences
of children, parents, teachers, students, and my own. It is
based, in part, on my previous book in this field, *There's
Music in Children,* revised in 1952. Among my most valuable
experiences were the years spent as a classroom teacher, and
it is through the eyes and ears of a classroom teacher that I
discuss teaching music and dance. I have been privileged to
work with colleagues and students at Teachers College who
were constantly looking toward children for insight and direction. My observations and attitudes have been further enriched by professionals in music and the dance, and also from
watching many and varied performances on the stage, screen,
and television. My teaching has also been deeply influenced
by writers such as Henry James, Alfred North Whitehead,

Robert Frost, Rainer Maria Rilke, William Butler Yeats, and Sean O'Casey who, in their poetry, letters, journals, and autobiographies, remembered so much that I had forgotten and perceived so much that I had not seen or heard. They have constantly inspired and awakened my thoughts and feelings and have opened new vistas. Indeed, one of the greatest joys in teaching is in being able to relate experiences of all kinds and from all fields.

Discovery is not enough, though it may be the *sine qua non* of a really vital learning experience. Guidance, too, is necessary. No system or method is promoted here, but there are ways of helping everyone to become more keenly aware of how children begin to appreciate these arts. I have tried to suggest some of the many possibilities for becoming acquainted with music and dance, and I have also included a variety of illustrations from classrooms in the hope that they may, in some measure, reveal the ways that children recognize music and dance ideas and how these ideas grow and bloom.

There are many kinds of music and dance, and there are many ways of learning them. Everyone has musical potentialities, but too few of them are recognized and nurtured. In their day-to-day living, children deal with sound and movement, the basic materials of these arts, in a vital way. Their interests and skills offer golden opportunities for teaching. Thus the more we know about and understand these arts (and I am not referring to performing skills), the more possibilities for guidance are opened up to us. Above all, it is skill in understanding children and not skill in the techniques of music that will bring the greatest rewards in fostering a child's love for music and dance.

To my students and coworkers I am deeply grateful. Some of their experiences are included in the following pages. From their explorations and pioneering and from my own, I hope that the reader may find at least a few places in *his* living with boys and girls that are touched and enlightened. For the stimulation and joy that have come from turning music and dance ideas over and over and from gaining fresh insights, I am thankful to my friends Senta Eckert and Lorene Marvel. I am deeply appreciative to Helen Lanfer who has done so much to open my ears and extend my perceptions in music and dance. The majority of the pictures in the book were taken by Irene Strauss under very difficult conditions. Children of all ages were brought in by members of a large college class so that children and students together could make discoveries about music and dance. This did not provide an optimum setting for a photographer! I am grateful to Miss Strauss for her patience, her agility, and her skill. And especially to Constance Rogers I owe so much for her understanding and her skill in preparing this manuscript for the publisher. Without my many years of association with *Parents' Magazine* as Record Review Editor my experience in this field could not possibly be as rich as it is.

E.D.S.

Teachers College
Columbia University
February 1959

CONTENTS

To Ginger

and

Jimmy, Johnny, Bobby, Dougie, Eddie

Music on their own

Chapter 1

CHILDREN AND SOUND

~~~~~~

Sounds are all around us. No matter where we are we cannot entirely close our ears to the sounds of today's world. And we have very different feelings about the sounds we hear. Many factors help to determine whether we accept or reject what comes to our ears. Nor are we consistent in our reactions. The roar of a train, the varied accents of speech, the whir of a motor, the cooing of a pigeon, the shrill voices of children playing outside our window—any one of these sounds may be welcomed at certain times and considered an annoyance at other times. Returning from a long summer vacation in the hills, the city dweller may be delighted and soothed by the reassuring sounds of buzzing city life—the very sounds from which at the end of a long, hard winter he fled to the country to escape. The time of year, the state of one's feelings (exhaustion or a sense of well being), the associations with sounds that have particular meaning, the degree of one's ability to be immune to what could annoy—all of these play important parts in determining whether a sound is music to our ears or whether it is noise.

There is no doubt, too, that age affects our feelings. I remember a summer visit, when I was nine years old, to a friend who lived on the town's main street along which the trolley ran. The clang of the streetcar bell was such music to my ears that I begged to be allowed to sleep in the front bedroom so I would be sure not to miss its six A.M. run. Every morning my ears waited for this music. This wonderful bell is about all I remember of a four weeks' holiday. Today I would give this same "wonderful bell" a very different reception.

Experience also affects our feelings about any particular sound or group of sounds. Some of us reject much contemporary music because our ears are tuned to the great classics and are unreceptive to different and strange rhythms, harmonies, and patterns. Rejection of the new has always existed. One of the most famous examples of disdain for new music was the violent reaction to Wagner's compositions by the leading classicists of his day. There is certainly no implication here that we must all like everything we hear; but it is one thing to lend an ear to the new and then still prefer what we have grown to love, and it is another thing to refuse to listen at all. The music that you and I like may constitute all music for us, but this does not say that our choices are those of others. All of this is very closely related to living and working with children, for their explorations in the discovery of the world of sound can irritate or please according as we "hear" the possibilities for extending their interest by the opportunities they present to us.

Some children are fortunate to have fathers who are high-fidelity enthusiasts. Now the members of this rapidly growing group may be motivated by various factors—perhaps the need to "do it yourself," to assemble and create with an ever-growing collection of parts, or the love of gadgets, or the desire to enjoy a hobby is the starting point. Perhaps a genuine desire to reproduce the sounds and music on records retaining as much as possible of the original may be the beginning and the final goal. At least, the high-fidelity enthusiast may convince himself that this is his goal, but his family and neighbors may be justified in feeling that the most important thing to this assembler of tubes, speakers, and turntables is a passion for the exploration and penetration of sound itself.

Nor is "sound" excursioning peculiar to the amateur. It is, of course, the business of the recording engineer to keep developing his skills in the techniques of sound perception and reproduction so that he can bring to the listener the highest degree of the inherent possibilities of any particular musical or spoken-word production. But the fabulous world of sound itself and its possibilities has been penetrated and recorded by such people as Jim Fassett who has been the supervisor of Columbia Broadcasting System's music for many years. Together with Martin Goldberg, CBS engineer, he is responsible for two of the most ear-awakening recordings I have heard—*Strange to Your Ears* and *Scandinavia,* both Columbia records. Here is the evidence of what happens when two imaginative experts combine both their ears and the almost unbelievable versatility of magnetic-tape recording. Enriched by delightful notes written by John M. Conly, editor of *High Fidelity Magazine,* these records offer a unique education in "sound." Some eleven- and twelve-year-old friends have been fascinated with this kind of education, which in turn has stimulated their interest in physics *and* in music.

Another interesting example of an adult's awareness of sounds found its way recently to the editorial page of *The New York Times* [1] where one column was devoted to a discussion of sounds.

The hammering of rivet guns as more and more tall new buildings stretch higher and higher. The clanking of subway turnstiles, the roar and rumble of trains and the sharp squeal of wheels protesting a curve. The clickety-click of women's high-heel shoes all over town, especially in front of shop windows. Taxi horns. . . . The rustling of pigeon wings in every block. The soft whizz as elevator doors open and close. Telephones shrilling.

Voices with accents from all over the world. . . .

[1] "Sounds of the City," *The New York Times,* April 25, 1957.

Voices of autograph fans, bright with excitement. The expectant electric air in studios as shows prepare to go on the air. The soft, fading flutter of envelopes spilling down skyscraper mail chutes. Calm metallic voices over the police radio keeping life on its track. The umpire's "Play ball!"

Squeals of laughter as boy meets girl through rowboat collisions in the park lagoon. The crack of target rifles in galleries on the square. The hoarse, tingling whistle blast of an ocean queen backing into midstream. Gaiety in the monkey house at the zoo. Church bells.

These are sounds heard by an editorial writer of a great newspaper. In describing them in his column he evidences his shrewd awareness of the "sound interests" of many adult readers. And here are some of the sounds that are heard and enjoyed by two eleven-year-olds:

SOUNDS

The wind blowing
Sleigh bells
A splash of water
Thunder
A squeak of a chair
The squeak of a door
The sound of money jingling
The sound of a horse's hoofs
The crackle of the fire
The sound of turning pages of a book
The sound of music
Tap of a pencil
The noise of a rifle
Different sounds you make when you walk
The motor of a car
Water running
Tick tock of a clock
A light switch going on
Hammering

Lynn Vasti

SOUNDS

1. Splashing of water
   Buzzing of a bee
All different sounds don't bother me.

2. Barking of dogs
   Buzzing of bees
I like all sounds from A down to Z.

3. Mewing of a cat
   Electric saw going
I like the sound of someone lawn mowing.

4. Crows keep on crowing
   Cattle keep lowing
Even televisions keep on going.

Shirley Lau

We adults like sound when we are the sound-makers. Witness the conventions of any one of our national fraternal organizations attended by *grownups*. Have you ever been registered at a hotel which served as headquarters for such a group? The problem of noisy juveniles in any home town fades into insignificance when compared with the "sound skills" of their elders. Political campaigns would fall flat without sound. Try to imagine a baseball or football game in a soundproof stadium! Even the most sedate person can seldom resist noise-making at New Year's Eve. "Sugar is not so sweet to the palate as sound to the healthy ear," quotes Emerson from an unpublished manuscript by Thoreau. In an essay on this subject he refers a number of times to Thoreau's sensitivity to sound, the music in the humming of the telegraph wires, and the "z-ing" of the locust. Thoreau's "eye was open to beauty, his ear to music."

Why is it that we are so unresponsive to this natural, early, and continuing interest in sound possessed by every human being? Why the broken continuity between it and the study of music in our schools? Music is sounds put together. To be sure, the way in which they are put together makes all the difference in the kind of music it is. But—and this is certain—there is no one right way, no one wrong way. Nor is there any one way of teaching music to children. But if we can, in one way or another, hitch this tremendous interest in sounds and sound-making to music and *start with the child,* we shall have gone a long way in encouraging a natural love for music.

Children not only accept sounds, but they also have a knack of adding to them until their elders cannot endure the din. Then, even though they are admonished and sent out of earshot, this passion of theirs is somehow never completely satisfied. Usually they are experiencing the elements of music in ways that are foreign to us because our ears have grown dull to the same kinds of experiences we had as children. Children's inventions in pure sound have vitality and offer us many and varied paths to music if we recognize and pursue them. To this end we adults must reawaken and extend our acquaintance with the "raw materials" of music, that is, we must teach ourselves before we can hope to teach others.

Primitive man made music, not by playing notes but by experimenting and listening. Today more than a few of our outstanding entertainers in the field of music have learned the same way. Children learn to talk by experimenting and listening; they can learn to make music by experimenting and listening—unless we stop them! Of course, with today's powerful communication systems, we can't really stop them, but we can encourage and nourish what has meaning for them and most certainly help them develop more fully than if they were discouraged. Our job is to seize children's enthusiasm at the flood tide. Few will turn out to be great musicians, but they will have a good time and they will most certainly develop a genuine love for music. They will learn a surprising amount about it, too. And if we do happen to have a musical genius in our midst, what better way of cultivating his creative powers than to develop at an early age the music he has within him?

Chapter 2

SOME WAYS IN WHICH CHILDREN USE SOUND

Is THERE ANYTHING that brings quite so much delight to his family as the babbling of the tiny baby? Unintelligible though it is, it tells us that this little bit of humanity is at peace with his world. He has discovered something he can do that thrills him. It isn't long before he stumbles into the delights of sounding easy syllables and repeating them endlessly. Gradually some of these sounds, like "ma-ma" and "da-da," take on meaning; at least we adults are always eager to attach meaning to them. But, meaning or no meaning, the baby happily pursues his babbling career. He gradually learns to talk through his experience in sounds and the meanings which have become associated with them.

Proust observed that habit removes the familiar from us. Those of us who live closely with children can let our senses grow dull (perhaps we even need to at times!). But it is refreshing to be awakened to the importance of what goes on in day-by-day living and the way in which bits are put together by the child and the learning that results. In relation to this discussion on sound let us read Harry Stack Sullivan:

Every important process in learning which I have been able to formulate is illustrated, at least in rudiment, before speech. I would like to emphasize again the fact that beyond any perchance, as early or before the end of the tenth month in many instances, so much learning of sounds by trial and error, or from human example, appears that the baby sounds to a person at a little distance as if he were talking to himself. This is a truly amazing instance of human ability. I would like to remind you that in your dealings with friend and foe, stranger and intimate acquaintance, modifications and stresses in the tonal patterns of your remarks can do things which no words qua words could do. When you see how very early and how extremely important this form of learning is, and how basically important are the things learned, oh so long before communicable thought can take place, you may perhaps feel a little more impressed with the importance of the phase of infancy.[1]

We do, of course, foster this early interest in sounds by the glow of approval that we show and by taking time to play back and forth with the child in words themselves. We are quick to entertain with nursery rhymes and songs, and nonsense sounds and phrases. Children revel in the clash and repetition of words. "Higgledy, piggledy," "Diddle diddle dumpling," "hickory, dickory, dock," "Bibbidi, bobbidi, boo," "Nickety nackety"—with their meaningless sounds and infectious rhythms—give endless satisfaction.

Children not only respond to the rhythm and alliteration in these sounds but they also enjoy experimenting with change in tempo and with unexpected changes in dynamics, pitch, and accent. Nor is this confined to little children. Recently on a warm evening, I listened from my window to a group of boys from about ten to fourteen years of age as they sang or rather shouted together a current popular song. Suddenly one of them took hold of a part of it, "Day-O," and

1 Harry Stack Sullivan, *The Interpersonal Theory of Psychiatry*, New York: Norton, pp. 156–157.

started teasing the others with it. His use of it became so contagious that everyone joined with him and the song itself was
lost for a time while the chant grew in intensity. This, in
turn, grew monotonous to the chanters and the song was
brought back and superimposed on the "Day-O" which several kept repeating. The listener with an ear for music heard
the use of counterpoint, harmony, dynamics, and variations
in rhythm and was exhilarated by the spontaneous way in
which these elements of music were used naturally, tried
out for their possibilities, and gradually put together in a
vital musical experience.

There came to mind certain familiar operatic selections,
ways in which folk songs are used and enjoyed, the ingenious
sound play with voices that attends the singing of many songs
on records, radio, and television, and the very charming voice
play that Miranda brings to the singing of Marais in their
concerts and on records. Here were boys on the street improvising and inventing and at the same time using important
elements of music and their voices in many ways. They
were, unconsciously, enriching their understanding of music
through inventions in sound. If we were working with such
a group, could we not increase their musical understanding
by supplying one or several of the experiences just mentioned?

Certain poets, too, have become famous because of their
genius in word sounds and word invention. The verse of
Edward Lear is frankly nonsense and does not pretend to be
anything else—and therein lies its charm. To enjoy it, one
must make it a part of oneself, and be able to roll it out on an
instant's notice. Children are never-ceasing in their demands
on someone who has a store of Lear verses. They may sing
along with the poetry, or be content merely to listen.

Children's pleasure in nonsense chatter can often be
turned into a constructive interest in what other people have
done with words.

There was an old person of Ware,
Who rode on the back of a bear;
  When they said, "Does it trot?"
  He said, "Certainly, not!
It's a Moppsikon Floppsikon bear!" [2]

Mopp-si-kon, Flopp-si-kon—how children like to lean on these words, play with them, invent more of their own, and go jingling on their way!

Laura E. Richards has delighted several generations of children and adults with her rhymes. She plays with words as a child does, and her nonsensical humor sends youngsters into gales of laughter. What is funnier than the mixing up of "elephant" and "telephone" to *telephant* and *elephone*? And is anyone's education complete without skinny "Mrs. Snipkin" and fat "Mrs. Wobblechin"? [3]

Every home, every school should possess copies of the poetry of Edward Lear and Laura E. Richards. We all remember Lewis Carroll for his delightful play with sound and nonsense. But reading to the child from these books is only a substitute for the ability to draw upon them at will wherever one is. We cannot, of course, have at the tip of our tongue all we could wish, but the more quickly we can say or "sing" these bits, the more vital will be the experiences we can give to children. For, with young as with old, seizing the mood is the secret of interest and enthusiasm, and if we have to go to a book or a piano for everything we sing, we miss the spontaneous joy that comes to those who sing as they work or play, whether it be poetry or music.

Poetry *is* music. Sidney Lanier, the poet, stated that poetry is basically *sound,* not sense, and that in reading it the "eye merely purveys for the ear." It is music in words. Surely Shakespeare is also remembered for the sound of his words.

---

2 Edward Lear, *The Complete Nonsense Book,* New York: Dutton.
3 Laura E. Richards, *Tirra Lirra: Rhymes Old and New,* Boston: Little, Brown.

But poetry is not necessarily music to children. Not long ago Bobby's mother told us that he disliked poetry. She had been accustomed to reading poems to him at bedtime, but he resisted so much that she finally stopped. Then she said: "Bobby has been coming home from school recently, bubbling over with snatches of Lear, Richards, Milne, and Carroll—so I told him *that* was poetry, too." "It is not!" he shouted; "I don't *like* poetry!"

"Will you please," pleaded Bobby's mother, who has a genuine love for literature, "will you please tell Bobby that what he is enjoying so much *is* poetry?" "Not now," we suggested, "for we don't care what he thinks it is. Names are 'noise and smoke.' " We knew our young Bobby too well to risk spoiling his fun by telling him something he did not want to hear.

The mature adult enjoys poetry for its construction, its meaning, its figures of speech, as well as for its sound and its rhythm. Little children judge poetry and song with their feelings, not with their intellects. This does not mean that we should expose them only to so-called children's poetry. If we go back in our own memories, we may be surprised at what we find. One recalls the magic-sounding words in Coleridge's *Kubla Khan*, in Noyes's *The Highwayman* with its impelling rhythm, in some special psalm of David, or in Shelley's *The Cloud*. No doubt these had little meaning for us at the time, but they are remembered for their sounds, their rhythms, and their associations.

Children's lives are made rich with these experiences if those with whom they live have a genuine love and appreciation for the music of poetry. Play with children as they play with words, give them stories and verse to stimulate their imaginations, and, especially, let them enjoy it all in their own way. The fun of living poetry with father and mother, with teacher and friend, will take care of the learning process.

Children have an uncanny ability to imitate the sounds of their environment. Their ack-ack guns or their fire sirens can be so realistic as to startle us. They reproduce these sounds naturally and with little conscious effort. Take the time to listen thoughtfully, and you will be amazed at the flexibility of their voices, the control they have over them, and the skill with which they use them. Many a trained singer would fail in an attempt to follow such youngsters' vocalizations.

In his autobiography [4] Roland Hayes tells of his childhood interest in sound and its influence on his musical career. His father spent a great deal of time wandering through the woods and along the streams. He loved nature, lived close to it, and was able to reproduce any animal call at will. Roland Hayes learned this art as a young lad from his father, and he attributes much of his later success to this early use of his voice. He acquired, naturally, the flexibility and control that most singers have to acquire through years of exacting exercises, and with (he believes) far less strain on his vocal organs. Children have unlimited imagination; their ability to identify themselves with an idea provides sufficient motivation to accomplish the "impossible." The "how" does not stand in their way. When Roland Hayes's father called a deer, he became a "buck" himself.

Not many have the genius of a Roland Hayes, but children have plenty of hidden ability that we grownups do not see or hear. Listen to a child or a group of children anywhere, in their make-believe play or in their sheer physical exuberance, and you can catch innumerable uses of their voices. Then if you still have little respect for this natural ability of children, try to reproduce some of these sounds yourself!

A fire siren, for example. Musicians work hard to achieve the crescendo and decrescendo that children emit without even trying. The whir of an airplane motor, its gradations of intensity, its rhythmic rise and fall; the call of the bullfrog; television, the radio, and their sound effects—all these sounds and countless others children can "turn on and off" at will.

Children continually use sound to make their play more

4 *Angel Mo' and Her Son,* Boston: Little, Brown.

realistic. They do not imitate: they *become* a steamboat, a train, or an animal at the drop of a hat. The child who will not sing a song beyond the range of his speaking voice will spontaneously produce the sound of a high-pitched whistle or horn. With younger children especially, the most effective musical guidance may come in connection with this type of play. Recognition and encouragement of it, and *sometimes* participation in it, provide a real opportunity for furthering children's interest in sound.

What parent or teacher has not at some time been driven to exasperation by the incessant "click-clack-clucking" sound that children make with their mouths? This particular form of recreation has a way of turning up at rest or mealtime, and it has a higher rate of contagion than any other childhood disease yet known. A design for tormenting grownups? Yes, it may be, for any smart youngster who gets such a reaction will not miss an opportunity to make it just that. But for the child it is, essentially, *fun* to be able to do all these tricks, and he is constantly discovering new and strange noises he can make. We ask children to stop, we tell them it is time to rest or time to eat, and not the time for such monkeyshines— that they can pursue this activity later. We have a right to make this request, but *too, too* often we forget about the later time. And since these children want someone to listen to them (that being nine tenths of the fun), we must do our share and take the time to pay attention and *experiment with them.*

In writing of his childhood, Igor Stravinsky says:

One of my earliest memories of sound will seem somewhat odd. It was in the country, where my parents, like most people of their class, spent the summer with their children. I can see it now. An enormous peasant seated on the stump of a tree. . . . He was dumb, but he had a way of clicking his tongue very noisily, and the children were afraid of him. So was I. But curiosity used to triumph over fear. The children would gather round him. Then, to amuse them, he would begin to sing. This song was composed of two syllables, the only ones he could pronounce. They were devoid of any meaning, but he made them alternate with incredible dexterity in a very rapid tempo. He used to accompany this clucking in the following way: pressing the palm of his right hand under his left armpit, he would work his left arm with a rapid movement, making it press on the right hand. From beneath the shirt he extracted a succession of sounds which were somewhat dubious but very rhythmic, and which might be euphemistically described as resounding kisses. This amused me beyond words, and at home, I set myself with zeal to imitate this music—so often and so successfully that I was forbidden to indulge in such an indecent accompaniment.[5]

One little group of five-year-olds made up a "sympathy" (as Miguel called it) by combining their "cluckings"! It was in three "movements": in the first, sounds were made with their mouths wide open; in the second, sounds were made with their mouths partly closed; and a combination of the two with clapping hands constituted the finale!

What do we do about this ability, especially in our schools? We clamp down on it and try to teach our children "music." We give them a course of study that has been logically worked out—a course that is simple and harmless, but usually too anemic to hold children's interest. We are blind and deaf to the vigor and vitality of the music children have within themselves. Many a youngster is labeled an "out-of-tune" and is the despair of the conscientious teacher or parent. How about turning the tables, how would it be if we ourselves got in tune with the "out-of-tune"? We might well consider Ruskin's idea: the only way to help others is to first find out what they have been trying to do for themselves, and then proceed to help them do it better.

One of these "out-of-tunes" was five-year-old Mary. When she sang with other children, she never seemed to be able to stay with them. She had a sweet, lovely voice to which she consciously listened when she sang, and the thoughtful way

[5] *Stravinsky, an Autobiography*, New York: Simon and Schuster.

she used it and her feeling around for a pleasant effect in sound restrained us from urging her to sing on the same pitch as the rest of us. One day, while we were singing *Ach, du lieber Augustin,* Mary's voice suddenly came through clear and steady. She was singing a third higher than the group, and she was able to go through to the end. Her eyes shone with delight—she had hit the spot that satisfied her and gave her a thrill, and "the moment of passage from disturbance into harmony is that of intensest life." [6]

Of course, Mary could easily sing on the same pitch as the others if she wished; her mother told us that she sang a great deal at home. It happened, however, that at the time she started to school she was interested in singing in a different way and—as children so often do—she had accidentally tumbled into a significant musical experience. She would wait until the song was started, then she would feel around with her voice until she found a comfortable place.

If Mary had been placed in an "out-of-tune" group or been compelled by adult pressure to sing on the same pitch, not only she but the entire group would have lost something. For this episode offered an ideal opportunity for teaching the children about two-part singing. They had come upon an important aspect of music. As they all tried to sing Mary's way (with varying degrees of success), they experienced and recognized—at five years of age—the essential element of harmony. This was therefore the time to tell them that when different sounds sound well together, we call it harmony. We did not care whether or not they remembered the word—though most of them did; but we "harmonized" off and on throughout the year. Most of this experimentation went on informally on the playground, during the work period, and at home. Singing simple two-part rounds with an adult supporting each part helped to enlarge experience and give much pleasure. Do we wait until second grade to introduce two-part singing?

6 John Dewey, *Art As Experience,* New York: Putnam.

Again let us listen to children. One summer day two-year-old Jonathan was riding high on his father's shoulders as he walked around the lake. "Ooh!" Jonathan squealed, surprised and startled, as his head was brushed by a low branch. "Ooh!" his father called back, so quickly that Jonathan forgot his fright in his enjoyment of this new game. Father found himself going back and forth under the trees at the young man's demand, so that more "oohs" would be forthcoming. And even though their pitch was occasionally varied, Jonathan was able to reproduce the call every time.

Several days later, a cuckoo clock arrived at Jonathan's home. But he was disappointed by the cuckoo's unpredictability: it simply would not "cuckoo" when he wanted it to, and usually when it did perform he was not nearby. After a few frustrated days, Jonathan was observed one morning standing in front of the clock and calling repeatedly: "Cuckoo, cuckoo, cuckoo!" It was so like the clock that his mother found the place on the piano in exact tune with Jonathan's voice, and later, when the clock struck the hour, she discovered that he had imitated it exactly in pitch and interval.

Perhaps this was an accident, but it was no accident that Jonathan could usually find some member of the family to play back and forth with him. On rainy days he and his older sister used to love playing a singing "question and answer" game, the long hall between their rooms being an excellent conductor for their voices.

We are told [7] that the artist Artur Rubinstein used only "song language" until after he was three years old, refusing to tell what he wanted or to call on other members of the family except in a singing voice. It is just as natural for little children to relate their doings in this way as in any other, and we find them doing it continually. They sing about their play, washing their hands, going to bed, getting dressed—in

[7] Amram Scheinfeld, *You and Heredity*, New York: Lippincott.

fact, about everything they do. Unfortunately, but for obvious reasons, they lose this natural ability as they grow older; for children do what others do, and people usually do not go around singing in this fashion.

But there are more than a few pioneering and imaginative grownups who are alert to the possibilities in sound that children bring. Here is an experience related by a teacher.[8]

It began almost two weeks ago when the class and I experimented with city sounds, animal sounds, and bird sounds. Last week, we followed it up with train sounds, bumble-bee noises, and I ended one session with some samples of some of my old college chants [cheers] we used on every Saturday afternoon in the fall. "Ooooo-H-IIIIII-OOOOO-ooooo," I chanted. I chanted another: "It's round on the ends and high in the middle—O—hi—O." We spent the rest of the day paying tribute to the seventeenth state to enter the Union. Yesterday I was surprised to see how well ready these eight- and nine-year-old people were for this type of singing. Danny broke the ice by showing us one he had made up about Kansas. "There's *Cans* at the first and *Us* at the end: "K-A-N-S . . . A-S." It caught fire: "It's *O.K.* to start with, *La* in French, and *Homa* is where we all go at the end: OK—LA—HOM—AAAaaa." And so on.

The incident happened because this teacher of some years of experience had recently been reawakened to his own "sounding" possibilities and therefore discovered the interest which his group had all along. He made it possible for their talent to be used in school.

In the following pages a preservice student gives us a vivid description of the fear and trepidation, and the joy and excitement, that accompanied her exploration into the unknown. She was privileged to do her student teaching with an understanding and imaginative cooperating teacher who likewise was interested in exploring with her third-grade children.

8 Used by permission of Charles Reasoner.

I am now a student teacher in third grade and have chosen to present a log form of my experiences with this group. I did not take detailed notes for my intention is to show my growth and to evaluate my work with children. I feel that my thoughts on how to teach music have changed immensely. I began the log on March 1.

March 1. I tried having the class listen to sounds, such as the radiator, and those from the other rooms. Since this was the first attempt at this kind of experience, many of the children thought I was doing this just to quiet them! At times this happens to be a valuable result, but in my opinion it is not sufficient reason for doing it.

March 2. Before leaving the classroom to go to the art room, I suggested that the class listen to the sound of their feet on the steps. Some of the children took advantage by stamping loudly. (It might be argued that stamping loudly is valuable psychologically as a way of expressing oneself and releasing aggressions, but I cannot forget that I am being evaluated on my ability to handle a class at all times, and too much noise in the hallway tends to disturb other classes!)

March 5. Had the class listen to silence. Not too successful. Some of the children began to wonder if their student teacher were a little crazy—she was beginning to wonder the same thing!

March 6. Class was very noisy. Quieted them down and we discussed the blessings of silence! Realized how relaxing silence can be and how beneficial as far as a break in a busy day is concerned. After the discussion we all listened to silence and then discussed it some more; this was the first time the class showed any growth in this type of activity.

March 9. At the height of a noisy session one child raised his hand and asked if we could listen to silence. As a result of our previous discussion on silence, we realized that it was something that required teamwork by the whole group. The class quieted down and we all gratefully listened to silence. We realized that there is no such thing as complete silence for even silence has its own peculiar sounds.

March 12. Before we left the classroom for the art room, a child asked if we could listen to the sound of feet on the stairs.

This time the whole class cooperated. Upon returning to the room we discussed the sounds we heard.

March 16. · During the past week, the whole class showed signs of real growth in this type of activity. I was quite encouraged.

March 21. After we had seen a film on sheep, I asked the class to sing *Mary Had a Little Lamb,* being careful to choose the boys who were likely to feel silly singing such a "sissy" song to sing a chant of bass. Didn't work too well. However, from my past experience with sound-making, I realized that experiments of this sort need working at, so I was not too disappointed.

All of these were fairly incidental experiences—none being longer than five minutes—and all occurred between regular class periods or new activities. However, a definite sign of growth was apparent both on the part of the class and on my part. I realized that the class must be oriented to this type of activity (that is, in school), but that once the project was launched, they loved doing it. When I first began this type of musical activity with the children, at times I wondered what the educational values were. Now I feel that I have found some of the answers to this question and they will be discussed later in the paper.

April 3. The teacher with whom I work played some rhythm records and to my amazement the whole class got up and danced as freely as birds in the sky! I have never seen children less inhibited while dancing to all types of rhythm waltzes, ballet music, jazz. The teacher explained that they had done some dancing at the beginning of the year but not since. The boys were just as uninhibited while dancing to ballet selections as they were dancing to really rugged numbers. I made quite a few observations as a result of this experience.

First of all, there was a boy new to the class and he could be spotted right away. He was not as free as the other children and he felt awkward. However, after a few more such sessions he loosened more and more. It was also quite obvious which girls studied ballet, for none of them seemed as free and uninhibited as the others. They seemed more concerned with the correct positions and looking graceful, than with really moving to the music and expressing themselves. I will not conclude that ballet lessons are therefore bad for all girls, for that would be too much of a generalization. In my own case, however, I started ballet lessons at an early age and, as a result, my dancing has been inhibited ever since. I believe that there is a definite relationship between starting formal music lessons or formal dancing lessons too early and musical inhibition. (I also studied the piano, flute, and harp —it seems that I am the perfect example of how to inhibit one's child!)

I also realized that this type of activity, although appearing to be completely unstructured by the teacher, actually requires quite a bit of directing. Such rules as not bumping into each other and how to move to and from one's seat with the least amount of commotion and in the quickest time are all necessary, especially when the space is limited and a free atmosphere must still be maintained. All of this takes ingenuity and planning on the part of the teacher.

April 9. Today the teacher and I discussed with the class the idea of presenting an assembly program based on rhythms and sounds. I began to tell a story and the class performed the sound effects. This lasted for about ten minutes. We all realized that this was still in an experimental stage.

April 10. The children came to school after having listened to sounds while walking to school, while in bed, while riding in a car, and so on. We had a session during which we experimented with the different sounds. Then the teacher suggested that a few of the children write stories which could be read while being sounded out in the background.

April 12. Stories were presented but ran like this: "I was walking to school and I heard dogs and cats and cars and people." The teacher and I realized that although we two could write stories better suited to what we were aiming for, we still wanted this program to be the children's. They tried again and again. Finally stories evolved such as: "I slammed the door when I left home and started running to school. All of a sudden I stopped for I heard a strange sound. It began getting louder and louder."

April 16. During this week, we worked on various stories such as a trip to the zoo, a walk along Fifth Avenue, a night in the country. As the project proceeded, we found ourselves dividing the class into groups for different sounds: for example, one group supplied bird sounds; another group of about six kids made sounds of people; another, animal sounds; and so on. The children chose the group for which they felt best fitted. We found this grouping arrangement was suited to our needs, especially if we were going to present an assembly program. As a sideline of this activity we played a record of bird calls to identify the sounds of different birds.

April 26. We went into the auditorium so that we could get an idea of how the different sounds would carry in the large room. We decided to keep the curtain closed and the children behind it while one came forward to read the narrative. I sat in the audience to get an idea of how it would sound and I was torn between hysterics and amazement. If I hadn't known that the 25 children with whom I work were behind the curtain, I would have sworn I was at a farm or that real animals were behind the curtain. I also could not stop laughing—the tears ran down my face. As a result of this session, we changed some of the sounds a little, made some louder, others more continuous, and so forth. As of this writing we have gotten no further but we all feel that this will be quite an assembly. It is far from completed but we think it will be effective. Each day brings a new discovery or change which stems almost entirely from the children's work and creativity. We two have just been steering while they have been the real writers, actors, critics, sound effects. It will be interesting to see how this experiment turns out. Certainly we have learned how much can be done with the human anatomy alone.

A few pages earlier, I mentioned that I felt I found some values on my own as a result of this musical activity. From my experiences thus far I have found the project to be very worthwhile for the following reasons: First of all, it is a great aid to those teachers who do not know how to play any musical instrument, for no instruments are needed. It is also good for those situations where no instrument is available. In these two instances a teacher who is unaware of this type of musical possibility might shy away from giving children any musical activity at all as a result of her own feelings of inadequacy. Then, too, such an experience is, in my mind, a truly creative one, for the children are producing sounds and movements without the aid of instruments, objects, music. Experiments with sounds can also expand into many other creative fields, such as story writing, as seen in our assembly project. I also feel that this is valuable educationally, for children become more aware of the sounds and life around them —and is this not an aim of education to make people *aware* of their environment?

Group cooperation is required for, in order to listen to silence or many of the other sounds, we must be quiet first. There is also much group cooperation in the type of assembly program we are doing. There is an opportunity for much incidental learning, such as that in listening to the bird records. These children are receiving wonderful musical training in that they are learning to be *active listeners*. They are also not as likely to be as inhibited as people who have not had this type of experience. As I mentioned before, this type of activity can also be used to help with the discipline problem occasionally! And I feel that the teacher who can give the children other musical experiences as a result of her own training is going even one step further.[9]

The above step-by-step development of a beginning teacher is very encouraging. What went on has musical implications but, of far more importance, is the willingness of a person to work towards the discovery of sound with a group of children—to sense what is important to them, to recognize the opportunities presented for further learning.

This takes courage, for there are many "ups and downs." The "downs" may show up more sharply when measured against the teacher's expectancies in relation to a specific product which she envisions; but the "ups" will far outweigh the "downs" when checked against the learning that evolves when children are released and encouraged to follow the pattern of their own growth.

A teacher has to be willing to gamble on being a bit insecure. One of the most comforting and reassuring comments on insecurity I have heard was made recently by a student: "Security is something that can never be permanently learned." But we certainly can become more secure in our attitudes towards the truly experimental—and become more

[9] Used by permission of Enid Shoobe Topchik.

accustomed to and thus more secure in our feelings toward the unpredictable.

We have described a few, a very few, of the many ways in which children use their voices. What can we do, as we live with them, that will insure the maximum of enjoyment and learning from these experiences? What guidance can we give, in the home and in the school, that will best contribute to their musical education? "Music" is a part of children's everyday living. Half-hour lessons and music periods can build on, ignore, or give perfunctory recognition to the *real musical* interests of children. Older boys and girls will welcome special times set aside for music in direct proportion to the willingness of those responsible for these times to identify with what has meaning for children. But music at any age cannot be relegated to *only* special times. Children use music functionally and, unless we have a broad understanding of it, we are likely to "educate it out of them."

We must have confidence in ourselves and respect for the music that is in us. We must blow away the air of mystery with which it is surrounded for many of the uninitiated. But no one is utterly devoid of music in some form or another. It is contagious; if we feel the need for it, then those who live with us will not go untouched by it. If we are trained musicians, so much the better, provided we are truly broadminded and flexible in our use of music.

If we provide for children, at home and at school, a simple, happy environment and freedom to use it, our first effective piece of guidance is accomplished. Children also need some form of recognition for what they are doing. This may be only a smile in passing, or a friendly interest, or, if in a group, help in finding a quiet spot where they can *hear* what they are doing.

At times, our actual participation in what a child is doing may be exactly what is needed. That participation may take the form of following his lead entirely, or we may feel that the time is ripe for helping him see the next step ahead.

Whether we do this or not depends essentially on our sensitivity, on our perception of his readiness for something more. If he loses interest because of our participation, we have taught him nothing; but if we do not attempt such participation, we may miss a rare opportunity to plant a greater interest in him. Sometimes, in our desire not to overstimulate children, we do not live up to the possibilities they have. Children are constantly reaching out for more, and if it is not given them, "problems" may turn up.

Making a child aware of what he is doing or has done is part of the learning process. If he can repeat at will what has happened, he has taken a step forward. The group's introduction to harmony that started with Mary's experimenting is an example.

Many opportunities for this type of guidance occur in a child's make-believe play. "This is the way your train whistle sounds," we may say, imitating his voice.

Going a little further, we may sound our whistle on a different pitch or with a change of intensity. "Listen to mine —it is far away." He will enjoy this game and gain much from it provided it is carried on in a spirit of play.

Here are some suggestions—more possibilities for guidance in voice play. They are not a set of procedures nor a sequence; rather they should serve to refresh our memories so that we have more to draw upon musically than we thought we had. When and where they are used depends entirely upon their appropriateness and the opportunity they offer to help children learn more than they already know.

• Match the child's voice sound with your own voice. *We* must be willing to experience failure, especially when working with older boys and girls.

• Take the same rhythmic sound as the child's and change pitch. Children like extremes in pitch.

• Find a different sound than child's—one which sounds well or harmonizes when both are used together.

• Add to the sound of the child, such as a "playback" or cadenza or contrast in pitch, dynamics, or rhythm. This is dealing in phrases.

• Talk in sound only—question and answer phrases, nonsense sounds or syllables, or words, numbers, and so forth.[10]

• Find the pitch of a sound on an instrument.

• Sensing the mood and rhythm of sound play, supply song material in the mood of play—such as *Turkey in the Straw, Nickety-Nackety, Woolie Boogie Bee, Fiddle Dee Dee, Deck the Halls, Three Dukes a Riding,* and so on.

Central to the thinking expressed in this chapter are two basic factors: first, the need to focus on children and discover what they already are familiar with and have skill in doing; second, the need for all of us adults to broaden our definition of music.

If we are not musicians, we should familiarize ourselves with the fundamental elements of music. In recent years, a number of excellent books about music have been written for the layman. They are interesting and easy to read, and they open up to the reader many of the "mysteries" of music. One of the most immediate ways of cultivating our ears is through a new awareness of how sound is used on television, radio, and recordings. In addition, if we can find the time and an understanding teacher, we should plan to spend half an hour a week with him, and at least a few minutes a day with ourselves, in exploring the world of sound. No matter what instrument is our choice—piano, voice, guitar, harmonica, or drums—and this may be exactly the relaxation we need to bring down our blood pressure or unjangle our nerves.

These suggestions may help increase our awareness of sound and confidence in ourselves.

1. Recall your earliest "musical" experience—your earliest "sound" experience.

---

10 If you have seen and heard Danny Kaye communicating to children all over the world for UNICEF, you will experience the power of sound and movement in and of themselves.

2. Recall ways in which you used sound as a child.

3. Try to remember the last sound you heard last night before you went to sleep, the first you heard this morning. Try this with children.

4. Go on a "hearing" excursion; concentrate on what can be heard.

5. Close your eyes at intervals and listen.

6. Listen to the *sounds* (not content) of people talking (children and adults). Is there a recurring rhythm to these sounds?

7. Listen to *Millions of Musicians* (Folkways).

8. Look at television or listen to radio commercials. In what ways are sounds used to heighten the impact of a particular advertisement? Are they effective?

9. What songs do you recall primarily for their sounds?

10. What poetry do you recall for its sound?

11. If you have a tape recorder, quietly record sounds of voices during work and play, in the home, on the street, in school. Play them back.

12. Try "talking" in pure sound as Danny Kaye does.

13. Reproduce some of your environmental sounds with your voice.

14. From listening to television, radio, or records, observe the ways in which voice sounds are used to support or elaborate on a song.

15. Can you find new and interesting ways of combining your voice sounds with those of another person?

16. Do you *hear* such voice sounds as buzzing, groaning, sighing, hissing, teasing, chanting? Do you recognize any form in the use of these?

17. Listen to music of other cultures through records to enlarge your "sound" experiences. (See Chapter 9 on phonograph records.)

18. Search for songs in which nonsense sounds or simple repetitive sounds are used, such as those found in Gilbert and Sullivan operettas, in certain familiar operatic arias (for ex-

ample, in *The Marriage of Figaro*), and especially in folk material. Inexpensive and prolific sources for folk, camp, and community songs are the pamphlets published by Cooperative Recreation Service, Delaware, Ohio.

19. Listen to *Mother Goose* (Caedmon) read by Cyril Ritchard, Celeste Holm, and Boris Karloff, and *Nonsense Verse of Carroll and Lear* (Caedmon) read by Cyril Ritchard, Beatrice Lillie, and Stanley Holloway.

Chapter 3

MORE ABOUT CHILDREN AND SOUND

〜〜〜〜〜〜〜〜〜〜〜〜〜〜〜〜〜〜〜〜

I T IS AN OLD SAYING that any unwanted sound is noise. Some-one has observed that there are no noises in the country—only sounds. Whether it is noise or sound that comes to our ears, we adults need to keep prodding ourselves continually if we are to be objective about our observations of how children use, play with, and learn about sound. Otherwise we will miss many of the musical implications that are there. In the previous chapter we have tried to reawaken our sound per-ceptions by focusing on a few of the ways in which sound is explored through the voice.

Children not only use their voices in experimenting with sound. They also have ready ears for environmental sounds— the little ones that you and I no longer hear. They also find out about sound through the use of objects around them—in most cases, the "percussive" use of them. The purpose of this chapter is to turn our attention more specifically to the per-cussive sounds. Actually, these do not necessarily exist sepa-rately from voice sounds.

All too soon for mother the baby discovers that dropping things from his crib or carriage is great fun. Of course, he enjoys the attention he gets when his plaything is picked up and given back to him, but he also likes the sound it makes when it hits the floor. Only we grownups tire of this game, and in order to escape so much bending exercise we think up other ways of satisfying the child without wearing ourselves out. So we tie spoons, clothespins, metal cups—in fact, anything at hand—to the sides of his crib or high chair so that he can toss them about and retrieve them at will. For him, it is not quite so much fun as having grownups do his bidding, but he will accept it, and will entertain himself for a long time.

Even when the baby is still in his carriage, we can begin to think about making it possible for him to play with and hear a variety of sounds. We may not be able to go as far as Montaigne's father, who had his son awakened every morning with some instrument in the hope that this practice would influence his character and disposition! But every home has many possibilities if we open our ears to them. One father whose job it was to brush up the crumbs around the family dining table decided that the family needed a new dust pan and announced that he would buy it on his way home from work. His choice was determined not by size, cost, color, or even durability, but by the fact that it pleased his ears as he tapped on it. Pleasant-sounding rattles and different types of bells are always enjoyed by the little child. Tiny bells sewed securely on a piece of elastic or tape that can be slipped over the wrist are fun. Sound boxes can be made by putting different articles in boxes small enough to be handled easily by the child, and then gluing or nailing on the tops. One nursery-school teacher used little toy wooden kegs for this purpose. After putting nails in one, dried beans in another, and so on, she screwed on the tops, which had previously been brushed with glue. The idea here is to achieve contrasts and differences in sounds so the child will be offered a variety of experiences.

A teacher of eleven- and twelve-year-olds who is alert to

the sound interest of children set up a "sound" table in the classroom, contributing a few small boxes and an assortment of objects such as paper clips, pennies, and pebbles. She suggested that her class might be interested in adding to this collection. And they did. Boxes of varied sizes, from band-aid to cereal boxes, were contributed along with nails, rice, marbles, tiny bells, and all sorts of small metal objects. The purpose here was to encourage different combinations of boxes and objects and thus become more discriminating in sound. These boys and girls used certain types of sound boxes to accompany some of their songs and also used them as sound effects for stories and dramatic play.

Children of any age thrive on interest and approval. It would indeed be a hard-hearted mother who refused to let her son investigate the kitchen pots and pans, and she would miss a lot of fun if she did not occasionally sit down and play with him. Even if she has little time and must keep close to her work, she can at least pay attention to this sound-making, for the toddler has ten times the fun if he knows that someone is enjoying it with him.

And here is an excellent opportunity to help the child learn more about sound. Instead of asking him not to make such a racket with his spoons and pans, give him a stick that is padded a little at the end. He cannot strike a pan lightly, and besides, he doesn't want to; but the padded stick will produce a pleasanter sound even if he uses the same force in striking with it. (We should never miss an opportunity to substitute a pleasant for an unpleasant sound *provided this does not interfere with the child's play*.) He will probably prefer a loud crash, but we hope that he will gradually get interested in the *differences* in sound. It will be less confusing to him and his interest will last longer if he uses only a few pans at a time, to say nothing of how much easier it will be on his mother! But also see that from time to time he has a change in the number and size of utensils. (Pots and pans have their utilitarian value for adults, too—musically speaking. A well-known dance accompanist and music teacher tells me that one of her special "instruments" is the cast-iron cover of an iron pot. She finds its gong sound specially appropriate for certain focal points in dance.)

Helping children to be *alert to the similarities and differences in sounds* is one of the ways we can guide this early interest. As a child plays on a pan, the mother may listen and ask if she, too, may have a turn. Then picking up his pan and tapping it *his* way, she can say: "Listen—this is the way your pan sounded when you played on it." Or again, she may pick up a utensil of another size for herself and tap it, asking the child to notice the difference between the two.

If we listen, we shall find that it is not long before a child can repeat the sound he makes with a certain regularity. At first he does not make a conscious attempt to do this, but he falls into the pattern during the course of his play because he likes the sound, and he keeps repeating it. Even as simple a movement as "tap-tap" repeated regularly is a rhythmic pattern, and when the child can consciously produce this at will, learning has taken place. We can show our interest in what he is doing and help him be more aware of it by repeating what he has done. We should not hurry this stage of playing *his way,* for sometimes in our eagerness to go ahead we expect the child to listen to *our way* before he is ready. Then he loses interest.

An assortment of mixing bowls can produce lovely sounds. (Obviously, it is necessary to wait until the child is old enough to have attained a certain amount of control over his experimentation before putting these at his disposal.) The kind of shoe tree that is tipped by a wooden ball makes an ideal tapper; the steel body is flexible and makes a pleasanter sound when it strikes the bowl than does a rigid stick. Other members of the family will enjoy playing on these bowls, and perhaps they will be able to collect a set whose various tones enable them to be arranged in scale sequence, and so lend themselves to simple melodies. "Tuned" water glasses or bottles are often used in this way as a substitute for a piano, but they are not recommended for small children because they break too easily. A ten-year-old who has a keen ear for tonal differences recently challenged the patience of his family by insisting that they sing and play *Oh, How Lovely Is the Evening* before they started to eat their dinner. He had tuned the glasses with water to one, three, and five of the scale and instructed each person when he was to play his glass.

This calls to mind an experience, a few years ago, when I helped tune one hundred water glasses for a college dinner party. All of the glasses at a table were tuned to the same interval and numbered. Each person was given a "score" indicating when his number was to be played. The entire group sang the song first with only the piano accompaniment; the next time the tuned glasses were added. *Jingle Bells,* the favorite song, was played four times: I will never forget this music time in which one hundred players participated.

In the following pages, a teacher who has cultivated her hearing perceptions responds to classroom situations involving sound in ways that promote a climate of good mental hygiene and in ways that offer unexpected opportunities for hearing in many areas as well as in the materials of which music is made.[1]

It was the third week of school for my second-year class. We were doing a social-studies unit entitled "We Go to School!" This unit included a trip around the school building to note the different rooms of importance. We passed through a narrow, enclosed staircase.

"Our voices sound different here," said Teddy.

"Our voice, it sounds like—like an echo," piped Phyllis.

The steps were made of metal and it was so nice to stamp our feet on them. Suddenly, we heard a child whom we couldn't see, but could certainly hear, run down the steps.

[1] Used by permission of Phyllis J. Corsbie.

"Sounds like a wall tumbling down, Miss Corsbie," said Deborah. Then soon we heard a class on their way down to assembly.

"The whole school's coming down now," laughed Stephen. We certainly had a grand time going up and down those staircases.

It wasn't nearly as much fun in the hallway though. The floor was made of a soft material. We couldn't hear our feet. Our voices didn't carry as far out here either. What was good about this? It certainly was no fun.

In the classroom we could hear our feet on the wooden floors. We could make all kinds of sounds here. But some liked the sound on the metal staircases better. The voices didn't sound as nice here as they did on the staircase either.

During the penmanship practice period, William was singing *Papa Loves Mambo* very softly to himself.

Since the song was infectious, Pat began to hum along while writing. Bradford looked at them, then at me, smiled, and began to move his body and give out with a "dum dee dee dum dum" sound. Pretty soon, quite a few joined in making different sounds with different parts of the mouth. Ronald tried to whistle, but he wasn't very successful. We stopped.

"This sounds very interesting," I said. I asked different children to sing the song the way they liked to do it best.

"Everyone is singing that song different," said Phyllis.

"How do you mean 'different,' Phyllis?"

"I can hardly hear Mamie. She does it so quiet." Mamie tried to hum the song.

"Bradford, he's too loud," said Leticia. Bradford decided to "La-la-la-la" the song.

"Let's see how many different kinds of sounds we can make to the melody of the song. Just use your mouth. What sounds do you think go nicely together?"

"Whee-ee-ee-ee" sounded the Little Red Fire Engine as it rushed down the street to reach the fire in time. At this point, everyone began to give his interpretation of a Little Red Fire Engine. How does a fire engine sound when it is about three blocks away from you? How does it sound when it is on the same block you are on? How does it sound as it rushes right by you? These questions fostered interesting thoughts and results.

"What are some other sounds that you hear on the street? Can you make any of them? Describe what kind of weather we are having today by using sound only."

Apparently rest period was not necessary this particular day. All the children were extremely restless. James began to beat on the desk with his hands. Ronald began to beat the metal part of his desk with a pencil in the same rhythm James had elected to use. Chuck began to scrape his heels. Patsy tapped her feet. Other assorted drumming sounds joined in.

"All right, class. Heads up. James, let's hear what you were tapping on your desk with your hands. Ronald, will you join in with James using your pencil just as you did before? Now everyone, think of something you can do with what you have around your desk."

Everyone found something with which to accompany James —paper, hands, feet, notebooks, crayons. Most of the children used hands and feet, however. Louis pounded his notebook in such a manner that it required a great deal of effort and energy to keep up with the pace he had started. Tiring, he had to slow down and make a softer sound. A discovery! There was a burst of energy again and then a subsiding of energy. The class returned to the "penmanship lesson" with interest and concentration.

"Teacher, listen to this," called James several days later during a work-play period. He had made a cone-shaped object out of some oaktag and was talking about it.

"Listen to James, Teacher," said John. "He sounds funny."

"Miss Corsbie, my voice sounds far away." Everyone wanted to try it. They all made cone-shaped objects out of different materials. Some were happy with their results. Others were not. They discovered through experimentation just what kinds of materials would give the most satisfying experience. We had empty carton boxes which they used to talk into whenever they got the chance. They began to cup their mouths. This was very effective in getting a friend's attention. They discovered that length, width, height, thickness determined the type of sound you could get.

Experimentations with rubber bands, combs, edges of paper emitted wondrous sound discoveries.

"Hey, Teacher. Wanna hear somethin'?" Pulling a rubber band very tautly, Chuck plucked it.

Dennis loved to rub his thumb over a small five-cent comb. It got to be quite an annoying habit as far as I was concerned but he was delighted with it.

Let chalk squeak on the board to the delight of some of the children and to the annoyance of some of the others. The next chance Deborah gets to write on the board, she will work unceasingly until she accomplishes the same feat.

With all the new things they seemed to have found out, they will be ready to try out these experiments on our instruments when they arrive. Undoubtedly they will discover something new.

I realized that these incidences were true experiments and not merely noise to annoy the teacher. I saw an opportunity of using these experiences in the curriculum. Social studies was involved all the way. They learned how to embellish and complement each other in making a satisfactory sound. They learned how to share their ideas. That's learning how to live together.

Mathematics played an important role also. The concepts of length, width, volume constantly reminded the children that sound depended upon these factors.

A genuine increase of vocabulary was evident. They discovered more words with which to describe different shades of sound. There were no longer ordinary words like loud, quiet, funny, or nice, but soft, sweet, booming, swishing, and numerous others. Children were interested in the sounds they could make. They learned to read and write new descriptive words. In other words, the language arts prospered.

Science not only prospered but was genuinely practiced. They practiced experimentation in a true scientific fashion. They worked with something they thought might work. If results were not to their expectations, they tried again with something else until the desired results were obtained.

Of what value were these experiments? They offered release of pent-up energies and an opportunity to let off a little steam. Next, there was a notable increase of vocabulary—descriptive vocabulary at that. Bradford would not only sing "loud," but he would sing in a great booming voice. Mamie wouldn't just sing "soft," but in a little, tiny voice.

These experiments gave aesthetic pleasure as well. It made some of the children appreciative and responsive to the fact that different sounds can produce a pleasurable experience. It was also, in my opinion, a rudimentary step in manifesting taste. A child has to use judgment in estimating the amount of sound needed to render a satisfying experience. In other words, he begins to judge quality as well as quantity. He also realizes that tastes are relative in nature. What Norma likes to hear, Roy may not like to hear. Yet who is to say whether Norma is right or wrong.

The knowledge of sound profited also. It progressed from a general attitude toward sound to a specific one. Any baby can create the miracle of noise by just opening his mouth and yelling or by stamping his foot or by banging away at objects. But to earnestly localize your sounds, to restrict their volume, to limit their frequency, to narrow them down for specific, concrete, and special ideas or purposes—that's the apex of life *at that particular moment*.

Then, from the viewpoint of sheer enjoyment, it seems to have been of inestimable value. There is gratification and a sense of happiness in basking in the luxury of wondrous sounds of your own creation.

This teacher who has a special skill in bringing children's talents into focus by working *with* children will certainly have a much more receptive group of individuals for the kinds of learning that are a part of the curriculum for seven- and eight-year-olds, than will the teacher who does not accept children's natural inclinations.

It is well for parents to be aware of the great variety of opportunities that teachers and children have in the cultivation of listening and sound discrimination. And, likewise, teachers' memories will be refreshed by the ways in which parents in the home enjoy sound with their children. A mother who has become very aware in this matter of sound observes that [2]

I noticed that *Anne noticed* the squeak she made with wet fingers on her balloon. She can identify every creak, squeak, and

[2] Used by permission of Susan Ginsberg.

sound she hears in our apartment from rooms far away. I also noticed the other day, as I was using the egg beater, that Anne was stamping her feet in a sort of Mexican dance in time to the rhythm of the beater. I tried the technique used in class of "talking with feet." Anne (two and a half years old) caught on immediately and now uses this not only as a game and a test of whether I can recognize her stamps but as a sort of transposed stamping that might be used in a temper tantrum!

I have tried to attack this on many fronts: by reading a great deal of poetry to the children (which was always read to me with more emphasis on the content than on rhythm or sound), by singing songs and playing music from different cultures, by letting the children make "real music" with all the odd instruments I never used—pans, glasses, table tops. And I have observed their body movements not just in terms of dance expression but as indicators of feeling and mood. While Sally does this to a certain extent, I have found that Anne *never* cries standing up—when she starts to whine she crumples at the knees and relative to that posture I can pretty much tell what kind of a mood she is in by the way she is moving.

I have found that my new awareness is reflected in heightened sensibilities on the part of the children. They are more likely to point out nuances in sound—we are more likely to talk about them now.

Is there anyone who does not remember the pleasure of running a stick along a fence? Can you recall the differences in the feeling of the vibrations depending upon where you held the stick? The lasting impressions here are probably the kinesthetic ones although the "sound" of the experience is not forgotten.

In reflecting upon his early childhood days, Henry James constantly recalled his sensory impressions—the smells, sounds, tastes, the touch of all the many and varied experiences that he stored away. He had a "treasure house of observations lodged in his memory" and it was added to all during his life. It is surprising how we grownups can gradually recapture our early sensory impressions.

Not long ago I took a fairly long automobile drive with a father and his three boys, aged four, six, and nine. "Shut your eyes; we're coming close," called the driver. Immediately the boys' eyes closed tightly and stayed shut until we had passed over a bridge. These boys knew their bridges—not only by the kind of construction but especially by the kind of sound that was made as the car passed over them. This was just one of the many sound games they played when riding in the family car.

One memory leads to another. Reminiscing with a friend will bring back memories buried for years. One person remembers manipulating her bedroom door in such a way that it squeaked the first phrase of *Good Night, Ladies*—though unfortunately the family oil can thwarted her music career! Another remembers his interest in the different sounds made by the train on rainy and on clear nights. Still another recalls as her first sound experience the satisfying lapping of the puppy drinking his milk. And to another, summer vacation brings up an immediate childhood association with the insect chorus in the country.

The suggestion here is that the reliving of our early sound experiences will contribute to a more sympathetic understanding and appreciation for the ways in which children use sound. Let us have respect for *our* "treasure house of sound observations lodged in *our* memory." Children are sound-conscious—acutely sensitive to all of the elements of sounds. If we wish music to have real meaning in their lives, we shall educate *through* this interest.

These suggestions may help to refresh memories and stimulate new discoveries.

1. Does sound annoy us or can we relax, at times, and listen?

2. What association does sound have for us—content, form, rhythm?

3. Are we aware of the ebb and flow in sounds made by people individually or in groups, such as at a ball game?

4. Are there any particular sounds that have a pleasant association, such as the "hollow" sound of a heavy refrigerator door closing, the increase and decrease of intensity of sound as an automobile or airplane passes, the inflection and accent in certain voices?

5. List the sounds that are acceptable, the sounds that annoy.

6. Listen to the following records:

a. *The Lonesome House.* Douglas Moore, chairman of music department of Columbia University, records sounds in an empty house, such as banging shutters and dripping faucets, and arranges these sounds in a composition (Children's Record Guild, 78 rpm).

b. *New York 19.* Tony Schwartz picks up the sounds of things and people in New York's postal zone 19 (Folkways).

c. *Strange to Your Ears.* Jim Fassett records and combines sounds creating an entirely new experience (Folkways).

d. *Millions of Musicians.* Tony Schwartz records the music in people's voices and in environmental sounds so that we may hear anew our everyday experiences (Folkways).

7. Do you like to "doodle" in sound, such as playing with a key ring, clicking the fastener of a purse, tapping fingers or feet?

8. Do the above experiences *contribute* to your *real* understanding that sounds put together can make music?

9. Are you becoming more accepting of the exotic sounds of modern music or music of other cultures?

10. Do you find yourself more and more curious and *entertaining of* sound?

Chapter 4

SINGING

Children enrich their understanding of music through inventions in pure sound. Many of these inventions take on aspects of singing and, at times, some of them are snatches of song. In the foregoing chapters we have directed our attention toward rediscovering sounds that have had meaning for us in the past so that we can be more alert to the sound track on which children move. It is suggested that in these early experiences is what John Dewey calls "art in germ." In his discussion on art, which for many years has been a highly rewarding source of enlightenment for me, Dewey states that "in order to understand the esthetic in its ultimate and approved forms, one must begin with it in the raw; in the events and scenes that hold the attentive eye and ear of man, arousing his interest and affording him enjoyment as he looks and listens." [1]

Commenting on domestic utensils, the furnishings of tents and houses of earlier times, examples of which we find in our museums today, Dewey says these were "enhancements of the processes of everyday life." Then he goes on to say that the "esthetic is no intruder in experience from without . . . but that it is the clarified and intensified development of

[1] John Dewey, *Art As Experience,* New York: Dutton.

41

traits that belong to every normally complete experience."
Is it worth our while to ponder the implications of these state-
ments in teaching the art of music?

Chant

Do we hear music, at least "music in germ," in the sound-
ings, the snatches of song, the chants that accompany day-by-
day living with children? "The whole idea of the origins of
music is new to me. I have listened to children's chant from
such an unmusical frame of reference that I feel robbed,"
observed a graduate student recently. Have we forgotten that
chant is found not only among children but among men
everywhere? For a most enlightening discussion on chant the
reader is urged to study the Pillsbury Foundation pamphlet
presenting the research in this field with young children by
Moorhead and Pond.[2] This valuable and informative study
brings to our attention the nature of chant and the ways in
which children use it. The authors remind us of the need
for association "with chants of the Tunisian Dervishes, with
the American Indian dance rituals, with the Haitian voo-doo
chant, with the litanies of the Christian church, if an accurate
estimate is to be made of the real musical value of the chant."

Does the minor third chant, evocative, immediate, and
universal, which children use so frequently and which is
highly contagious, threaten us or are there times when we
allow it to resolve itself or, even more, can we find ways of
extending the musical values of children's chanting? A vigorous minor third chant such as "I want some ice cream!" is
easier to accept from an individual child than it is from a
group. In the beginning it may be more comfortable for the
adult to test himself with a single child. The first major

2 Gladys Evelyn Moorhead and Donald Pond, *Music of Young Children—Chant*,
Santa Barbara, California: Pillsbury Foundation for Advancement of Music
Education.

accomplishment for a grownup is the *acceptance* of a chant. It is pretty certain to increase in intensity, but more important, it will also *decrease*. The more we resist it the more the child senses our feelings and the longer it will take for resolution.

It is fun to surprise the child and play with him. For example, catching his pitch and rhythm, chant with him a phrase as *"not now* but *later."* Or join in with a staccato reply, such as *"here it is,"* slowly on one pitch, or catch the interval between his chants with a quick *"no"* or *"all right."* The important idea is for us to *feel* and *hear* our way with our voices as we play both soundwise and contentwise with a chant. It isn't long before even the uninitiated musically finds himself exploring and enjoying the forms of music such as counterpoint, harmony, phrase. Are we aware of how often we use this minor third chant? The mother, in a relaxed mood, calling *"John*-ny, *John*-ny, *John*-ny," or the crowd at a ballgame chanting "We want a hit," rising in intensity and pitch, are expressions that come so naturally that we are unaware of them. Is there any association of sadness in this use of the minor key, and yet how many of us were introduced to the minor mode as a sad or mournful key? Probably the most famous example in musical literature of a minor third theme is in Beethoven's Fifth Symphony.

Recently I visited a group of six-year-olds who suddenly blew up into a chant "We want a story." The teacher took her group by surprise and chanted back, "dee dee dee-*dum,"* on the same pitch as the children's chant but with the rhythm of Beethoven's theme. This was so much fun that the children took up the teacher's chant. Then the teacher said, "I'll sing your song—'we want a story'—and you answer with my song." The storytime became a music time with many variations and combinations of sounds evolving because of the inventiveness of both children and teacher. Was this not an "enhancement of the process of everyday life"? What better time could one find to highlight a musical experience and to get acquainted with a great composer by illustrating this theme on a musical instrument or by playing an excerpt of the Fifth Symphony on the phonograph?

Adult Leadership

Chapter 11 gives some suggestions for developing group sounds and chants. Many of these are applicable to groups of children. Basic to this kind of musical adventuring in a group is the authority of the teacher—the kind of control that encourages spontaneity and freedom. For a teacher with firm control knows that she has the immediate response of her group when necessary. A teacher who does not have control cannot allow for freedom of ideas of any kind. Usually it is very important for the inexperienced teacher to hold the reins tightly until she becomes more sure of herself and of children. But the thoughtful person will surely *work towards* the kind of living with children where they will respond when asked because both teacher and children have built together an understanding of the importance of responding when asked. A young teacher of six-year-olds tells of her experience in establishing this kind of social organization. During the first week of school she discussed with the children the need for some kind of signal that would mean that she wanted to say something to them. Together they made out a list of "sound-makers" to be tried out—a triangle, a whistle, a cow bell, a press bell, a flashlight, a clicking frog, and a "stop and go" light. They decided to try each one and give it a fair trial before choosing one to use all of the time. This would take time. The children brought in the "instruments." They found out through trial that the cow bell was the best signal! They were very much a part of the decision and were most responsive, says the teacher, "as long as what I told them, after they had responded, was worth listening to!"

Each teacher works in her own way toward establishing with children the kind of social living where freedom is permitted—a freedom that encourages spontaneity, invention, and creativity, in this case, in music and dance.

The teacher is not afraid of children going beyond the boundary lines (and into the realm of creativity) because this is a group where response to the leader is respected and observed. "I was amazed to discover," relates a teacher of fifth graders, "that since there is more freedom in my class in regard to sound and movement, the boys and girls are *more* responsive to controls when needed." I have never known a group, and I have worked with many, that was not willing to accept this responsibility for the privilege of learning in the way that has meaning for them.

In recent years I have had many opportunities to test the validity of this last statement. For a long time I had been reluctant to work with a group of children whom I had not known before. In workshops with teachers in various sections of the country I dodged requests to arrange a music period with children. What I thought these teachers were asking for was a demonstration lesson and "demonstration" lessons are not my way of teaching. Then one day, after a request from a group of teachers in Ohio, I faced myself squarely. Was I afraid of children? "No," I could answer quite honestly. What I really feared was the measure of my ability, in a short time, to create an environment in which children's spontaneity can be released. I felt—and still feel—that the full extent of this kind of living with children is built day by day and is not the result of a fiat. Nor does the presence of several hundred or even twenty-five adults in the room make it easier.

Here is what happened. I agreed to work with five- and six-year-old children. A few minutes before we went into the gym, I met with these boys and girls. We got acquainted with each other as far as names were concerned. I told them there would be a large group of teachers in the gym and I hoped we would be able to sing some songs and ask the teachers to join us. I also said that whenever I raised my hand that would be the signal for all of us to stop what we were doing. Then we went into the gym and sat down on the floor (not on the platform), the adults already having been seated around a good-sized open space.

Several of the children recognized friends in the audience and waved. "Wave to your friends," I suggested, and everybody waved, and the audience responded immediately by waving too. We were all together in this, and there was no use pretending that there was no audience! Let us make the most of it, I reasoned. We were off to a good start and I relaxed. Then a casual (?) question—what is your favorite television program—and we embarked on a "panel discussion" which could have taken the entire half hour. Favorite songs? Yes, there were many. After hearing several (and I not knowing any of them!) I picked what sounded like the easiest to learn and suggested that they teach it to me and to the teachers. We tried hard but we didn't learn very quickly. By this time the children were very much at ease.

I felt a need to be a bit more secure so, after the children had their turn, I taught them a song, *Hush, Little Baby, Don't Say a Word*,[3] which they joined in, before I was finished with the first verse, even though they didn't know it. Everybody learned this song and also the old English humorous folk song *Aiken Drum*.[4]

Together with the audience we had made a good start in creating a place where children could be their natural selves. The remainder of the half hour was spent exploring children's ideas and several of my suggestions both in singing and movement in a setting of enthusiasm and enjoyment. This experience gave me courage. Since then I have worked with many "new" groups, from five to twelve years of age.

[3] From Ruth Crawford Seeger, *American Folk Songs for Children*, New York: Doubleday.
[4] From Walter Crane (ed.), *The Baby's Bouquet*, New York: Warne.

Several summers ago a student who was doing a study of "music on the streets of New York" asked if she could bring in a group of boys and girls whom she had been observing. This group of twelve, from eight to thirteen years of age, gave a class of one hundred and eighty experienced teachers what I believe was the most important single contribution of the entire course. The student valued their ability to make music and she made them understand that we too would appreciate it. They responded readily to the signal for response which we had set up, because they quickly discovered that we were doing everything possible to create a place where they could do and enjoy what was important to them musically.

A place where singing can go on—the kind of singing that has meaning for children—is not easy to create. We need to free ourselves of so many of the well-intentioned but thwarting technicalities that have been associated with teaching music. And, as a friend observed recently, "it is truly frightening how an adult can lose his spontaneity and flexibility and not even be aware of it."

Burl Ives, the well-known ballad singer, was once asked to tell how he learned to sing. "I started singing about as soon as I could talk. It was just something that went on in our family," said Ives simply. Folks were poor where he came from, but they were singing folks, and it wasn't possible for a youngster to grow up without singing too. This way of life was as natural and as necessary to his people as eating and sleeping. And, when children anywhere are happy and satisfied, it is natural for them to sing, but they are indeed lucky if they live in a family where singing goes on day after day.

Songs

Musically speaking, today's child is very different from the child born fifty or twenty-five or even twenty years ago. He is exposed to more records, to more radio, and to television, and we have no real measure of what he absorbs. His diet may be good, bad, or indifferent, depending upon family tastes, the current enthusiasms of his peers, and the breadth of his own listening experiences.

Many people are seriously concerned about the kind of songs that are "right" for children, and rightly so. But, at any age, we must build taste and discrimination for ourselves, and they result from choices—choices made from a great variety of experiences. Sometimes we underestimate our own repertory of songs; at other times we forget some of them. There are, of course, some songs that have a particular appeal and are every child's rightful heritage. But, there is one thing that some of us have learned with respect to choice of songs: you cannot be too sure in advance what a child will or will not like!

Music cuts through all age levels. In this field there is, thank goodness, no such thing as a "chronological age." If we sing the songs that have pleasant associations for us—folk, popular, classical, service, or college songs, ballads or hymns—we shall soon discover our children's favorites. Our first concern should be to have confidence in our own musical competence, limited though it may be, and then to broaden our interests in every way we can. We should never overlook our own stockpile of songs in enriching children's repertory.

Folk Songs

We hope that children will learn many songs that are the lasting kind. The chances are good that the majority of these will come from our vast resources of folklore for as Ben Botkin defines it "this is the stuff that travels and the stuff that sticks." [5] Folk songs grow out of the needs and aspirations of people. Their very essence is change and adaptability both in melody and words. They are evocative in nature and they encourage invention. The rhythm and melody are

5 Ben Botkin, *A Treasury of American Folklore,* New York: Crown.

simple and basic, providing a flexible frame within which
stories and emotions are easily expressed. We sing them because we need to sing them and not for entertainment of
others, although that may be a by-product.

These songs are heard over radio and television, on records, and in the theater, and increasingly fine collections are
available in books. The bewitching melodies of *On Top of
Old Smoky, Skip to My Lou, Jim along Josie,* the many
beautiful Negro spirituals, the great jazz songs such as *I Got
Rhythm* and *St. Louis Blues,* calypso from Trinidad, and
countless others have an irresistible appeal. These are songs
that sing themselves, and they are loved by young and old.
They are songs that stick.

There are so many ways of singing the same folk song. I
know of no better way to encourage invention and experimentation at any age level than through a folk song. Recently
I divided a class of a hundred teachers into groups of five
each. We all sang, with the conventional piano accompaniment, *Way Down Yonder in the Paw Paw Patch.* Then I
asked each group to take the same song, explore it for about
ten minutes, and then present it anyway they wished. It
would take pages to relate the variety of responses—improvi-
sations in words, accompaniment (sound and movement),
rhythm, harmony, pantomime, and so on. The only musical
instrument in the room was a piano which all were free to
use but none did. The kinds of sound accompaniments that
appeared from pockets and pocketbooks and from the use of
walls, floor, chairs, various parts of the body, and unusual
registers of the voice were truly amazing. Creativity, invention, I care not what you call it. There was more of it in those
one hundred teachers than anyone dreamed of, and what fun
this is for boys and girls of any age!

A large variety of the folk songs of the past, songs that
have social significance, songs that sing of personal emotions,
songs that tell of heroic deeds and the history of a country,

work songs, sea chanteys—and the folk songs that are being created today—all of these are an important part of a child's musical heritage.

Songs in Other Languages

Is there any happier way of becoming familiar with a foreign language than through song? A little child will enjoy the "sound" of unfamiliar words and if the song is a lasting one, its sounds slip naturally and easily into place and are a part of its rhythm and flow.

Songs like *Sur le pont d'Avignon; Frère Jacques; Ach, du lieber Augustin;* and *Il était une bergère* jump right across our adult barrier of literal-mindedness and find an immediate response in the sound-loving and sound-making propensities of children. If we are not at home in any language, we should explore our immediate friends, neighborhood, and community. The ability to speak other languages than English is frequently overlooked by those teaching in localities where parents or grandparents are foreign-born. Naturally the school is primarily concerned with helping children in the correct use of our own language, but if we consistently overlook the cultural significance of these broader contacts in children's lives, we are neglecting not only a wonderful educational opportunity, but even more the human-relations value of promoting better understanding among peoples.

All countries have their favorite and significant songs. If by good fortune we can bring to our children some of this musical literature, their lives will be that much richer.

Somehow it seems so much easier for the younger generation to "take on" a language through song than for most adults. We so often let the meaning of the words get between us and the sound of the song. A child values and uses his sensory impressions—meaning is of secondary importance. In Hesketh Pearson's biography of George Bernard Shaw,[6] he

6 Hesketh Pearson, *G.B.S.*, New York: Harper.

tells us of Shaw's early youth in a home where "operas, concerts, and oratorios were constantly being rehearsed." Shaw "knew by heart many works by great masters from Handel to Beethoven, to Verdi and Gounod, and could whistle them from beginning to end or sing them in a language that would have been mistaken for Italian by an Irishman, for Irish by an Italian. . . ." But seriously speaking we should never discount the extension of vocabulary a child experiences through songs.

We are fortunate in having so many good recordings of songs in other languages. Folkways has an outstanding catalog in this field. Some of our major companies such as Columbia and Decca, as well as a few smaller companies, have made excellent contributions (see Chapter 9). A great variety of accompaniment is used in these recordings, thus providing delightful instrumental and harmonic experiences in addition to the singing. A few school music-series publishers also press recordings to accompany their books which provide a good representation of folk material. If these are to be used in a school, it is suggested that variety in musical accompaniment and also in voices be seriously considered before making a choice.

Patriotic Songs

A mother recently asked her nine-year-old son to name his favorite song. "The baseball coming-on song," was his immediate reply. That *The Star-Spangled Banner* means "baseball coming" to this youngster evidences the child's sensitivity to the *associations* built up around songs, and this is especially true of our patriotic music. Our national anthem takes on its peculiar meaning according to where it is heard— at a concert, the theater, a public gathering for any purpose, even a boxing bout viewed on television. Long before he can understand the full meaning of the words of *The Star-Spangled Banner,* the youngster feels himself a living part of its spirit, and will join in lustily but with great dignity when it is sung. Certainly this is a difficult song to sing, not only for children but for most adults, but the child's inability to stay on tune and to reach its "musical top" are far outweighed by the profound feelings called forth by his experience. *Anchors Aweigh, The Marines' Hymn, When Johnny Comes Marching Home, The Battle Hymn of the Republic, Yankee Doodle, My Country 'Tis of Thee,* and many other songs of this character all have a way of helping to make a child feel a part of a larger world.

Community Songs

These are songs that are associated with happy times when people get together. In this group are *Sweet Adeline; My Bonnie Lies over the Ocean; Goodnight, Ladies; Reuben and Rachel; K-K-K-Katy; Row, Row, Row Your Boat; Oh, No John; Loch Lomond; Home on the Range,* Stephen Foster's songs, Negro spirituals, songs from current and past musical shows—*Oklahoma, South Pacific, My Fair Lady;* songs from successful films, some of the popular and bewitching Walt Disney melodies, popular songs of today and those that have come down to us from the past. Children pick these up quickly. All is grist that comes to their mill. The best of these are songs to be enjoyed both at home and in the school.

Holiday Songs

Holidays, too, come in for their share of celebration in song. Tradition plays a great part especially in relation to such a holiday as Christmas. We sing the same old familiar carols, year in and year out; indeed for many little children they are year-round songs. To such children there seems nothing incongruous in singing *Silent Night* in midsummer. These carols belong to all, regardless of race, color, or creed. "Carol," by the way, originally meant a kind of dance, and "to carol" meant to dance in a joyous manner. In days long ago Christmas carols were exclusively associated with the village or community celebration of the birth of Jesus. It was a day of festivity and gaiety, and it was not until much later that the Church recognized the value of the carol as a part of religious worship.

The First Noel; Adeste Fideles; Good King Wenceslas; Bring a Torch, Jeannette, Isabelle; and *God Rest You Merry, Gentlemen,* are only a few of the more familiar carols. For those of us who feel the urge to go exploring further, there is a wealth of carol folklore that is only beginning to come to light. One or two new collections of these less-known carols usually turn up each year at Christmas time. Occasionally we run across an edition of carols in the original languages, while some collections give both the English and the foreign versions. And if we can sing them in the original language, so much the better.

Hanukkah, or the Festival of Lights, is celebrated in song. The gaiety of this happy Jewish festival is reflected in the charming song, especially for children, *I Have a Little Dreidl* —a dreidl being a small spinning top. More important musically are some of the lovely old folk songs associated with this holiday such as the hauntingly beautiful *Oh Hanukkah, Oh Hanukkah, Come Light the Menorah.*

The most personal of all holidays to a child is his birthday and no birthday is complete without *Happy Birthday to You.* You may be interested to know that the words of the birthday song were written by Patty Smith Hill, professor of education at Teachers College, Columbia University for many years, and a pioneer in the field of early childhood education. No other birthday song has ever taken its place. The melody, by the way, is an old folk tune.

Halloween is celebrated by songs about jack-o'-lanterns, pumpkins, witches, and black cats; Easter, by songs about bunnies and Easter eggs, and, we hope, by songs expressing the rebirth of nature in the springtime.

Then we have the patriotic holidays such as Independence Day and the birthdays of Washington and Lincoln. There was a time when teachers felt that special songs must accompany all these occasions, and as a result songs were "manufactured" by the music companies to fill this need. Almost without exception such songs are forced and artificial, and have no value musically. Children find these holidays of interest, but they should be made conscious of them in a more natural way. For the very young child a picture and a comment or two on Washington, for example, may be all that has meaning to him although we should be guided by the amount of interest he shows and give him as much information as he shows readiness for. Such holidays for older boys and girls will be made significant in many ways. Songs which were popular in Revolutionary days and during the Civil War period would be of real interest.

Songs of the Seasons

Songs about the seasons of the year have always been sung, and here again folk music gives us some of our most delightful melodies: *The North Wind Doth Blow; Tirra, Lirra, Lirra;* and *All the Birds Have Come Again* are examples. Younger children are fond of such songs as *Swish Go the Leaves* [7] and *The Weather Is Warm.* [8] And was ever a song more beloved by young and old than *Jingle Bells?* The melody of this song, written in 1856 by James Pierpont, was not considered seriously in its time; it was classed as what we today would call a "pops" tune!

Gilbert and Sullivan have given us some easy to remember songs that are seasonal in character, such as "Titwillow" and "The Flowers That Bloom in the Spring." Folk music is

[7] From Clara Leyden, *Seasons and Such,* New York: Grosset and Dunlap.
[8] From Satis Coleman and Alice G. Thorn, *Another Singing Time,* New York: Day.

also a rich source for this type of song; for example, *Early One Morning* and *It Snows in the Night*.[9]

Humorous Songs

While it is not possible to touch upon every kind of song enjoyed by children, one type certainly must not be omitted: the humorous song. There are far too few of these, and even these few are not brought to children often enough. The pure nonsense song is enjoyed tremendously, providing a welcome outlet for a youngster's love of fun. Folk-music literature is a rich source for this type of song.

Some funny songs, like *This Old Man* and *Willy, Willy, Will*, depend for their humor upon an infectious repetition of syllables. Others, like *Aiken Drum, Polly Wolly Doodle, The Bear Went over the Mountain,* and *The Gingerbread Lady*, appeal largely because of their ridiculous content as do *I Went to the Animal Fair, The Monkey's Wedding,* and many others.

Many of the old "cumulative" songs such as *I Had a Cat* which are so quickly learned by boys and girls, much to the embarrassment of adults, would also be classified as humorous songs. Singers like Burl Ives, Alan Mills, Shep Ginades, and Marais and Miranda are constantly bringing us long forgotten humorous songs and new inventions.

Lullabies

Lullabies, the first songs a mother sings to her baby, are in turn sung by small girls to their dolls. We should not want any child to grow up without being at home with *Rock-a-bye, Baby; Sleep, Baby, Sleep;* Brahm's *Cradle Song;* the old Southern *Hush, Little Baby; Go to Sleep, Pierrot, Little Brother;* and *Away in a Manger*. Each country has its own lullabies, and if our children can hear some of these in the

[9] From Davison and Surette, *140 Folk Songs*, Boston: E. Schirmer.

original languages their musical experiences will be much richer. A song such as the Italian *Fa La Nana*[10] is easy to sing even with no knowledge of the language.

Older boys and girls may be especially interested in lullabies from other lands. Childcraft's *Music for the Family* has a fine representative group both in the original language and translation. Another source is Dorothy B. Commins, *Lullabies of Many Lands* (New York: Harper, 1922). Caedmon, Inc., has recently issued an unusually beautiful album of lullabies, performed by artists whose voices are best suited for the lullaby which they sing. The long-playing record is accompanied by a book containing descriptive materials and the music and words for the lullabies. *Golden Slumbers* is a distinguished contribution from every standpoint.

Action Songs

Not a few songs evoke an action response in terms of movement. Boys and girls who have been to camp usually come home with quite a repertory of songs such as *John Brown's Baby Had a Cold upon Its Chest* and many of these songs are also taught in our schools. They are good fun and it is easy for youngsters to outdistance the skills of their elders in singing them. From the toddler, who has been entertained with finger plays, to the adult, this type of song has been popular.

Finger plays have been used by many teachers and for various reasons. Unfortunately, they are used far too often when children begin to get restless as a method of holding the group under control. Anyone who has worked with children in groups has experienced times when some such "tranquilizer" is welcomed. But it is unfortunate that this kind of action is used as a substitute for a more vigorous type of movement which growing children need, and it is even more unfortunate when it is turned to as a palliative for the effects

10 From *Music for the Family*, Vol. II, Chicago: Field Enterprises.

of a curriculum that is not in keeping with children's real needs.

Another aspect here needs to be considered. Songs to which certain actions are taught tend to become routine. Children respond with certain physical movements but their own imaginations and creativity are not encouraged. Recently a group of thirty-five seven- and eight-year-olds were taught *This Old Man.* The song was sung in the traditional way, and then the children divided themselves into small groups. Each group worked out its own way of singing and acting this song. The groups varied in size from two to five children each. And what a *variety* of ways of enjoying the same song were presented! While it is fun to do a song in the traditional way, is not the spirit of this type of song essentially a creative one? Why, then, limit the creativity to the originator of a particular kind of action?

Another thought on action songs: Give a group time to learn the song—plenty of time—before introducing "actions." Not all "action" songs need actions, and some songs that are not usually thought of as action songs may in any particular group or by a certain child eventuate in action.

Certain music teachers have acquired considerable skill in encouraging children to act out songs, usually folk material, and have been lauded for the creativity of the children whom they teach. One has to consider thoughtfully whether it is *the teacher who is creating by using children* or whether she is the kind of person who really releases children to *create in their own ways.*

Rounds

Singing rounds is a musical experience usually associated with older children and adults. It has been our experience, however, that while little children cannot alone carry the organization of round singing, five and six year olds greatly enjoy being a part of this type of group singing. If there are two grownups with a group, the children can be divided and can follow their leaders in a two-part round. One of our kindergarten Christmas celebrations was remembered especially by the children because the visiting parents and friends joined the children in singing *Frère Jacques* in round form. This was so much fun that long before Lincoln's Birthday the children planned to ask their fathers (who were to visit the school on that day) to sing *Row, Row, Row Your Boat* with them.

Rounds offer one way of familiarizing children with part singing. They are also used by music teachers in introducing certain musical forms such as the fugue. The record *Round and Round* (Children's Record Guild) offers a delightful experience in showing the relationships between a round and a Bach fugue.

Another interesting way of part singing is to combine two songs, half of the group singing one song and the other half another song. For example, *Three Blind Mice* may be combined with *Row, Row, Row Your Boat; Are You Sleeping,* or *The Farmer in the Dell; Ten Little Indians* with *Skip to My Lou; Blue Tail Fly* with *Shoo Fly* (choruses only); *Solomon Levi* with *A Spanish Cavalier; Darling Nellie Gray* with *When You and I Were Young Maggie; Keep the Home Fires Burning* with *There's a Long Long Trail.*[11]

Other Ways of Part Singing

Little children, especially, offer us many opportunities to sing a song "differently." When, for example, *She'll Be Coming Round the Mountain* is mentioned in a group, someone almost immediately starts chugging—"chug, chug, chug, chug"—or tooting the whistle or blowing a Diesel-engine horn. Almost instantaneously it becomes a chant and goes on and on. Relax and let the chant get established. It soon becomes rhythmical. Then catch the rhythm and the key with

11 Songs suggested by Lorene Marvel.

your own voice and sing the melody on "top" of the chug. It isn't long, even with a tiny bit of encouragement, until all kinds of combinations of sound and song will evolve.

One of the most exciting experiences I have had in composing the "associative" sounds of a song with the song itself was with a conference of 200 teachers and parents and 50 young men from a music school. What fun we had rediscovering the sounds that are associated with *Jingle Bells* and sleigh riding—crack of the whip, jingling bells, whoa and giddyap, wind blowing, singing voices, laughing voices. The entire group was divided into half a dozen groups and each group practiced its own sound. One group sang the song. After several trials of putting sounds together we found that laughter—just hearty laughter—supplied by the young men gave us a wonderful underpinning and together we discovered the right degree of intensity of each group sound *so that all could be heard.*

Sometimes such an experiment doesn't work too well at first but rather than be discouraged we should keep on. *Listening* and *discriminating* are the essence of making it successful and whenever a degree of success is achieved, what fun it is. This type of experience is the opposite of ready-made part singing in which parts are assigned according to the form of the song. Is there not room for both? And is not the appreciation of the "ready made" enhanced by these inventive experiences?

Experience Songs

One way of encouraging and supplementing the child's early efforts at song making is to bring to him some of the songs that have been written about him and his world—songs about swinging, running, and jumping, songs about dressing and undressing, songs about animals, boats, trains, and airplanes, and simple festival songs.

A few collections of this type of song have lovely colored

illustrations that appeal to little children and that help to stimulate their interest in singing. Children like to have someone sit down with them and sing through a book, repeating over and over again their special favorites. Many of these songs are arranged so that the child can sing about his name or his particular interest; the song merely provides the framework for his personal experiences. Moreover, little children are just as likely to be stimulated to singing by any favorite picture book as by a song book; to them the absence of music makes no difference.

Nursery Songs

There is really no dividing line between folk and nursery songs, but there are many songs that we associate especially with early childhood, such as the Mother Goose rhymes, many of which are in song. Surely no one would deprive a child of these. The experience sung about, because many of these songs are so old, comes to the child only through pictures but regardless of the "here and now" theory the child takes some meaning from them; probably the predominant "meanings" are sensory and associative. Both words and themes are traditional. Occasionally new words are set to old tunes or new tunes to old words. The most successful illustration of the latter is found in *A Cat Came Fiddling* by Paul Kapp (New York: Harcourt, Brace, 1956). There are some delightful musical experiences in this book for boys and girls in elementary school.

Singing Games

When we observe a group of little children playing *The Farmer in the Dell, London Bridge, Little Sally Waters,* or any other familiar and simply organized game, we are almost certain to see every member of the group singing. Even a child who is not likely to sing easily at other times will lose himself in the game and sing. This is a truly functional experience, for singing is needed to keep the game going. Then, too, the character of the music and the words of the song make it very easy for each child to do his part. A great deal of repetition both in words and music makes these songs easy to sing and hard to forget.

Little children learn many game songs long before they are able to participate in a group game. They hear older boys and girls singing them in their play, and a few of them are usually included in collections of traditional songs for children. Edna Potter has compiled and illustrated a collection of singing games.[12] Little children will enjoy this beautiful book as a picture song book, or will occasionally "play out" a song in their own way. For example, a four-year-old asked to play *The Muffin Man;* she wanted all the girls, holding their skirts straight out in front with both hands, to stand at one end of the room, and all the boys at the other end. She asked the adult to sing the song, and then the boys were told to walk over and take muffins out of the little girls' skirts!

This simplification of a game is a perfectly satisfactory way of playing for the younger children. In *London Bridge,* for example, passing under the bridge and singing the song are much more fun than standing behind the bridge-holders after having been caught. Children use this song in many ways. A small group of five-year-olds playing on a seesaw had a hilarious time improvising on the verse "Build it up with iron bars." Nothing was too ridiculous to fit into this framework: "Build it up with bacon and eggs," "with shoes and stockings," "with toads and mice," and so on.

In any group there is likely to be one "conformist" (we hope it won't be the grownup) who insists on following the rules of the game. If the adult with the group feels that the traditional organization of this particular game is beyond the children's social development, it is well to direct their play to

[12] Edna Potter, *This Way and That,* New York: Oxford.

a simpler form, saying that there are different ways of playing the game. Here is an excellent opportunity to tell children how folk songs have come down to us and why it is that the same song may have several variations.[13]

As I have observed the kinds of singing games children play outside of school, the majority seem to fall into a different pattern than the circle games taught in most of our elementary schools. Recently I asked two New York eight-year-olds to teach some of their games to a group of over one hundred teachers from all over the country who were in summer session at Teachers College. Several of the games started with "1 2 3 and a zing, zing, zing," [14] followed by a singing chant. Each person had a partner and all participated at the same time. A few of these contemporary folk games were indigenous to New York; others such as "Who you gonna marry—what you gonna feed him" have unusual implications! Even grownups could learn to play these games at once. The fact that we all participated *actively* and *immediately* and that this participation was the main factor contributing to our enjoyment gave us a great deal to think about in evaluating the usual games taught to children in school. There is room for all kinds of singing games but surely we should be aware of how the games we teach are used outside of school; we should also give thought to the values of children and the reasons they turn to *today's* folk material for games.

Make-up Songs

Much has been said and written about the child's creative songs, and a number of songs illustrating his free and spontaneous expression have been recorded. Some of these first songs have a charm and freshness all their own, but their

13 For a discussion on games for younger children see Emma Dickson Sheehy, *The Fives and Sixes Go to School*, New York: Holt.
14 Recorded from street singing for Folkways by Tony Schwartz.

importance lies not so much in their intrinsic musical value
as in what happens to the child as he sings them. We may
choose to record a few of them quietly and unobtrusively, or
help the child to find them on an instrument, and then sing
or play them back to him. If this procedure serves to stimulate him to more music-making, well and good; but if, as
happens many times, the adult takes to refining and polishing
the product, or if the child becomes unduly conscious of his
own genius and basks in the reflected glory of his creation,
it is obvious that it is not only his musical development
that suffers!

It is important that these beginnings of music-making
should focus on the constant encouragement of this *way of
expressing himself* and not on the product itself. As the child
grows older and is consciously interested in composing songs
and having them recorded, and even learning how to record
them himself, he becomes more aware of his ability to create.
If, however, this stage of development (which belongs to a
later period) is forced on him prematurely, he is likely, in
his preoccupation with the symbols of music, to miss the core
of the art that the symbols represent. What is important is
not the preservation of any special song that a child creates,
but the preservation of a way of life that will keep on inspiring him to experiment freely.

One of the most successful music teachers I have known
tells me that she has become very cautious in recording the
spontaneous evocative song of younger children. She finds it
difficult to catch it just as it is sung and when she asks for it
to be repeated, it so easily loses its vitality.

Creativity in song evidences itself in many ways. Invention in pure sound, variations both in words and melody of
songs already known, chanting, repetition of phrases or words
that fall into a simple form, singing words that are the
natural expression of a mood or result from an experience
that has particular meaning, experimentation with a melodic
instrument—all of these and many others are ways in which

children tell us that music is an art which is functioning in their lives. We need to be on the alert to *hear the creativity that children bring us.*

A skilled teacher may be able to record some of this creative singing in notation, note by note, or catch the beginning and ends of phrases, or more simply, record the general line of direction of the melody in the way our earliest musical "notation" was recorded. Children, too, are interested in the way notation grew.[15]

The most accurate, direct and satisfying way of recording creative song is on a tape recorder. One can hear it as often as one wishes. Discriminating listening may bring changes and refinement resulting in a satisfying permanent record. Or the creative song may be transferred directly to a melodic instrument and then recorded in notation. Some boys and girls become highly skilled in doing this. Occasionally someone has such a keen tonal memory and an ability to reproduce accurately what he hears that he can give back to the child or group the song as it was sung. Frequently the interest in the song itself may change into a very real interest in the process of notation itself; when notation has *real* meaning for children it arouses their curiosity and they are eager to learn about it.

Accompaniment for Songs

From time to time there have been heated arguments as to the merits of teaching songs with or without an accompaniment. Singing does not take place in a vacuum. It is a part of the total setting and there are many factors influencing this setting. A song can be supported in many ways, the most necessary and always important one being the *encouraging climate* of the group, either in the family or in school.

A great deal of the time, especially with little children,

[15] Marion Bauer and Ethel Peyser, *How Music Grew,* New York: Putnam.

we sing without an instrument, informally, and when the mood is upon us. Children enjoy the attractively illustrated song books both in our own language and in foreign languages. Many parents and nursery-school teachers make a practice of sitting down with a child or a small group every day for storytelling or reading. A special time for singing each day is also welcomed by the nursery-age child. One, of course, never forces a child to be a part of such an experience but it is our responsibility to make the experience attractive and inviting. It is very important that music for the youngest be more than accidental. At times the child will be so engrossed in the picture about the song that one wonders if he even hears what the adult is singing. At other times he will join in with enthusiasm.

Aside from the musical value of this experience there is also the opportunity of getting acquainted with attractive books beautifully illustrated. Some of the picture song books listed at the end of this chapter are illustrated by famous artists such as Willebeck Le Mair, Walter Crane, and Boutet de Montville. Collecting singing books including those from other countries is a good hobby for parents and teachers to cultivate. These books will be used more frequently if they are kept in the child's library rather than just on the piano. There are many times, too, with younger children, when looking up a song in the index turns into a reading experience. *Attractive books* then invite singing and make a fitting accompaniment for songs.

Many teachers have found the *autoharp* and *guitar* to be specially appropriate in accompanying songs. The autoharp is easy to play, even younger children being quick, through their own experimentation, to learn when to play the right chord. The guitar is, of course, more flexible and even more useful than the autoharp. If the teacher plays no musical instrument, this is a good one to learn. A few lessons and *steady* practice will give the adult not only enjoyable recreation for himself but also a valuable accompaniment for supporting songs. Both the autoharp and guitar are informal instruments. They do not get between the teacher and children and they can be carried anywhere. An accordion, too, is a wonderful accompaniment for certain kinds of singing.

If children are encouraged and given an opportunity, they become very adept in choosing accompaniments for their singing. All types of percussive sounds from those on temple blocks to the snapping of fingers may be used for certain songs. As they listen, children find that at times the restrained use of such sounds serves to make the song more interesting than if used steadily. They pick up many ideas from television and radio and also become very inventive. Trying this, that, and the other encourages listening and discrimination. Older boys and girls enjoy working in small groups with a song, each group using its imagination and resourcefulness in accompaniment. From six or seven such groups in a classroom will come a great variety of sound accompaniments.

If we think back to our own experiences we may recall some *strange ways* in which we accompanied our singing. One recalls the "perfect" accompaniment of the treadle of an old-fashioned sewing machine. With a hymn book open on the leaf of the machine the singer went through the book from beginning to the end with the rhythm and sound of the treadle which she worked as she sang. Another remembers the satisfaction of playing songs on the porch-rail "piano" with many pianistic flourishes to accompany her singing. The composer Grétry sang his songs as a child to the music of his grandmother's singing tea kettle. And a recent student [16] recollects the singing that went on when she and her sister fed the chickens—"the louder we sang the better we felt, and the better we felt the louder we sang, so you see how this thing can build up." Then, too, haven't we all found songs to be wonderful traveling companions, accompanied by the sound of the automobile as it whizzes along?

16 Jacqueline Oleson.

Songs on radio, records, and television are not only a stimulus for singing but also give us real support. In this case we accompany the song with our voice, hands, or tapping of feet or sometimes with a simple instrument. An interesting adventure in sound is the Concord record of the music of Gilbert and Sullivan's *H.M.S. Pinafore*. The libretto of the opera goes with the record and the listener can sing along with the music.

Movement can also be used very effectively in enhancing a song. The viewer with an eye for movement will find many examples of this on television and in musical plays. Again this is a fruitful field for experimentation.

The *piano* is probably the most widely used and most valuable accompaniment for singing. From the use of the melody only to help the child learn the song to the use of the entire musical score as a support for group singing, the piano is an indispensable instrument, providing it does not drown out the voices of the singers. Many classrooms do not have a piano but we hope that the school piano can have a visiting schedule to individual classrooms so that there is an opportunity to enjoy its possibilities in accompanying singing in classrooms and not only in assemblies. Other musical instruments such as the *recorder, flute,* and *violin* provide a delightful variety of accompaniments for singing.

There are many ways, then, of accompanying songs. The world of sound as explored through the media just discussed is a vast resource that can evoke children's ingenuity and offer genuine musical ways for promoting listening, discrimination, and musical growth. There is no one right way to accompany a song—there are choices, many of them, and the thoughtful decisions by children and adults are a real part of a musical education. When children live in a rich musical environment, they acquire an almost uncanny ability to sort out the good from the poor. They may go overboard at times for an insignificant song or inappropriate accompaniment, but in the long run their taste—if it is the result of many experiences—tends to stand up unusually well.

Child Voice

The "high, sweet voice" so often attributed to little children is a myth so far as most youngsters are concerned. The average range of tones is from around middle C to C or D above. For the nursery-age child, songs within five or even three tones are more easily learned than those that have a wider range, but not all children are alike and some very young children show uncanny skill with their voices. Naturally, a child should *hear more* than these songs, but if his singing voice is to be encouraged he should be exposed to many songs that are easy for him. That is why folk material has a great appeal.

Jersild and Bienstock report [17] that while children sing more easily when a song is changed to a lower pitch, they tend to use higher tones in the spontaneous use of their voices. This study emphasized the importance of helping children discover their singing potentiality at least by the end of the third grade; otherwise there is a danger of their falling into the habit of not using their singing voices—a habit difficult to compensate for later.

When it comes to singing ability, some people are born lucky, having a keen sensitivity to pitch plus a natural ability to sing easily and accurately. At the opposite end of the pole are the persons who are called "tone deaf." It has been estimated that in any given group one child may be two hundred times as sensitive to pitch as another. This by no means implies that every person is aware of his full potentiality; intelligent training can be of inestimable value if it is directed to the full exploration of that potentiality.

[17] Arthur T. Jersild and Gregory Bienstock, "A Study of the Development of Children's Ability to Sing," *Journal of Educational Psychology*, October 1934.

It is unfortunate that children who use a limited range of their voices are often called "monotones." There *may* be real monotones, though in our experience with many children over a period of years we have not encountered a single one. True, some children's singing voices tend toward monotony, lacking flexibility; usually their speaking voices show the same tendency, lacking inflection. If we have sharp ears we can notice that these same children frequently use a different register of their voices during spontaneous play. In other words, the motivation of the play spirit calls forth from the child a higher pitch of his voice than any singing experience would do. We have found it helpful to utilize, *at the time it happens,* this type of experience—not in a formal way, so that the child is conscious of the fact, but by joining in his play. High places may stimulate the use of the higher register of the voice.

It is not, then, specific vocal training that will encourage a child to find "different places" in his voice so much as the way in which we encourage him to "play" with his voice and gradually help him be aware of its possibilities. What these children need most of all is to be helped to get a "spring" in their voices, to be encouraged in the sheer manipulation of sound. They should at the same time get acquainted with many songs that are easy for them to sing. There is nothing quite so frustrating to anyone, young or old, as to be constantly confronted with experiences in which they cannot achieve conscious success.

Yet we have thoughtlessly exposed so many, many children in school to experiences in singing with the expectancy that if they try hard enough they can "reach" the song taught. A student recently expressed her dilemma. "I have a low voice and I couldn't learn to sing alto, so I just stopped singing." The class reaction was appalling. At least fifteen teachers had had similar experiences! Is there anything wrong with a low voice and does a low voice have to sing alto in order to sing? Certainly if that person wishes to be in a choral group, she will have to sing with the voices that are in her range. But the majority of people do not sing in choral groups. Should they therefore stop singing?

Listen to any group of adults singing in church. What happens when the hymn soars? The choir carries it with a few high voices in the congregation. The majority wait for it to come within their range. Why is it that the popular singers on radio and records and television "teach" songs so quickly to the listeners in the home? Their songs are within an easy singing range that most people can cope with. So the listener hums or sings along and almost unconsciously he learns the song.

Having worked with children and teachers for so many years, I thought that I was aware of the great variations in voices and of the fact that the majority of people, young and old, have "middle" rather than high voices. It was, however, brought home very realistically to me several years ago in a series of television programs for children which I conducted. I sang songs usually in the key of F or G and sometimes in D, depending on the song. Almost immediately came telephone calls and letters—many of them; I was singing too high! Mothers and children could not sing the songs. I protested at first but one doesn't protest long in such a situation. One listens to one's audience and since I wanted my viewers and listeners to sing with me, I took their objections seriously. So I listened carefully to folk singers and others like Rosemary Clooney whose singing on records, radio, and television "invited" the listener to sing, too. I discovered that they used almost exclusively a middle range of tones. I tried singing in a lower key and immediately received enthusiastic response.

Voices are different. Not all voices are low or middle range but neither are all voices high. Let us then be sure that we have songs suitable for all and songs that will encourage everyone to keep on singing. Many with "middle" voices have not touched their potentialities in this matter of range, but they will do it only when they are comfortable where they are and when we have respect for what they can do.

On returning from a tour of the Near and Far East, Eleanor Steber commented on the low range of the Eastern voice and said that "the Indians have difficulty in understanding the western female voice." Indian voices are trained in the lower register and the emphasis is on quality—purity and timbre of tone. Is not this an interesting observation?

Another characteristic of children's singing for which we must be prepared is that it is more vigorous than exact. There are times when a youngster feels like giving all he has, and that can be a great deal! He is full of robust feelings, and the sweet, light voice so often demanded by singing teachers in no way measures up to these feelings. Children's moods, however, are not always dynamic. If they have a legitimate amount of outlet for their strong feelings, they will tend toward a balance, so that there will be many times when they find it natural to sing less vigorously. It is our job to see that they have music to fit all their moods and to recognize the *importance of balance* in their experiences.

Skills in Singing

All through this chapter on singing, we have tried to keep in the reader's mind not only the characteristics of children's singing but also the ways in which we can help children to a better use of their voices. We believe that skills in the use of the voice are developed primarily by the many informal day-by-day experiences rather than by specific training.

What then of the techniques that have been the music supervisor's stand-by in training the child's voice? For example, is there no place for the tone drill (matching tones of another voice or of an instrument), the echo game, the pass word, the singing names, the question-and-answer, and other exercises?

If we are observant, we can find the roots of practically all these techniques in the daily play of children. Not that it is wise to utilize every opportunity, but there are many times when a child will welcome this variation of his play so long as the adult is careful that it does not become forced or artificial. Occasionally with older children some of these games can be carried over to a "music time." If the child welcomes this, well and good; but if he becomes self-conscious, the procedure defeats its purpose.

As children gradually become aware of their own skills and also their lack of skills in singing, they begin to reach out for and become receptive to specific help in the use of their voices. It is then that we have their cooperation and we can work, and *work hard,* together with them on the skills needed. When such training is well timed it is successful. If, however, it tends to make the boy or girl more self-conscious, nothing is gained. Rather, a great deal is lost.

In our concern for developing skills we must always keep in mind the following:

• Remember that love of singing is of first importance.

• Use specific training only if you have the child's interest and cooperation.

• Be careful to differentiate between improvement and accuracy.

• Do not resort to competition in order to raise standards.

• Encourage children to listen to their own voices and to the voices of others.

Teaching Songs

We don't really know too much about teaching singing, that is, the experts don't! There are many methods and all singing teachers have their favorite method, but as one famous music critic has observed, "a unique hazard of vocal study is that in many cases the longer one studies the worse one sings." Certainly this should not be true where teachers are imaginative and understanding and adapt their method to fit the individual.

The most effective teaching of songs occurs when the song fits the mood of the children. This does not mean that every activity a child engages in must have a song experience related to it. Though a song about a train may sometimes be just what a child will welcome if he is engaged in building a train or is studying transportation, this is not invariably true. Music is not of the intellect, and a sensitive person will feel the mood of a child in bringing him a sensory experience. The adult must *know* the song, and present it free of mannerisms and dramatic affectations; what is required is good enunciation and simple directness together with a pleasant quality of tone.

Songs are made to be sung, not to be talked about, and *preliminary* explanations and discussions are thus not only unnecessary but inartistic. The song should be sung through from beginning to end, and we must not be disturbed if children's enthusiasms urge them to join in even before they know what is coming next. *After* they have participated, they will usually be willing to listen to the song several times without trying to sing it. The piece-by-piece method of teaching a song, whether by words or by phrases, does not hold up in the light of our knowledge of the psychology of learning. If there are parts of the song that give difficulty, these can be worked on independently *after* the listeners have heard the song in its entirety at least a few times. A good song is a moving, flowing thing and isolating parts of it *before* the feeling for this movement is established hinders rather than helps in the learning of the whole.

Many times we adults try to direct children's lives before we find out in which direction they are going. Parents in the home are usually pretty well aware of the songs that are important to their children. In schools, however, we may work on the application of a music program and ignore what children actually know. So one of our first important jobs is to discover their musical interests. This is not easy and each person has to find his own way. Can we live with children in school so that we can know about their favorite songs, so they can tell us something of themselves in music, *so* we can have something to take hold of?

Teachers encourage boys and girls to bring their favorite books to school. Why not favorite songs, too? A teacher of eleven- and twelve-year-olds made this request and suggested that there were many ways for doing this and all would be welcomed. The ways used by these resourceful and imaginative children included playing the song on an instrument, singing it, clapping its rhythm, dancing to it, pantomiming it, humming or whistling it, drawing a picture of it (others would have to guess what song was represented), bringing another person to play or sing the song, or bringing a recording of it. Most important were the interest and enthusiasm generated by this opportunity and the resulting imagination in song accompaniment utilized with the songs taught in school. Children can be on a single track musically (so can we), but if we are aware of that track, we can do a much more intelligent job in enriching their experiences in song.

Children enjoy bringing songs to school. Unless the kind of songs we teach them are those which are remembered and can be "taken home," our music program is on the wrong track. We are thinking, of course, about the songs they know and that have become a part of their lives. A few years ago, a teacher of five-year-olds initiated an idea that spread throughout the entire elementary school. At the end of each school year, she chose about a dozen of the children's favorite songs of that year, cut stencils of the words and melodies, mimeographed them, and enclosed them in gay folders. Each child had his own song book to take home. As this class proceeded through the school, there was no question about an end-of-the-year music book for each grade!

Wherever the child is, at home or at school, his singing environment must be free of tensions and conflicts. Pleasant, "easy" surroundings are an absolute requisite if we wish a child to develop an interest in and love for singing. If all of us who are interested in children's musical development concern ourselves less with "the teaching of singing" and more with seeing to it that singing is something that goes on in our family or in our school, the results—the kind of results that really count—will bob up of their own ccord.

SONG BOOKS

Illustrated collections of songs intended especially for the very young child are marked with an asterisk (*). It would be very unfortunate, however, if the other books listed here were not recognized and explored as sources for songs for the younger as well as for older boys and girls and adults.

* Abeson, Marion, and Charity Bailey, *Playtime with Music,* New York: Liveright.

Ames, Russell, *The Story of American Folk Song,* New York: Grosset and Dunlap.

Association for Childhood Education International, *Songs Children Like,* Washington, D. C.

Attaway, William, *Calypso Song Book,* New York: McGraw-Hill.

Best, Dick and Beth, *The New Song Fest,* New York: Crown.

Boni, Margaret Bradford, and Norman Lloyd, *Fireside Book of Favorite American Songs,* New York: Simon and Schuster.

——— and ———, *Fireside Book of Folk Songs,* New York: Simon and Schuster.

Botkin, B. A. (ed.), *The Pocket Treasury of American Folklore,* New York: Pocket Books.

Brand, Oscar, *Singing Holidays: The Calendar in Folk Song,* New York: Knopf.

Chase, Richard (ed.), *American Folk Tales and Songs,* New York: New American Library.

Coleman, Satis, and Elkin K. Jorgensen, *Christmas Carols from Many Countries,* New York: Schirmer. Original language and translations.

* —— and Alice G. Thorn, *Singing Time,* New York: Day.

Cooperative Recreation Service, Delaware, Ohio. Inexpensive paperback pamphlets of a variety of songs.

* Crane, Alter (ed.), *The Baby's Bouquet,* New York: Warne.

Dearmer, Percy, R. Vaughan Williams, and Martin Shaw, *The Oxford Book of Carols,* New York: Oxford. A classic collection of carols.

Eisenstein, Judith, and Frieda Prensky (eds.), *Songs of Childhood,* New York: United Synagogue of America.

* Elkin, R. H., and J. Röntgen, *Old Dutch Nursery Songs,* New York: McKay. Out of print.

Greenberg, Noah, and others (eds.), *An Elizabethan Song Book,* New York: Doubleday.

* Hader, Berta and Elmer, *Mother Goose Picture Book,* New York: Macmillan. Out of print.

* Hunt, Evelyn H., *Music Time,* New York: Viking.

Ives, Burl (ed.), *The Burl Ives Sea Songs,* New York: Ballantine. Paperbound.

——, *The Burl Ives Song Book,* New York: Ballantine.

Johnson, Margaret and Travis, *Early American Songs,* New York: Associated Music Publishers.

Kapp, Paul, *A Cat Came Fiddling,* New York: Harcourt, Brace.

Kolb, Sylvia and John (eds.), *A Treasury of Folk Songs,* New York: Bantam. Interesting background comments on songs.

Krugman, Lillian, and Alice Ludnig, *Little Calypsos,* New York: Van Roy.

* Landeck, B., *More Songs to Grow On,* New York: Sloane.

* Lloyd, Norman, *The New Golden Song Book,* New York: Simon and Schuster.

—— and M. R. Beatty, *Songs We Sing from Rodgers and Hammerstein,* New York: Simon and Schuster. Simple piano accompaniments.

* MacCarthey, Ellen P., *Songs for the Nursery School,* New York: Willis Music Co. Excellent collection.

Marais and Miranda, *Folk Songs from South Africa,* New York: Hansen Music Corp.

* Mason, Agnes Leckie, and Phyllis B. Ohanian, *God's Wonderful World,* New York: Random House.

Morehead, James and Albert (eds.), *101 Favorite Hymns,* New York: Pocket Books.

Newgate, Leslie (ed.), *The Penguin Song Book,* New York: Penguin.

* Ohanian, Phyllis, *Favorite Nursery Songs,* New York: Random House.

* Potter, Edna, *This Way and That,* New York: Oxford. Twenty-four singing games. Out of print.

* Seeger, Ruth Crawford, *American Folk Songs for Children,* New York: Doubleday. Outstanding.

Taylor, Cyril V. (ed.), *The Hawthorn Book of Christmas Carols,* New York: Hawthorn.

Tobitt, Janet, *Sing Together,* New York: Girl Scouts.

* Van de Velde, Ernest, *Rondes et Chansons,* Paris: Marne.

———, *Chansons Danson,* Paris: Marne.

———, *Chansons Noël,* Paris: Marne.

Wilson, Harry Robert, *Songs of Hills and Plains,* Chicago: Hall and McCreary. Out of print.

SOURCE BOOKS AND HISTORIES
OF AMERICAN SONG

Botkin, B. A. (ed.), *A Treasury of American Folklore,* New York: Crown.

Lomax, John A. and Alan, *American Ballads and Folk Songs,* New York: The Macmillan Company.

——— and ———, *Our Singing Country,* New York: The Macmillan Company. Out of print.

Luther, Frank, *Americans and Their Songs,* New York: McGraw-Hill. Out of print.

Sandburg, Carl, *The American Songbag,* New York: Harcourt, Brace.

Scarborough, Dorothy, *A Song Catcher in Southern Mountains,* Boulder, Colo.: University of Colorado Press.

Shay, Frank, *American Sea Songs and Chanteys,* New York: Norton. Out of print.

Thomas, Jean, *Ballad Makin' in the Mountains of Kentuc',* New York: Holt. Out of print.

Chapter 5

INSTRUMENTS

People of all ages and from all over the world have found and are finding ways of nurturing and developing their interest in sound through a great variety of instruments. Composers and conductors of orchestras keep searching and trying to capture certain "sound ideas" by discovering and inventing new instruments. Their success as far as the listener is concerned is measured by the degree of one's tolerance for the unexpected, the new, and the strange. The musician or the musical listener who has long been a student of the classics may reject, or welcome, such experimentation.

Many composers of contemporary music have no hesitation in pushing beyond the conventional barriers in order to capture more firmly their musical ideas. A composer's working materials are the combination and movement of sounds. To the extent that he wishes to reflect the complexities of today's world with its sounds and movement, he will inevitably have to use a musical language that will convey these. Not a few composers invent new instruments that will give just the right effect. John Cage has been experimenting for a number of years to enrich music through inventions in sound. His abstract compositions call for strange sounds and

78

combinations of sounds in which a "prepared" piano is featured prominently. He has a small but devoted coterie of
followers, but many others feel that he has limited himself
in regard to melodic structure.

Edgar Varese depends on electronics for his sound adventures and uses tapes, transmitting them on stereophonic systems. The composer Ernest Toch invents new instruments
in order to reproduce his sound ideas. William Steinberg
conducted the Pittsburgh Symphony Orchestra recently in
Toch's Third Symphony. The score calls for a special use
of the Hammond organ, a rotarian—a rectangular wooden
box in which croquet balls are placed and moved around by
a hand crank—and a hisser, the hissing being produced by
releasing carbon dioxide through a valve. I did not find it
easy to follow certain parts of the symphony—at least on its
first hearing—but neither was I endowed with Mr. Toch's
sound imagination. Whether we welcome this kind of experimentation or not, we certainly cannot say that it has no
significance.

Several years ago I attended a series of concerts at the
New York Museum of Modern Art. The music was by modern composers and it was conducted by Leopold Stokowski,
a musician who has always encouraged the development of
the new in music. Stokowski is not only a great musician but
he also has an understanding of the psychology of listening.
The concerts were delightfully informal. After he had played
one particular new composition, he commented on it briefly.
"Would you like to hear it again?" he asked as he noted the
interest of the audience. Prefaced with just a few more comments by Stokowski the repeat performance of this work took
on new meaning, at least for a number of listeners. Although conventional instruments were used for the most
part, I was intrigued by three hollow boxes of graduated
sizes with one side open, resembling the nest of fitted hollow
blocks that little children play with—only much larger. These

were played by a tapper moved rapidly by the player from one side to the other on the inside of the box. A resulting liquid quality of tone was not unlike that of Far Eastern wooden temple bells.

A short while ago I visited the Carroll Musical Instrument Service in New York, on the search for different sounds in instruments that would be appropriate for children's use. The service collects, mostly for rental, instruments and sound effects from all over the world. For example, in just one category alone, bells, over one hundred and fifty different bells are listed in Carroll's fabulous catalog of sounds. Mr. Carroll, a graduate of one of our largest music institutes, played percussion in orchestras for many years. He had played percussion in the Stokowski concerts and was responsible for the sound boxes. His interest in sound and instruments led to the establishment of his well-known instrument service which produces any and every variety of sound needed. "Musicians and 'sound-effects people' do not ask me *if* I *have* a particular instrument or sound. They order it and if I do not have what they need, I search for it or invent it!" said Mr. Carroll. Certainly a knowledge of the vast resources in the field of sound does more in a short time than anything else to make one aware of the unlimited possibilities of the world of instruments.

The great variety of instruments from Far Eastern countries offers an unusually rich source of acquainting our ears with new and different sounds. In the Pillsbury Foundation studies (I, *Chant,* p. 3), the investigators chose sarons from Java and Bali, bells and gongs from China and Burma, and drums from Japan, Korea, and China, among other instruments, for children's use. These offered no technical difficulty and yet provided unique tone qualities and variations in timbre. The reader may be interested to know that the Pillsbury studies were carried out at the suggestion of Dr. Stokowski.

Occasionally television and radio offer an opportunity to

get acquainted with the music of other cultures through the playing of instruments. Some time ago, in a never-to-be-forgotten television program, Yehudi Menuhin introduced two of India's outstanding musicians who played the sarod (a string instrument) and tabla (drums). His interpretation of the Indian raga was skillful and his deep respect and fascination for this music was infectious.

Colin McPhee [1] reports the delight the Balinese take in using small bells. "In the sky, during the windy months, long kites, furnished with vibrant strings, throb in wiry chorus. Small bells are attached to everything—to oxen's yokes, weaver's shuttles, pony carts, even to the necks of pigeons, along with tiny whistles, to make shrill music when the birds are released to wheel above the trees."

I have introduced this chapter with illustrations of music-makers which adults are using as instruments, some new, some representing other cultures. Our awareness of the many varied kinds of instruments will help to free us so that, together with children, we shall reach out to and recognize new musical possibilities. Of course, we shall not attempt to emulate the skills, for example, of an Indian who plays the tabla or drums. His skill is the result of long training, and is rooted in the culture of his country and his knowledge of the intricacies and possibilities of Indian music. But the drums can be played by the smallest child in his own way. Should not the resourcefulness of people like Stokowski, Toch, Cage, and countless others give us courage to explore in different and hitherto unthought-of ways of making music? If boys and girls know that we have such an interest, we do not need to worry about supplying ways and means. Encourage the curiosity of children and it flourishes like mushrooms. Nor should we underestimate the influence their curiosities can have in keeping alive our own sensitivity to the joy of discovery.

[1] *Childhood in Contemporary Culture*, edited by Margaret Mead and Martha Wolfenstein, Chicago, Ill.; University of Chicago.

Drums

The choice of instruments for little children and the way in which they are used demand just as much thoughtful consideration as selecting instruments for older children. If we have respect for the learning capacities during these early years—when they are greater than at any other time during life—we shall not be likely to choose just any instrument that pleases our fancy. Most toy instruments have as little intrinsic worth as toy tools or toy cleaning sets, which appeal to the adult because they are cute, little, and inexpensive. But this does not mean that children's instruments need be expensive, for it is a matter not so much of cost as of careful choice.

Drums are among the most satisfactory instruments for children, and some of the best ones can be made at home. Large cans, wooden mixing bowls, acid pails, butter tubs, nail keys, and large barrels can be used. (Little children cannot make these drums alone, but they will love to help other members of the family make them.) The inner tube of an automobile tire stretched tightly across one end of a tub or barrel gives a deep, resounding, primitive sound. Better still is a skin drumhead which can be secured at a musical-instrument supply store; "seconds" are less expensive and just as satisfactory as new ones. When buying a drumhead, either new or secondhand, hold it up to the light to detect thin or weak spots. Also the skin diameter must be two inches wider than the diameter of the keg.

How to Make a Drum

First prepare the keg or pail or bowl by sanding and filing down the rim if it is thick. Too broad a rim offers resistance to the vibration of the drumhead and affects the sound. Soak the skin for one to two hours (or longer if necessary) to soften it. Stretch it fairly taut across the top of the base and then anchor it with thumbtacks placed about an inch apart but pushed in only part way. Let the head dry overnight and if the next day is not humid, test the drum. If the head is stretched too tightly, the sound will be sharp and brittle; if too loosely, it will have little resonance. If you are successful the first time in getting a good drum tone, secure the skin permanently with upholstery tacks. If not, the skin will have to be soaked again and the process repeated. Recently some students have had considerable success with a new kind of glue in securing the skin to the base. The drums have not been used long enough to determine how this will hold. Large fiber containers bought at a cooper's or salvaged from supply rooms give a beautifully resonant tone. The skins have to be laced or glued on or held taut by a metal band. These are lightweight and less expensive than wood. A screen-door handle attached to the side of the keg makes it easy to carry the drum.

Some people prefer to use leather or nylon thongs to lace the drumhead on. In this way a metal container can be used for the base. Creative Playthings, Inc., of New York sells a "do-it-yourself kit" including wooden keg, drumhead secured on a wooden hoop, and lacings. This drum has the advantage of responding to tuning when needed, according to weather conditions. Substitutes for skin drumheads, such as chamois or paper parchment, are often suggested in order to save money. The result looks like a drum but does not have a satisfactory sound, since these materials do not have good sounding qualities. The emphasis in this discussion is on securing the best possible sound quality and not on appearance!

A head made of skin is superior to a rubber one because it is easier to control the sound; when rubber is struck rapidly, the sounds overlap and are muffled. Both kinds, however, are useful; in fact, a variety of sizes and shapes of drums will add more interest to children's experimentation. A pair of "bongas"—two small but different-sized drums attached to each other in Siamese fashion—offer an interesting contrast in sound. These are used in many small orchestras and can be purchased at instrument stores.

One of the most satisfactory types of commercial drums is the large Chinese tom-tom that can be placed on the floor or on a low table. These drums are strong and sturdy and stand up remarkably well under use. Their pigskin heads seem to be less affected by atmospheric pressure than other kinds of skins. It is difficult to secure these today but occasionally one may be picked up at a secondhand shop.

A pair of regular timpani sticks padded with lamb's wool (they can be bought at a music store) will prove a very worthwhile investment. If it is not possible to get these, they may be made by wrapping the ends of two sticks with firm padding. Try out the padding in order to find the kind that will produce the best sound, for it must be neither too hard nor too soft.

Besides the large drums, there are, of course, a variety of small ones of the snare and tom-tom type that are usually sold for children's use. They enjoy carrying these drums around and using them in dramatic play, as in parades and processions. The regulation small boy's parade drum is suspended by a cord around his neck, and swings along in front of him as he walks, making it difficult for him to play on it with any degree of regularity. The Indian tom-tom, made from a tree trunk and small enough to fit under his arm, is much easier to manage. The wooden mixing-bowl drum, in the center of which a hole large enough for a forefinger has been bored, is also easily handled. The snare drum is more appropriate for the older child's use than for the young child. Skill is required to play it effectively and so it does not lend itself to the kind of experimentation that the young child brings to drumming or, shall I say, the kind of sound exploration that most adults can accept!

Use of Drums and Other Percussion Instruments

Experience leads us to believe that the most thoughtful experimentation is best encouraged when the drum is placed in a convenient position so that the child is free to use both hands in playing. Moreover such a position allows the child to develop his feeling for rhythm more freely because his body can move naturally as he plays, and all this, in turn, helps his playing as a whole. Perhaps the best results are obtained when the child is standing and the drum is placed at a level so that his stick or hands will drop on it easily. Or he may prefer to sit down, or kneel, or sit on the floor when using it. In any case, his body should be free and uncramped.

The outdoors is an ideal place for little children to use drums. Their first attempts are sure to be full of vim and vigor, and this is as it should be. We must not ask for control too soon, for children do not want to play "lightly." Remember, too, that a hard stick used vigorously on a drumhead can make a very unpleasant sound, whereas a padded stick can be used with full force and yet be free from harshness.

It is a good idea, especially in nursery, kindergarten, and primary groups, to set aside for the use of instruments special corners that are off the line of traffic, removed from the noisy activities of woodwork or block building. Then the young musicians are not distracted and they can *hear* what they are playing.

Children should be given every opportunity to try out these instruments in their own way. By this we mean *legitimate* experimentation for the purpose of sound- and music-making. Obviously, musical instruments should be respected as such, and not rolled around like balls or pounded with hammers.

Older boys and girls can plan for special times of the day when individuals may have an opportunity to get acquainted with instruments. A few well-chosen drums and other percussion instruments available for a short time each day during a general activity period may be a possible solution. The first use of these will probably be noisy but except for the tense child (for whom this may well be excellent therapy) the player or players very soon become interested in a more controlled use of the instruments.

Here are some of the things children discover about drums:

1. Not only the head but also the sides and the edges of a drum can be played on.

2. Weather changes the sound of drums, because of its effect on the skin.

3. The sound of the drum comes from the vibration of the head which moves the air. This vibration can be *felt,* on a large drum, by putting the hand very close to it as it is played, and *seen,* by putting a small amount of sawdust or sand on the head and watching it move round as the drum is played.

4. Different drums have surprisingly different sounds. After a child is familiar with the sounds of several specific drums, he may enjoy playing a game in which he only listens, trying to decide which drum is being played. This is a good test of ear discrimination and can be made increasingly difficult when the child is ready for it.

5. The same drumhead sounds different when struck at different places. Usually a spot near the side produces a better effect than does the exact center, that is, the spot which allows the skin to vibrate most freely.

6. The hands may be used in various ways to play a drum, and some drums respond better to hands than to sticks.

7. Children can gradually be helped to *feel* and *hear* that when a sound is "pulled out" of the drum it is much better than when "beaten in." A quick staccato touch allows the skin to vibrate. Children are often helped to understand this principle by pretending the drum is "hot."

8. Drums may be played loud or soft, fast or slow. Much experimentation is possible not only with rhythm and intensity but also with combinations of drums.

It will not be long before a child falls into a regular rhythm when playing on a drum, and we must be sure to let this happen naturally. The opportunity comes when we hear it happen; we can then register it for him by repeating what he has done or by helping him repeat it. When he has established a rhythm, he may enjoy having us play with him, either on another drum or on his, provided we do not run away with the show. If he can maintain a steady rhythm, it is fun to pick it up, carry it along with one hand, and improvise a secondary rhythm with the other. This relieves the monotony of the steady beat and gives the child a new experience; sometimes he will be able to take over the "orchestration" while we provide the primary rhythm. Older boys and girls enjoy "talking to each other" with drums. They are interested in the way drums are used in primitive countries for sending messages. They frequently develop some very interesting forms in sound.

For another interesting experiment, place four or five drums at varying distances from each other in a circular formation, leaving enough space in the center so that the child can move freely from one instrument to another. The rhythm produced as he moves from one to the other, dropping the end of his stick (or his hand) on each instrument in turn, is determined by the placement of the drums. The movement of the body provides the primary rhythm, and the instruments the secondary one. This type of experimentation has endless possibilities in contrasts of sound and rhythm, and grownups will enjoy it too. It is just another way of discovering and developing into form the rhythm that we have in us, instead of approaching it from the mechanical end of "counting out."

(Speaking of adults, especially those who do not play an instrument, there is no group of instruments that offers such a thoroughly good time as percussion. Some of the "unmusical" faculty members of one of our large eastern colleges have had an interesting time the last few years in a percussion orchestra. Great music is not the aim nor the result, but there is a tremendous amount of "self-expression" and fun in it.)

With little children, we are concerned with the individual use of instruments. They like to be near adults or other children, but each one likes to play his own way, whatever activity he may be engaged in. As they grow older, however, they become more interested in playing with others. In music, as in any other activity, this stage cannot be hurried. Usually between the ages of five and six, however, children begin to show interest in playing in a small *informal* group. Occasionally one of their number has sufficient initiative and ability to hold the group together. At other times an older person is needed to help organize their ideas, and supplement these if it is felt that the time is ripe.

The music corner of an outdoor playground lends itself particularly well to this first group playing; there the other children are not disturbed and the players are much freer to experiment with sound than they would be indoors.

Here is a typical example of the way in which group interest may develop and be enriched by guidance. The first important thing is to see that the interested children are protected from the noisy play of the rest of the group. Much of the time children will be sufficient unto themselves, but they like to know that a grownup is interested. You can always tell when you can add to what they are doing.

A group of three five-year-olds had been playing off and on together every morning for a week. They came to school early each day to help carry the drums to the playground, but especially to get a first turn in playing them. One day I heard them chanting as they played, in well-accented rhythm: "You better watch out for your whole life!" It kept getting louder and louder, and it seemed that it would never stop. Finally I suggested that music changes, has different parts, and that in an orchestra the instruments sometimes take turns in playing. Perhaps they might try something like that, using their voices part of the time and instruments part of the time.

The shouting, however, went on as before, only with more vigor and enthusiasm, and the next day's performance was the same except that almost all the rest of the group had joined in! Evidently the moment of readiness for the next step was not at hand.

On the third day, however, there was a variation in intensity, and just a beginning of a feeling for form. The children were really thinking about what they were doing; they experimented in various ways (sometimes with an adult helping and again by themselves), and after three days came through with the following arrangement.

DRUMS AND VOICES:
> *You better watch out for your whole life!*
> *You better watch out for your whole life!*

VOICES ALONE:
> *Better watch out—better watch out!*
> *Better watch out—better watch out!*

VOICES ALONE (hushed):
> *Shoo, shoo, shoo, shoo,*
> *Shoo, shoo, shoo . . .*

DRUMS AND VOICES:
> *You better watch out for your whole life!*

VOICES SHOUTING (finale):
> *Watch out!*

As the year went on, other instruments were *gradually* made available to the children but not until I felt that these instruments would enlarge their musical interests. For example, as the children became conscious of climax as part of form, they were given a large gong suspended on a stand. When I felt they would profit by new contrasts in sounds, Korean temple bells (hollow wooden bells) were introduced.

Placed on a table covered with a mat, they gave out a pleasant, "liquid" sound when tapped with a striker that had a hard rubber tip. Gourd rattles were used frequently, especially by the dancing members of the group, for very often the players were joined by dancers.

In the beginning these instruments were used without a piano, but later I occasionally added piano accompaniment in the form of simple improvised chords or music that would fit into the children's plan. In working with a group I sometimes found it helpful to ask one child to start playing, the others listening, until he had established his rhythm, then each one joining in when he *felt* the music would sound better by the addition of his instrument. Gradually, a feeling for the whole was built up, and children began to plan ahead and to repeat what they had already done. Basic to this type of group work is *long and unhurried time for individual use of instruments*—that is, if we are working honestly for children's progressive music development and not simply for products. The very different kinds of music that result depend on what instrument and what child take the lead.

This is the way children can work in a truly creative way with sound and rhythm. It is a slow process, but a rewarding one—at times even a thrilling one. We believe that the limitations lie in us grownups rather than in the children—in our inability to find material for music in the great variety of sounds that children make.

After the children have worked for some time with instruments, they enjoy "orchestrating" music that is played for them; this becomes a thoughtful musical experience, not an occasion for merely beating time. Often they work out a plan with their instruments and then ask for music to supplement or reinforce it. It is not uncommon for a child to go to the piano and either "improvise" the music himself or play enough to show us the character of the music he wishes to have.

But this is only *one* of the ways in which children develop

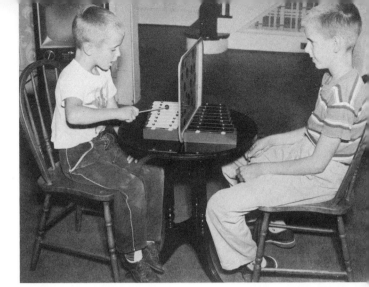

Raup Photo

Experimenting with percussion sounds—a resonator
game (above) and a marimba (below)

Irene Strauss

A drum composition offers opportunity for the discovery of sound vibrations

musically through the use of instruments. Unfortunately, we have found that all too frequently the procedure is to tie up the children's first experimentation with ready-made music— either by chanting nursery rhymes or with piano music. Children then depend on these accompaniments and, in turn, the rhymes or music become the stimuli without which the child is unwilling to play his instrument. A sensitive teacher will have to decide which she is working toward—quick sounding results or musical growth through child-initiated listening and creativity. Too often the only musical aspect stressed is "keeping time," which completely ignores the child's need to acquaint himself with all the elements of music.

Time and opportunity for children to find themselves and what they can do with a musical instrument are needed equally as much by older boys and girls. In the following illustration a teacher of eleven- and twelve-year-olds reports her classroom experience with drums.[2]

When we began using instruments we used just a few drums first—various children taking turns using them. Without my directing them those who did not have instruments improvised and used their hands, their feet, and so on, just as they had done in their previous experiences in sound without instruments.

I observed one particular boy who has many emotional problems. He attacked that drum with complete abandon and afterward was relaxed for the rest of the day, which was most unusual for him. Since then I have watched him and he constantly will tap out rhythms with anything that is available—a jar of marbles, a pencil, a piece of wood. This was particularly interesting to me as this is a child whose entire family is involved in music and yet he, up to this time, would not take part in any musical activity. He has an excellent voice, but he refused to sing. Now he not only sings with the group, but he volunteered to sing with a trio. The child had to develop his own desire—parent pressure obviously could not awaken this boy. Originally I had wondered how I would follow up the "sound" sessions, but I was pleased to find

2 Used by permission of Georgianna Teaford.

this was never any problem as the children always thought of something new to try. I was also very happy to see that all of the children were taking part. This was something that they could lose themselves in very easily and no one held back.

And then she goes on to comment on the carry-over into singing.

I found that when we sang, the children were trying out new variations—experimenting with new types of endings, patterns. They were keeping time to the music by clapping their hands, by moving their feet in various ways. Once we all took off our shoes and listened to the effect. We varied it by keeping one shoe on and taking one shoe off. Gradually the sounds which they discovered previously were now employed in their singing. I was tremendously pleased not only with the results or the products which were obtained but also with the experimentation that was continually taking place. Here was a group that was certainly developing, through continual experimentation, creativity and a wonderful open-mindedness. I don't believe that I am being far fetched in my last statement. Certainly this group, with its exposure to all types of sound, was not going to insist that modern music was the only good music, nor that classical music was the best, but that each had its own appeal.

Here is another example of children with percussion instruments. A class of ten-year-olds had a "jam" session with a variety of instruments in a gymnasium—a completely new experience for them. It was fascinating to watch individual reactions to this session. Some spent the first part of the time trying out the possibilities of all instruments, others stayed with their first choice. One became so delighted with a two-toned Indian bell from which the tapper had been removed and a hard rubber tapper supplied that he stayed with it the entire time, listening to it himself. Taking it from person to person, he held it close to each one's ear as he tapped it so all would have an opportunity to hear. One little girl discovered she could feel the sound vibrations while others played drums by holding her ear to the floor.

The first use of these instruments was individual but within a few minutes small groups of two to five children each began to form. Nor were these static groups. As they became more alert to sounds, individuals would move to another group with their instruments and join in. Various rhythmic patterns developed, contrasts in intensity were experienced, pauses came naturally, and the boy with the Indian bell never failed to use one of these pauses by punctuating it with a tap of his bell. This was a delight to everyone, and pauses no longer were accidental but were consciously sensed always with the expectancy of making a place for the bell.

This group became so interested in the percussive sounds that on their excursion to the park the next day they brought back to the classroom a variety of objects, all having been tested for sound. Flat stones that could be tapped together, an assortment of sticks for tapping or rubbing (some with notches) and a variety of small metal objects were the starting point of a steadily increasing group of sound-makers. These, together with one homemade drum and the borrowed Indian bell, were a part of the regular classroom equipment which the children used individually and in groups from time to time. Their teacher reports that much of the time in group experimentation only one or two instruments were used, the children turning to percussive use of hands and feet and their voices to make up the ensemble. Different children took turns leading with an instrument or with hands or feet or voice, the remainder waiting until the "theme" or rhythm was established and then feeling their way into the whole, thoughtfully and consciously, and "hearingly" made a composition. This group had no opportunity in school for learning to play usual musical instruments but certainly any kind of sound experiences that evoke such thoughtful and discriminating listening and choosing and sensing of tone relationships has real value musically.

The record *Exotic Dances* (Folkways) was supplied by the

teacher because of the interesting use of percussion instruments in the selections recorded, especially one in which the bell was featured. At times the children just listened to parts of the record, at other times they played their instruments (very thoughtfully) along with it. This record had real meaning for it added to and enriched their own discoveries.

In this classroom the experimentation was carried on with "quiet" instruments. It is not the kind of instrument that is important but the ways in which the teacher allows the children to use imaginatively what they have. A class which has no musical instruments can have a more creative musical experience in sounds than a class equipped with the latest and best, but with no permission to get acquainted with and use this musical equipment in ways that have musical meaning. It would indeed be unfortunate if this comment were interpreted to mean that a school does not need good, yes, the best of musical instruments!

I recall the experience of five- and six-year-olds with a camel bell that a child's father had brought to school. The next day I added a pair of elephant bells and a Swiss cowbell. Then bells of all sorts began to appear. Our bell table, covered with felt, was of great interest. Since the clappers inside the bells made it difficult for the ringer to control the sound, I removed them from the larger bells and suspended each bell on an improvised stand high enough for the children to stand in front of and play comfortably. I supplied sticks with hard rubber tips. For these children this provided a more creative musical experience. The stand became a testing rack for all kinds of objects—teacups suspended by handles, long nails, spikes, stones netted in twine, horseshoes, and so on. How exciting it was when we discovered that the sound of bottles could be changed by adding water.

In addition to the percussion instruments and objects used for producing sounds mentioned, there are a number of others, such as cymbals, tambourines, gongs, rhythm sticks, wood blocks, castanets, gourds, triangles, chimes, marimba, glockenspiels, and the assortment of orchestral and band drums—timpani, snare, bass. We hope that even the youngest children will be able to become acquainted with most of these. Special visits of a kettledrum, for example, to the classroom, where children have time to touch and play and find out what they can do with it, pay big dividends musically. Many classrooms have tambourines, triangles, wood blocks, and rhythm sticks. The point is: are these made available to children in the same way as other materials in the room—art, books, blocks—or does the teacher think of them only as parts of a rhythm band?

Not a few boys (and some girls, too) in elementary school have ambitions to become percussion players and they dream of possessing the entire range of percussion instruments. Naturally they see themselves as part of a band, but how unfortunate it is that the usual bands need so few percussion players. Whatever motivates them, the need to be part of the group is a persistent one.

A percussion instrument which achieves contrasts in sound (and in a quiet way) is the Ghana marimba. This has the usual marimba appearance, except that it has fewer tones. The bars, however, are not tuned to our scale nor are they intended to be. This is a good instrument for classroom use since it is not noisy and can be made by a teacher or older children. The different-length bars need to be mounted on felt placed on the base and must be attached *loosely* so they can vibrate when tapped. This should not be confused with our marimba which is tuned to the diatonic scale.

Simple Melody Instruments

Tonal instruments that give opportunity for melodic experimentation offer still another type of musical experience for children. Among these are a few that are easily moved from place to place. One of the most satisfactory portable instruments is a set of resonator blocks made of metal bars attached to blocks of wood. When struck with a hammer the bars produce an unusually lovely sound. Because each block is separate, a little child may be given only a few at a time or even one if that seems better. The resonator blocks are accurately tuned to the diatonic scale and are constructed in such a way that it is almost impossible for them to get out of tune.

When these blocks are to be used, it is important that they be placed in correct scale sequence, with the lowest tone to the left, corresponding to the arrangement of the piano keyboard. A set of eight comes in a box designed to hold them, and it is better to leave them in this box when playing them so they will not get out of correct order. If only 1-2-3 or 1-2-3-4-5 of the scale is given to the child first, it is a good plan to find a box into which either of these groups will fit snugly.

Each child will use these blocks in his own way and should be left free to do so. His first playing is likely to be haphazard, but soon he will discover certain tonal arrangements and sequences, such as thirds, high and low, or various rhythmic patterns. Occasionally he will enjoy having someone repeat to him what he has just played, or he may like to take a turn repeating what someone else has played. At times they may be used simply as a percussion instrument with no concern for their melodic nature.

We should let his ear be his guide when he begins to try out familiar melodies. He will find that not all of the songs he knows will fit on these blocks, unless he has the complete set, but there are many songs within the range of the five tones or the eight tones in the set, and a few use only three tones. We can encourage him to sing along when he plays if that seems to help him find the tune. We should not, however, urge him too much to play songs that he already knows, for one of the values of this instrument is that it encourages him to make up his own melodies. Both of these experiences are important, but unless we show continued interest in his own inventions, he is likely to give them up. One of the things we can help him learn is that if the tip of the hammer is *dropped* on the bar, a much more musical tone will result than if the bar is *struck*. Again, we cannot ask for this control too soon, for it is not as easy as it appears, but since we are concerned, in musical guidance, with acquainting a child with pleasant rather than unpleasant sounds, it is well to encourage it whenever the time is opportune.

The resonator bells are recommended rather than the small marimba or the xylophone because they have a larger striking surface, the bars are not as close together as those on a xylophone, and they have excellent tone quality. Little children's lack of motor coordination makes it hard for them to play on an instrument in which the tones are close together. The entire chromatic-scale sequence is available in this instrument. In schools where the classrooms do not have pianos, this should prove to be a very worthwhile investment. It is not inexpensive, but the blocks can be moved easily and, even with only one set, many children, over a year's time, can have opportunity to find out about tonal relationships and also to accompany some of their songs with this good musical instrument.

If it is not possible to secure resonator bells, a well-constructed and accurate xylophone can be used. The importance of tonal accuracy and sound construction cannot be overemphasized.

Tuned bells attached to a standard make a delightful instrument. Though fairly expensive, they are practically indestructible—an excellent investment for a school, especially when pianos are not available. They can be used by a number of groups. There are two types: In one, the bell is regulation bell shape; in the other, it is round and flat, like an old-fashioned doorbell. The bells are screwed to a standard and are easily removed, so that their number can be limited for the younger children. If one end of the clapper is attached by a long string to the standard, it will be on hand when needed! At the present time, neither of these instruments is being made, but I am recommending them in the hope that some enterprising instrument maker will manufacture them.

Bowls, tuned glasses, and bottles have been mentioned as suitable for older children. If the glasses are placed on a piece of felt in a long, narrow tray, they can be moved about easily. Sometimes, if one is patient and has a good ear, it is possible to select a set of glasses that are tuned to the scale, making it unnecessary to tune them by using water. Tuning glasses is good ear training, and its value is evident for older children; but it cannot be done unless one has a reliable ear or can check with another instrument. Corked bottles suspended from a stand are, for purposes of accurate pitch, more satisfactory than open glasses, since the water in the glasses evaporates quickly, destroying the proper tuning.

Younger children use melody instruments individually since it is beyond their ability to play melodically in groups as do older children. It is always of first importance that these instruments be accurately tuned, because *there is no substitute for correct tonal relationship.* Melody instruments offer interesting possibilities in experimenting with melody and with similarities and differences of pitch. Just before Christmas, four-year-old Dorothy, taking off her snow suit in the hall, overheard us arranging the resonator blocks and testing them by playing down the scale. As she came into the room, she said, "That sounded like a candlelight song, but it wasn't quite the same." She had heard part of a Christmas-carol service the day before, and when we played the first phrase of *Joy to the World, the Lord Is Come,* her eyes danced with the thrill of recognition; she had caught the melodic progression even though the rhythm was different.

When children enjoy finding the same pitch of a tone on another instrument, they begin to be ear conscious of an instrument's timbre as well as of intervals—the distance from one tone to another. All of these tonal instruments give excellent ear training, and that is the foundation of a sound musical education. Too often instruments are placed in the child's environment, and no more attention is paid them. His musical growth is hit or miss, and many opportunities for musical development are not even recognized. What music occurs is accidental, and remains so. When music education is thought to begin with piano lessons, there is no appreciation of the value inherent in these earlier experiences. Musical impressions gained during children's pliable early years have a way of staying with them, and all during their lives a feeling of at-homeness with music is never entirely lost. Later on, music lessons will have more meaning if this important early training is recognized.

Other Melody Instruments

The guitar and autoharp, which have been mentioned earlier, the psaltery, and the ukulele are well known for their use as accompaniment for singing. These informal instruments may be played by both adults and children. Several years ago a kindergarten teacher who was learning to play the guitar took it to school after several lessons. She played what she could and the children enjoyed her progress as much as she did. But, more important, she made this instrument available for the children's use. These children respected their privilege. All of them tried the guitar from time to time, some more interested than others. One little girl, however, found such satisfaction in strumming and plucking its strings, listening and improvising voice sounds and songs, that she returned to it over and over. Because she was one of a large family, this little affair she had with the guitar afforded her not only a rewarding musical experience but also a private time for herself which was hard to come by at home. The teacher made several tape recordings of this child's music for her parents and for her own records. She explored an amazing variety of tone and range in pitch, mood, and rhythm. She continued her "music with the guitar" during her first grade year and, when in second grade, she became interested in the autoharp and learned to play it. One usually thinks of the autoharp preceding the guitar, but one never knows! This child found great satisfaction in the guitar because she could do so much with it in terms of exploration of sound. After this experience, however, she welcomed the chordal structure of the autoharp because she was able, through chords, to give the songs of others a harmonious accompaniment.

There are the blowing kinds of simple melody instruments—recorders, harmonicas, ocarinas, tonettes, flutophones, clarinets, and the like. The hygienic aspect of these instruments needs supervision when they are made available to children in a group. For this reason they are not as satisfactory with the younger children, but older children are usually fairly responsible about care of the mouthpiece. The recorder offers a wide tonal range compared with the tonette, for example, and certainly offers greater musical possibilities than an instrument of limited range.

It is necessary to consider our purpose in making these instruments available to boys and girls. Do we think of them as a way of teaching notation, or are we concerned with the musical values that attend them? Certainly the two may go hand in hand, but too often the child sees the instrument only as a lesson in reading music. Music is an aural art, and the truly musical way to it is through the ear. Just as a child has years of experience in speaking and being read to before he starts reading the printed word, so in music he needs extended experiences to find out what it is like and what he can do with it on his own initiative. When reading the notes of music has meaning in the child's life—meaning that is *real* to *him*—then it is the time to give him consistent help in notation, no matter what his age.

Let us consider this matter of notation. Certainly one

needs this skill if he is a member of a choral group or if he plays an instrument. Its value lies in its use. Unfortunately, the teaching of notation has become a mechanical routine in many schools. All children are expected to read music whether or not they will use this skill. We all know the result: "Children and adolescents spend hundreds of millions of man-hours presumably learning to read music. But they don't learn to read. Let us face it." [3] In the light of this report and our own observations, we need to consider very seriously the waste of time involved, to say nothing of the unpleasant association built up for many children because of the identification of note reading with music. A child needs to be taught notation when his knowledge of reading music will promote his further development. There are many aspects of notation that are of interest to children—even young children—for example, the rhythmic pattern of a song, its general line of direction and movement, its "ups and downs," its phrases. A discerning and thoughtful teacher who knows her music and can roam freely in her knowledge of it will find many opportunities to interest children in notation all through elementary school. I believe that a broad understanding of music is necessary to teach notation intelligently and musically. Unless a teacher has this I suggest that her time with boys and girls is better spent in the enjoyment of music through the many media which we have today than in struggling with the bare mechanics of notation.

Now let us get back to our discussion of instruments. The strings, woodwinds, and brasses used individually, in small ensembles, or in orchestras, in addition to the piano (discussed in a separate chapter) constitute our important melody instruments. No one of these is easy to play, but then there are different ways of playing! The three-year-old who has an opportunity to get close to a bass fiddle, to pluck its

[3] Gerhert D. Wiebe, "The Evaluation of Research Studies in the Psychology of Music," *Volume of Proceedings of the Music Teachers National Association,* Forty-second Series, Pittsburgh, Penn.: The Association, 1950, p. 232.

strings, and to draw a bow over them, *is playing* this big instrument. The twelve-year-old who is large enough to handle the same instrument will be interested in playing it in an entirely different way, for he sees himself and his fiddle as a member of a group. The nursery-school teacher who brings her violin to play for the children plays it one way, but as each child has an opportunity to pull the bow across a string or pluck a string he, too, is playing it. Nor should this opportunity extend only to the youngest. What youngster of any age does not welcome the experience of making the acquaintance of any band or orchestral instrument in *his* way? Instead, our usual procedure is to give the kind of lesson that stresses the "proper" technique from the start. There is an assumption here that no one can learn to play without this kind of lesson. Yet how many people have taught themselves —witness the accomplishments of many of our greatest jazz players.

But there are *other kinds* of lessons and teachers, and not only in music. The teacher who gives a child ample opportunity to do for himself in any area and who, sensing where help is most needed and where it will be welcomed, brings everything he has to do a skillful job of teaching. How the child can learn for himself and how the teacher can help him do a better job requires more thought on the part of the teacher than merely applying a system, but the rewards are much greater for both the child and the teacher.

An amusing but tragic story that illustrates my point is told by a friend. An earnest young teacher was giving a boy his first violin lesson. For ten minutes she worked on his proper stance, the exact way the violin was to be held, and the precise way in which to hold the bow. Then she stood back and, satisfied with her work, said "Play!" The child stood immobile and then finally was able to ejaculate, "I can't move!" Children are wonderfully resilient, and we hope that this yongster suffered no emotional disturbance from this incident! But we teachers are here to do the best job we can of encouraging music-making and not discouraging it through poor timing in giving what we have.

Our suggestion is that we adults, both in the home and in school, reach out in as many ways as we can to give children opportunities for firsthand acquaintance with as many instruments as we can find. The first purpose is to give them more and more musical experiences. Parents, neighbors, friends, musicians (amateur and professional), and the instrument resources of high school and elementary school are possible sources from which to draw. There is *no such thing as proper age level* in establishing a relationship with an instrument! From among the instruments we can bring to children, many of them will pick their favorite and want to learn to play it. Their motivations will be unique and perhaps not always musical, as illustrated by ten-year-old Jimmy's consuming desire to play a pipe organ when he grows up. Perhaps there is a musical reason back of his enthusiasm, but knowing Jimmy at ten one would hazard a guess that it is bigness in sound and size that determines his ambition!

When children have ample and unhurried time to hold, to touch, to try, to sound, to hear a variety of individual instruments in ways that are appropriate to them, do not these experiences help to make them more discriminating in their choice of an instrument should they want to study one seriously?

Guidance in the Use of Instruments

Guidance in musical experiences as in other areas is a many-sided thing. It is so much more than *giving* information. It is, of course, making information available, but there are many ways of doing this. We adults have such an enthusiasm for teaching that it is easy for us to pour information in rather than to pause, observe, and discover just how and what is being learned. Yet this is exactly what the greatest teachers of all time have done. From our knowledge of how any particular child or group learns we get our best clues for teaching. Guidance is an implicit part of the illustrations used in this chapter and of the discussion relating to them. In addition to the list of possibilities in musical guidance below, some of which have already been noted, each reader will see more and more possibilities unique to his own experience and skill from which he can draw at the opportune time.

1. Let the child find his way and be himself in the exploration of music through instruments.

2. Show interest in what he is doing and, if you feel he is ready, play with him. For example, play or sing his rhythmic pattern or melody along with him.

3. When he pauses, play *back* to him what he has played. Change pitch, use different instruments or the voice.

4. Play *with* him on a different pitch or a different instrument.

5. "Orchestrate" what he is doing. That is, let him establish a rhythm and then join him playing variations in and around his rhythm. Let him do the embellishments while you maintain rhythm.

6. Add to what he has played, as in a cadenza, the feeling, for example, that impels one to follow an ending with a final ending such as "boom, boom."

7. Play with question and answer in pure sound—"talk" with drums, hands, feet.

8. Use variations of dynamics to change the monotony of a pattern—loud, soft, crescendo, decrescendo.

9. Change the pace (rhythm) of what the child has done, keeping the same sound pattern.

10. Play with distance in sounds—behind a screen, in a closet, in the next room.

11. Take a turn at being the leader. For example, vary what has become a monotonous rhythm. Most spontaneous playing falls into a two-four or four-four rhythm. Try using a three-four time.

12. Tap out the rhythm of a song or phrase—a good guessing game. With younger children tell them it will be one of two songs which you name.

13. Encourage children to use these possibilities with each other.

Group Playing of Instruments

If we believe that effective group cooperation in any endeavor is predicated on personal satisfaction, then we will see to it that playing instruments in a group is the natural result of individual experimentation and learning. Is it not unfortunate that we so frequently think of a group playing instruments *only* in terms of certain types of groups—rhythm band, band, orchestra? In the eyes of the community and in the aspirations of children these become *the* groups. One "makes" the band or orchestra or one doesn't. And too often, failure to achieve membership in such a group may spell the end of one's musical interest. Now it is not the intention of any school music program to discourage music-making interest; but there is something dramatic and spectacular about a school band that appeals to all of us and we easily fall into the trap of identifying this with school music. The same can be said of trained choral groups. Instrument manufacturers contribute to this misconception by focusing their sales on certain groups of instruments and even by promoting expensive band uniforms. Surely it is fun to be dressed up—for those who get the chance. Whether this is a sound musical investment in the light of the musical needs of every child remains the decision of the school in regard to the size of its budget.

No bands, no orchestras, no choral groups? Certainly, these are important. We are not trying to make a musician out of every child but we are suggesting that our musical measuring stick has been an extremely limited one and that we have not really had enough respect for the great variety of ways in which group playing may be manifested and through which musical education may be advanced.

Consider, for example, chamber music in the professional concert field: duets, trios, quartets, quintets, small stringed groups, percussion groups, and, of course, soloists. We may prefer orchestral to chamber music, but we have respect for both. Should we not extend the same status to all kinds of instrument combinations which children may use? Children are quick to sense what we accept and encourage. Our knowing, accepting, and appreciating the many media through which musical growth is nourished inevitably results in a carry-over to children in the form of an enriched music program and the joy of living in a climate where music-making in its many facets is encouraged.

What then about the expectancies of the community—of parents, in particular? Perhaps we need to check on our assumption that all of the parents expect a school band and nothing else. At any rate, since we have been responsible in building music expectations in the form of a band, do we not have the responsibility of informing parents about a broader kind of program in the art of music, our reasons for it, and the many ways in which it is manifested in the lives of children? If we really believe this, and if we see to it that all through school equal status is given to serious music-making in many forms, parents, too, will understand. It is a sorry state of affairs when we, in the schools, rely on assumptions as an excuse for perpetuating a condition unfavorable to the growth of all children by discounting the intelligence of *informed* parents.

From time to time we read about the musical achievement of a group of little tots who give a rhythm-band show "led" by a young prodigy standing on a podium. Fond parents applaud, and all (except the prodigy's mother) secretly envy the genius of the leader. This may be a musical experience for the children who participate (though we doubt it), but it most certainly is not a healthy emotional experience. The children who are the best performers always play the important instruments, and the ones who need help the most are kept in the background with instruments that are not too obvious. Not that there may not be satisfaction to some merely in group membership; but it has been the unhappy experience of hundreds of thoughtful teachers that the frustrations and disappointments of the shy child as well as of the less skilled (to say nothing of what happens to the leader's ego) have far outweighed any compensations inherent in this kind of performance.

It is possible to train any group of little children to keep time, and they will accept direction from adults. Whether or not it is sound procedure from the standpoint of child development and musical development is another question. Certainly the value of a rhythm band in training children to keep time to music can be discounted. If children have plenty of opportunity to use their bodies in a free and rhythmic way, if they frequently use instruments individually and in small groups, and, above all, if they are relaxed and free of tension, then they need no training in keeping time. We can't keep them from doing it! It is as natural to them as running and jumping.

The instruments generally used in a rhythm band can be used by children in a creative way, as and when the need for them is evident. Tambourines are fun to play and to dance to; they provide the crashes of sound so loved by youngsters. Bells offer another contrast. The triangle is a gentle instrument, but because of its swinging movement it is not so easy to play. As for cymbals, we prefer a gong or a cymbal struck with a timpani stick to the uncertain effect produced by the crashing of two cymbals together. The latter are difficult for a little child to play, calling for care and skill if good results are to be obtained.

Let us take a look at the type of directions given to the teacher in order to introduce and organize a rhythm band.

Such procedures as the following are suggested: children should be seated quietly; the teacher should introduce and name each instrument separately and show how it is to be played; after the instruments are distributed, children should wait until a signal for playing; children should be told that they must play the same instrument during the entire period but that they will be given opportunity to try all of them during the year; if possible each child should have one opportunity to direct the band during the year. (As an experiment, try passing out a "set" of rhythm-band instruments to a group of adults asking them in advance not to play until a signal is given.) What about our knowledge of child development and the psychology of learning? Are we inhibiting children so they learn little, or do we release them so that they learn much?

Suppose we introduce other art activities such as painting, drawing, or modeling within such a framework of limitations! The teacher will have to decide whether the kind of procedure suggested above releases and works toward the unique musical potentialities of each child and the optimum use of each instrument. Is beating time the ultimate in music-making for even the very young child? Is three-year-old Karen learning something important about duration of tone and timbre when she discovers, after several days' use of a cymbal, that she can stop the sound by quickly placing the cymbal on her lap? What is four-year-old John learning from his first experience with a large suspended gong? He plays with varying intensities for an extended period, and after each tap he waits and waits and waits for the sound to end, getting his ear close, but not too close, so he could catch the tiniest sound.

What is six-year-old Jerry finding out as he spends time every day in trying out tappers—hard, soft, metal, wood—for the big homemade keg drum and choosing what he thinks are appropriate sounds for some of the songs the group is learning? Are seven-year-old Mary and her two friends learning anything about music as she uses a dramatic glissando, which falls into regular phrase length, on the xylophone to announce and to end the playing of this trio (xylophone, maracas, drum)?

Do such experiences as these help children to be more conscious of all the elements of music than is possible in a ready-made organization laid down from above? Organization is inevitable in any group of children or adults; as they use instruments spontaneously, individually, and thoughtfully, an organic structure will develop as each member of the group becomes conscious of other sounds. It is fun; it can't be stopped, and it is an organization that has meaning.

As this playing takes form we have rare oppportunities of opening new musical vistas. Perhaps we will join in with another instrument, perhaps provide an improvisation or a piece of music on the piano that catches the mood and musical feeling of what is going on. Perhaps a special recording will add to the experience or extend the group's musical consciousness. For example, percussion groups will enjoy selections from such recordings as *Africa* (Esoteric) or the percussion group from the Boston Symphony Orchestra in *Evolution* (Boston), both examples of what others more skilled have done with percussion instruments.

There will be opportunities for the adult to suggest that all the members of a group play together (the children may think of this first). We must remember that exciting percussive sounds are possible without formal instruments; the children may use their hands, feet, voices, or objects to produce musical effects.

A teacher of a sixth grade in Louisiana recently told of his experience with percussion sounds. Each year some of his twelve-year-old boys would discover that they could play intricate rhythms on the metal parts of their old-fashioned stationary desks. He would not openly recognize their tapping because he felt that it had no place in "school music." After a few sessions of playing percussion instruments with a large group of his peers, he allowed himself not only to show interest in what happened the next fall but to encourage it. The result was electric! No longer was this interest a clandestine affair. His fear that he would not know how to guide it disappeared as the youngsters themselves improvised and combined and composed out of the sounds they made. Although this teacher had a musical background, he frequently was unable to keep step with the intricate rhythms and counterpoints that evolved. He was truly amazed at the musical abilities of his group. Moreover, after he had recognized their skills and played along with them, he found that they were many times more receptive to the songs he taught them. Together they had a wonderfully musical year as the skills of both teacher and children were joined and became the starting point for musical creativity in many forms.

A different kind of group experience is illustrated in the following example. Four twelve-year-old boys, three of whom had had an unusually rich background in classical music, one with a flute, another with violin, and the third with piano, and, all having had a wide acquaintance with good musical literature, became passionately devoted to jazz. They bought records, listened to jazz on television and radio, and played it exclusively! A trumpet, horn, clarinet, and drums made up their band. It was obvious to the music teacher in the school they attended (the Dalton School in New York), that this was a tremendously serious interest. Arrangements were made to set aside a short period each day within the school hours and provide a place where these boys could pursue their musical development in this area. The school also offered to provide a teacher for guidance but this offer was politely turned down by the boys. They preferred to learn for themselves via records and experimentation!

One of these boys had been in my kindergarten group six years before and, knowing my interest in music, he persuaded his fellow players to come to Teachers College at Columbia and play for a class of adults. After four months of practice they offered to play. And could they play! It wasn't long before all of us were actively involved.

In a discussion following their performance, I asked the boys to tell us why this music meant so much to them. "You can do what you feel like doing with it—not what the notes say"; "It has guts to it," they explained. Two of them said they still played classical music, and now all four, who are in secondary school, participate in some form of classical-music group, at the same time holding on to their jazz interest. Here was a school that made it possible for a small group to develop musically in line with their maturity and ability to take on personal responsibility.

Do these examples, in addition to our knowledge of how children grow and develop through individual and group experiences in ways that are in keeping with their natural disposition, tell us something of the most important value of all, even beyond learning music—the development of sound mental hygiene for each and every child?

There are times when the teacher will feel it is right for her to take the lead by playing something and asking children to play with her. Thoughtful orchestration of any appropriate music can be an exciting and rewarding experience. Is the rhythm-band orchestration notated in the book the only kind of orchestration? The children may decide they like it better than their own or they may prefer their own way. They may find it of great interest to orchestrate a special record with the thoughtful control that is necessary in any group playing—the control that keeps each player conscious of the sounds of all of the others.

Let us summarize briefly some of the ways in which guidance goes on in group playing.

1. Let the group find "itself" as each member plays and becomes aware of the playing of others. (Be sure to establish a signal in advance so that the players will respond to you when you want them to stop.)

2. Out of the mass playing, listen for certain elements of music such as a repeated rhythm, the use of dynamics, a change of pace, feeling for phrase, introductions and endings, free counterpoint, contrasts in sounds, use of certain instruments intermittently so as to help in phrasing and punctuating the musical line.

3. Select certain ways of playing, either individual or small group, and ask the entire group to listen.

4. Suggest that group join in a lead after it is established. Use a variety of these. Do not hesitate to provide a lead yourself when things become monotonous.

5. Add instruments as needed.

6. Listen and listen and listen.

7. Wait and wait and wait.

8. Bring your musical resources and ideas to the group when they have real meaning.

9. Play music that will support and extend what the group offers.

10. Play music that will stimulate and bring new experiences to group.

11. Find time within the school program, together with children, when individual and small-group playing may take place.

12. Expose children in every grade to a variety of instruments.

Good instruments are not inexpensive and many families are unable to afford them. If an older child wishes to study an instrument seriously he should have had some experience with it before it is bought. Some schools are making instruments available so that they can be borrowed and taken home for a real tryout. This is a very valuable service. School libraries lend books, some of them extending the privilege over the summer vacation. Why should not a similar privilege be extended to the lending of musical instruments for the use of children? If the school cannot, perhaps the public library, or a church, or the community center might be interested in trying out such a program. The financial outlay would be comparatively small, and there are many ways of raising money; but the returns in satisfaction for children, especially those who have no instruments in their homes, would be great.

Through musical instruments, then, we find untold possibilities to guide the musical growth of our boys and girls. They provide the means through which natural interest in sound and rhythm may be developed. Through a variety of choices in instruments we can come closer to the needs and talent of individuals than through the practice of allocating a single instrument to a grade level. Today's world of communication in music is rich. Let us be certain that the school recognizes what musical capacities children already have and be especially careful that we provide them with a well-balanced music program in school.

SELECTED REFERENCES

Coleman, Satis N., *The Drum Book,* New York: Day. Out of print.

Mason, Bernard S., *Drums, Tom-Toms and Rattles,* Boston: Barnes. Out of print.

Pillsbury Foundation Studies, *IV. Free Use of Instruments for Musical Instruments for Musical Growth,* vol. IV in *Music of Young Children,* Santa Barbara, Calif.

Wilson, M. Emett, *How to Help Your Child with Music,* New York: Abelard-Schuman. Helpful in possibilities for the use and selection of instruments.

THE PIANO

WE HAVE DISCUSSED the development of children's musical interests through acquaintance with and study of a variety of instruments. Since the piano is probably the most widely used instrument, at least in the beginning study of music, and since it offers such a wealth of possibilities musically, it is worthy of special attention.

Is there anyone who at one time or another has not felt the urge to sit down and pour out through piano keys his pent-up feelings? Some people are "naturals"; they cannot remember when they could not play. Others have achieved the ability to make the piano do their bidding through long and laborious study. The vast majority of people, however, are shut off from this form of self-expression; moreover for many of them the piano has unpleasant associations. Ask any group of adults if they play the piano. The chances are that a large number will respond, "I took lessons when I was young," "I can play with one hand," "I can play in the key of C," "I hated to practice," and so on.

Learning to play the piano is not easy but it can be interesting. When children suddenly realize that "taking piano lessons" does not guarantee complete control of the instru-

114

ment within a "reasonable" length of time, they are confronted with one of the first great disappointments of their lives. They have big feelings and big emotions, and there are many times when picking out *Mary Had a Little Lamb* in no way measures up to the size of what is pushing within them.

Investigating Its Sound

For children, a piano is, first of all, a sound-making instrument, not an object to which one transfers notes read from a printed page. They do not wait to play the piano until they can read notes, any more than they wait to talk until they can read the printed word. In both cases they learn through their ears. When they are old enough, they are only too ready to learn to read from the printed page, either in music or in books.

Children are curious about a piano—all parts of it, inside and out—and nothing else offers them so much fun as exploring it. The piano is, of course, a precious instrument and one cannot afford disastrous accidents to its mechanism. But there are many things children can find out about its workings, under proper supervision, and not only will they do no harm to the piano, but their interest in music will be tremendously enhanced.

One day Susan's mother, a concert pianist, paid us an unexpected visit at school. For several days before her visit the children had been spending considerable time investigating the inside of the piano, and when she came into the room half a dozen of them were around it, standing on chairs, tables, or anything available to get as close as possible to the strings and the sounding board.

Diana had the advantage of being near the deep end, and she could "strum" the long strings and make the loudest sound; several were playing on the keyboard and watching the hammers; another was plucking the upper strings. Confusion—yes, plenty of it; and, besides, no one could hear the sound he himself was making. I suggested that each person take a turn so that he could *listen to his own music*. Susan's mother was as excited over what was happening as the children were, and soon she sat down at the keyboard to control the duration of the sound by the pedal. She had her turn, too, for, said she, "I have played the piano since I was a little girl, but I have never played the strings!" She was thrilled by the strange and lovely sounds. One of the boys said, "Her music is 'banshee' music, just like what I heard on the radio!"

Just before Susan's mother left she played a Bach gavotte, but this time the music was not so much heard as watched, for the children were intrigued by seeing the hammers bob up and down on the strings. As she left she said that never in her life had she spent such an enjoyable half hour or such a musically profitable one.

Time and again during the year the children experimented with the strings and hammers of the piano, always under adult supervision, since it was important for them to learn to use it carefully and thoughtfully. They looked forward eagerly to the coming of the piano tuner and listened while he worked; and, of course, there was always someone to help him decide whether he had just the right pitch! Usually a few of the children stayed by until the end; most of them went back and forth to the piano from their work and play; but they all had contact with some aspect of the experience. Our tuner, a friendly person, always took time to answer questions; there usually weren't many, for the children's own observations supplied the answers. He showed them how the tuning fork is used, and each child had a chance to try it.

There is no way of measuring what the children learned about the sounds of the piano during the year, for we did not quiz them. But if enthusiastic interest, thoughtful listening, and experimentation are any indication, we venture to guess that their understanding of the piano can be rated high.

The children were given many unhurried opportunities to try out and observe; then their questions were answered simply and directly; and, finally, new information was offered when the time was opportune. Words and names were not flung at them, but neither were they withheld when needed. That children picked up far more than we were aware of was evidenced by reports of their conversations at home and by overhearing their talk among themselves.

Here are some of the things children discovered about the piano:

- The vibration of the string sets the air in motion, thus producing the sound. The string is made to vibrate by the hammers dropping on it. Plucking the string will also make it vibrate. Strings of different lengths produce different sounds. We call the sounds made by the short strings "high" and those made by the long strings "low." Sounds are always higher or lower than a given sound.

- The length or duration of the sound can be controlled by the pedal.

- When the strings are played in certain ways, they remind us of other sounds, such as bombers, wind, motors, airplanes, witches.

- The effect of the vibration of the strings can be seen by placing a pencil or piece of paper on them, and then playing on the keyboard.

- Strings are made of various materials: some are copper, some steel. Some are thicker than others.

- In the upper register of the piano the hammer falls on three strings at once; in the lower register, on only one at a time.

- Intensities and duration of sounds may be experimented with by using the pedals, by closing and opening the top, and by using the hands with varying degrees of pressure.

The Piano and the Physics of Sound

One of the outcomes of our children's experimentation with the piano was continued interest in physics of sound. The classroom was very large and, being flanked on three sides by windows reaching from ceiling to floor, was well known (among adults) for its echoes. One day Anna objected strongly to the shouting of a group of boys who were playing war, saying that the noise hurt her ears. She couldn't understand why they did not wait until they were outdoors to play war. This same group of boys had been much interested in the piano experience, so I thought they might like to know something about the acoustics of the room. I called the children for a meeting and told them of Anna's complaint, and most of them agreed that we had been very noisy. Then we tried the following experiment:

I told the boys that we were going to *listen* while they played war again, and asked them to "shoot their guns" just as before. After the enemy had been annihilated, we all went downstairs to the soundproofed cafeteria (then, midmorning, not in use) and I asked the boys to continue their war while we *listened* again. The listeners immediately noticed the difference in sound. Then I pointed to the ceiling and told them that much of the noise was absorbed by it, whereas, in our own room, the ceiling was hard and had no little holes in it, and there were many glass windows which stopped the sound so that it remained in the room.

Then we went to the roof and repeated the experiment. I did not need to ask what happened to the sound up there, for one youngster volunteered the information that "it just goes up into the sky, and then away out into the ocean and drowns!"

When we went back to our room, I showed the children a soundproof block that had been given to us some time before. They could see the tiny perforations that absorb the sound.

The next day we experimented by listening to the tick of a watch, first placing a piece of porous cloth between it and the child's ear, then wetting a similar piece of cloth and using it in the same way. Water closed the holes of the cloth, and the sound of the watch tick was reduced. By using a strong magnifying glass, the children could see for themselves the differences in the cloth.[1]

Again a comparison of children's curiosities with those of certain adults may be of interest to the reader. Hull tells us that the composer Scriabin "derived all harmony from 'nature's harmonic chord,' and thus carried the science of sound triumphantly into the regions of art." [2] Cowell and Stokowski are both well known for their excursions into the science of sound as it relates to music.

Far be it from me to suggest that we had any musical prodigies in our group, or that there is a moral to this story so far as the noise-making proclivities of youngsters are concerned. Boys, and girls too, are not made to be quiet, but perhaps a request for quieter play in a room where others are annoyed by it might seem to them just a little less arbitrary when they understand what happens to the sound made by their voices. The mother of one of our "highly developed" noisemakers reported one day that, after she had asked Jack to be quieter at home, he responded with exasperation, "Why don't you give me a soundproofed room? Then you wouldn't hear me!"

Other opportunities for exploring sound occurred from time to time. For example, when Louise's mother brought her cello to school to play for us, we observed the difference in sounds when she played with the peg on the bare floor and when it was placed on a thick rubber pad, and what happened when the mute was used.

Not only the inside of the piano but also the piano key-

1 Wilmer T. Bartholomew, *Acoustics of Music*, Englewood Cliffs, N. J.: Prentice-Hall.
2 Eaglefield Hull, *A Great Russian Tone-Poet: Scriabin*, New York: Dutton.

board present endless ways of experimenting with sound. No wonder children delight in playing on the keyboard; high or low, tiny or big, soft or loud, dissonances or pleasing sounds —all respond to their immediate control. Even the tiny baby on his mother's lap can satisfy his urge for sound-making.

"But I will not have my children banging on the piano," said the musician-father of two little children recently. "When they are old enough, I'll see that they have lessons from the best teacher available, and until then they can listen to music and learn to appreciate it."

Using the Keyboard

What this father fails to see is that there is a vast difference between uncontrolled, haphazard banging on a keyboard, and thoughtful experimentation with it, even though the results may sound similar. In one case the child is not really interested or even thinking about what he is doing; in the other, he is making a *conscious* effort to produce sounds that satisfy him. Or, to put it simply, it is the difference between not using and using his ears. Surely no thoughtful person could call this second kind of playing "banging." The sounds produced may not please the father and he may feel it necessary to ask the child to turn down his loudspeaker, but much published music does not please either. In writing about sound in *Music for All of Us,* Stokowski says: "All sound can be music to some—to them every sound has some kind of tonal design, no matter how irregular." [3] Is it not possible, then, for us to see in this keyboard curiosity an opportunity for constructive guidance, and is this not far better than to prohibit the child's investigations?

Perhaps if we enumerate some of the ways in which children use the keyboard, we may see more clearly the elements of music inherent in this type of sound-making.

[3] Leopold Stokowski, *Music for All of Us,* New York: Simon and Schuster.

Groups of Keys

Playing the piano with the whole hand or even with the forearm is one of the ways in which very little children may experiment. This frequently tends toward rhythmic as well as sound play and, by the way, this use of the keyboard is not confined to children. One of our well-known modern composers and pianists, Henry Cowell, often uses his forearm in playing "tone clusters," and he also produces unusual and very beautiful music by playing on the strings. He has an exquisite sensitivity to sounds and a unique approach to their production, in addition to fine creative powers and able musicianship.

Black Keys

Quiet, sensitive, three-year-old Timothy used the school piano a great deal, and the interesting thing about his playing was that he used the black keys exclusively. No one had told him to do this, but apparently these sounds pleased and satisfied him. Timothy's mother was musical, and he was accustomed to hearing good music at home; even at the age of three he showed unusual discrimination in his appreciation of music. In talking with his parents, we came to the conclusion that the way he used the piano was only another evidence of his discrimination, for, in using only the black keys (the pentatonic scale), he encountered no dissonances. We are told that Mozart at the age of three showed a "pronounced liking for concords and [an] aversion [to] discords. He gave joyous gurgles when he put down a satisfying third." [4] Grownups as well as children can have a fascinating time in exploring the black keys only. No matter how we play them the sounds are harmonious. They afford an interesting opportunity for exploring rhythmic patterns and contrasts in sound.

[4] Dyneley Hussey, *Wolfgang Amadeus Mozart*, London: Routledge.

Intervals, Combinations of Sounds, and Rhythmic Patterns

Five-year-old Mary liked music and hung around the piano when the children were using it. I noticed, however, that she never played, and when I urged her to take a turn she refused, saying that she did not know how to play. This was a shock to me, for, in all my experience, I never had met a little child who doubted that he could play! There was no lack of volunteers to help Mary, but still she held back. Finally, she turned to me and said, "You show me how to play *Frère Jacques.*" I played it for her twice, at the same time saying: "You can easily learn to play that, but there are many more interesting things that you can play. Try playing all over the keyboard." I was especially anxious to have her use the keyboard in her own way, for it was typical of her to wait to be shown how to do things, never using her own imagination and ability. Finally she began to play with one finger, and advanced, key by key, until she had covered the entire keyboard; then she repeated the whole procedure, this time including the black keys.

By now there was no use for anyone else to try to take a turn, because Mary could not be pulled away. About ten minutes later, she ran over to me excitedly. "Come and listen!" She was playing in thirds (with one finger of each hand) up and down, first both notes together, later one after the other, in a rocking sort of rhythm. Then she played them in two-four rhythm with the accent in the left hand, and later on she discovered a three-four rhythm, playing the accent on one and the other note on three.

Hardly a day passed that did not find Mary at the piano, experimenting in a variety of rhythmic patterns, in various intervals, and in unusual harmonic combinations. Frequently I played back to her what she had just done; she would listen carefully and then play it again. Sometimes she would close her eyes, and I would play for her a very short bit, and she would repeat it. This game worked both ways, and I got

Grishkot

Getting personally acquainted

Time for everyone to have a turn

Irene Strauss

Parents' Magazine

The firsthand experience before the concert in Darien, Connecticut

Finding out about resonator blocks

Raup Photo

tripped as often as she did. We both found that it helped if we sang the melody as we tried to play it. Since Mary could count accurately, I named the intervals she played, showing her by counting the steps between the tones why they were so called: thirds, fourths, fifths, and so on. After letting her get considerable experience with this I told her to close her eyes and tell me—when I played a third or an octave—which was a *little* interval and which was a *big* one. She did this accurately and without hesitation.

Mary was alive to the excitement and joy that accompany the discovery and exploration of qualities and combinations of, as well as difference in, sounds.

Delight in harmony is characteristic of many children's experimentation. Grieg reported that at the age of five he was thrilled by "the wonderful mysterious satisfaction with which my arms stretched out to the piano to discover—not a melody that was far off—no, that there is such a thing as harmony. First a third, then a chord of three notes, then a full chord of four, ending at last with both hands. Oh, joy! a combination of five, the chord of the ninth. When I found that out my happiness knew no bounds." [5] As a mature musical adult, Grieg recalled his "discovery." Whether his family planned for time and opportunity for him to discover, we do not know, but it would seem that those of us who are responsible for children's musical education today—parents, music teachers, classroom teachers—would consider seriously a way of living with children, day by day, so that discovery *can* and will happen.

But let us follow through on Mary. Her interest was so intense that it carried over to the home, and her family decided that it was time to buy a piano. Knowing her mother's love of perfection in all things, I told her very carefully just what Mary had been doing and urged that Mary be allowed to use the piano in her own way, and that she should not be expected to play tunes all the time. Mary had learned to play

[5] Henry T. Finck, *Grieg and His Music,* London: Lane.

a few simple songs by ear, but she was much more eager to do "big things."

Now this story has a moral for grownups. Shortly after the piano arrived in Mary's house, her interest in it began to decrease steadily. Her mother was unable to see any musical value in what Mary had been doing and, determining to waste no time, started to teach her correct fingering, calling her experimentation silly, and insisted that she practice scales every day! In doing this, she destroyed her child's curiosity and interest, and especially her *enthusiastic persistence* in learning. Mary's mother failed to discriminate between musical techniques and Mary's interest in the essence of music itself and, no doubt, felt that Mary's interest would certainly follow the accomplishment of skills. It did not.

Sound Effects

In much of their make-believe play, children supply the necessary sound effects with their own voices, but occasionally they turn to instruments. They may ask an adult to supply the music, but more often than not they are self-sufficient. John was a backward child, graded "slow" by the usual school standards. He followed the lead of others, was friendly and amiable, but lacked the ability to make himself felt in the group. One day, shortly after Halloween, a small group including John were playing pumpkins and asked me to play some "night pumpkin music." "But," I said, "I am not sure what kind of music you need. Could you tell me?" "Oh, I'll show you," said John as he went to the piano and started to play in the lower register. Then he stopped abruptly and asked to have the lights turned off. How could he play night music in a light room?

John's music, in its feeling for weird sound and slow movement, was so completely fitting that there was no question of his showing me what to do; his effect was far superior to anything I could contribute.

This experience proved to be a milestone for John. His imagination had found an outlet, and he achieved recognition by the group. He was constantly called upon to contribute his talent, for talent he had and in no small measure.

Pitch

Ear training is fundamental to a sound music education, and the children's use of the piano can contribute a great deal to this. In pointing out the possibilities for development, we must remind the reader that they are only *possibilities*, and the way in which they are opened up depends entirely on the child's interest and on the guidance or furtherance of that interest.

High and low in music are arbitrary terms, and children have to learn that tones are high or low in relation to a given tone. Middle C is in the middle of the piano, the tones to the right are higher, and the tones to the left are lower. Repeated experiences in playing or singing a middle tone and then a higher or lower one, letting the child decide which each is, will help him to understand this. We must be sure—and this is very important—not to stick to middle C as our middle tone, but to use others as well.

After the child has a clear understanding of this, he will be interested in using only his ears in deciding whether the second tone played is higher or lower than the first, and it is important to use wide differences at first. Some children have very acute ears, and it is not long before they can distinguish even a half tone of difference. This game should be played the other way around, too: let the child take a turn to play, and the mother or teacher do the guessing.

Another game that increases awareness of pitch is singing a tone and then finding the same tone on the piano. Several

children can enjoy this together, each one taking a turn singing and the others helping to decide when the piano tone
matches.

Matching the tones of other instruments, tonal and percussion, with the piano is also good fun. An interesting experiment is to find the corresponding pitch of a drum on the
piano on a dry day, and compare it with the pitch on a damp
day; or, for an immediate contrast, to use the drum like the
Wigman, whose head can be tightened or loosened.

One of the ways in which ear training is developed in
music schools is through the use of two pianos. The pupil sits
at one and the teacher at the other. After the teacher plays a
melody or rhythmic pattern, the pupil repeats it on his piano
by ear. Many classroom teachers have found that two identical and accurately tuned xylophones offer opportunities for
ear development. Two children sit opposite each other at a
table, each with a xylophone. A screen or partition is placed
between the instruments so that neither child can see the
xylophone on the other side. One plays a tone or short phrase
or rhythmic pattern while the other listens. The game is for
the listener to repeat accurately by ear what has been played.
This game can be played to advantage by children of any age.
Even without any musical instrument two children can have
much fun by tapping out rhythmic patterns on a table. A
dividing screen makes a game out of this and, besides, it helps
to isolate the sound element.

Occasionally children show an interest in the names of
piano keys. They will enjoy finding all the C's on the keyboard or all the F's, and so on. After learning the names of
notes, they can play a game of closing their eyes, landing on
the keyboard with one finger, and naming the key.

The modern dance accompanist sometimes uses her fists as
tympani on the keyboard. Children can accompany simple
rhythmic movements in the same way, gradually becoming
more and more sensitive to the importance of *quality* of
touch and the ways of achieving dramatic effects.

Melodies

Children like to pick out simple melodies by ear, and they should be encouraged to do this, for there is no better ear training possible. "I started [playing the] piano by my own intuition. There were no lessons, no efforts to teach me. With one finger I was always seeking, always trying to find the melodies." This was Paderewski at three years of age.[6] The ease with which some children play a tune in any key on which they happen to land arouses jealousy in some of us older people who learned the hard way. They become truly versatile on the keyboard and avoid many of the difficulties that arise later when they read music. Their ears are their guide, and for the average child they are a reliable one. Good music teachers stress playing in many keys from the very beginning.

Many of these first melodies will, we hope, be of the children's own making. Sometimes they will have words but usually they are without. If our ears are quick enough to play back to children their own tunes, we will add much pleasure to their experience. They will also play songs that they know or hear others sing, and at times they will run into difficulties. It is important to help them over these hurdles and not let them become discouraged.

Children enjoy hearing the melody of the scale, and in the beginning we must be sure to see that they become scale-conscious *in their ears*—not in terms of letters, numbers, names, or syllables. Here again they can start on any key, letting their ears guide them. (Disregard fingering at the piano; the emphasis here is on ear training.) They will enjoy singing a simple scale song like "As I climbed up the apple tree, A big red apple fell on me"; or "It's fun to see the jolly clown, He shouts 'Hurrah' and tumbles down," in a major

6 Ignace Jan Paderewski and Mary Lawton, *The Paderewski Memoirs*, New York: Scribner.

key; or "The north wind comes, the north wind goes, But where he lives nobody knows," in a minor key. Some of the older children may make up scale songs, and they may also be interested in distinguishing between songs that go up and down, step by step, and those that skip tones.

Touch

Children have a highly developed sense of touch, for it is one of the important ways in which they learn about things. Certainly the qualities of touch of a skilled pianist are an integral part of his art. Naturally, children are not as highly sensitized as the artist, but we would be foolish not to encourage the "touch" explorations that are a part of their very being. In their beginning keyboard experimentation, and long before they "play a piece," they are interested in practicing different qualities of this same sound. The variations in intensity are the most obvious. The duration of a sound as related to touch, the use of staccato and legato, are recognized and used. The glissando, which the child does in his own way at first, is facilitated by showing him how to use the nail of the third finger on ascending and his thumbnail on descending the keys. The use of the entire keyboard and the contrasts in degrees of intensity of touch are exciting and fun. All of these kinds of thoughtful experimentation help to establish a *feeling of confidence* at the keyboard.

Music Lessons

"When shall I give Alice music lessons? Can you recommend a teacher?" Asked over and over again, these are among the most difficult questions to answer for the simple reason that there is no one answer. Music lessons might be exactly what six-year-old Ann needs, but an unhappy experience for

Alice, even though she shows the same interest as Ann. For children who go to a school where the teacher is able to give them many experiences in music and movement, or for those who live in a home that encourages and guides their interest, so-called music lessons would seem unnecessary before seven or eight years of age. For other children, who have neither of these privileges, fifteen or twenty minutes of *musical experiences* with an understanding teacher several times a week should prove very fruitful.

The home will have to be the final judge of whether or not the child is ready for music lessons. Perhaps parents will not have to worry about making this great decision; it may be taken out of their hands as it was in the case of the parents of little six-year-old Peter Tchaikovsky.

Very early in life he displayed a remarkable ear and quick perception. He could repeat on the piano all that he heard in an orchestration. He found such delight in playing that it was frequently necessary to drag him by force from the instrument. Afterwards, as the next best substitute, he would take to drumming tunes upon the window panes. One day, while thus engaged, he was so entirely carried away by this dumb show that he broke the glass and cut his hand severely. This accident led his parents to reflect upon the child's incurable tendency and consider the question of his musical education.[7]

The choice of a teacher is of paramount importance, for it is the quality of the relationship between teacher and child that determines whether or not the child has a happy and profitable time. We should not choose a teacher simply because she is a concert artist, or because she plays well. The only sure way to decide whether a certain teacher will bring out the best in the child is to observe that person at work with children. Any honest and sincere teacher is only too happy to offer that opportunity.

[7] Rosa H. Newmarch (ed.), *The Life and Letters of Peter Ilyitch Tchaikovsky*, New York: Scribner.

What are some of the things that we look for in a teacher? Does she have genuine respect for children's intelligence, and does she understand them? Is she aware not only of their possibilities but of their limitations in such matters as span of attention and inadequate muscular control? Does she have a broad understanding of music, and is she flexible in her use of it? Is the music studio equipped with a variety of instruments for music-making, and is intelligent and musical use made of these?

Does she see possibilities in children's curiosities about sound? Does she teach by a "system," tying herself and the child to a rigid lesson plan, or is she able to see more immediate and more important possibilities? Is she interested merely in training, or in sound progressive music development? Does she recognize signs of fatigue and lack of interest and proceed intelligently?

These and many more qualifications, depending upon the individual child's need, are essential. Today there *are* teachers who know and understand children and whose first concern is the child and not music. We should search until we find that person, tell her what we want, and then *be sure* that we do not handicap her by asking for immediate results in terms of performance. The results to be sought are of a different nature; they are sustained interest in and love of music, eagerness for "music time," creative use of sound and rhythm, and a happy relationship with the music teacher.

Serious music study demands long, hard work; there is no sugar-coated path to musicianship. As children grow older and begin to have an adequate understanding of what they are working for, even though they do not always feel like practicing (and who does?), they will realize that there are satisfactions to the hurdles they have to jump. When, however, children are too young to look beyond the present and can have no possible understanding of a goal in the minds of adults, the method of training for training's sake becomes the surest way of antagonizing the child and making him lose interest. An intelligent teacher knows this but often has to set aside her better judgment or lose her pupil. She is constantly on the lookout for opportunities to encourage technique, but she will not stress technique at the expense of interest. Has she no plan, then? She most certainly has a plan—a large plan that includes both child and music, a plan that demands the best possible all-round development of that child *through* music.

Egon Petri, Dutch pianist and teacher, gave a piano lesson to seventeen hundred people in Carnegie Hall. Among other things he discussed the value of practicing. "If," he said, "you work very intelligently, you don't have to work as hard as if you do it stupidly. . . . Mechanical keeping at the piano for hours and hours—that's old fashioned. Repetition in itself doesn't help, unless you are always experimenting." He also insisted that there is no one way to play, but that "pianists should play in the manner that is easiest and most natural." "Work intelligently" and "always experimenting"—these are exactly what we want for children, and they will do both if given a chance. In this advice Petri is reflecting sound knowledge of the process of learning.

Once the child and his family have decided that he will study music through the piano, is his pursuit of this to be left to incidental interest? Certainly not. There are many ways of motivating and sustaining interest. Successful teachers may use a number of different ways, and what one teacher finds rewarding may not yield results for another.

Since interest is closely related to learning, the pupil's self-selection of music to be studied should be given consideration. Just as self-selection of stories to be read results in improved reading ability, so the child's musical choices will provide genuine motivation. A wise teacher will see to it that a variety of music within the child's ability is offered so that he may make choices. There are many kinds of music, and over a reasonable period of time, a child should become acquainted with all of these.

Many teachers find that a guide book kept jointly with the pupil is helpful. This may have a record of past achievements, plans for the next lesson, *and* plans for the future. It should stimulate and have space for recording all kinds of musical interests. Did you hear a new song during the week? Did you learn a new song? Did you hear a new instrument directly, or on television or radio or recording? Did you hear any new music? Did you make up any music? Can we write it down? Did you hear any new sounds? Did you find out anything about a composer during the week? The piano teacher who recognizes the musical value of these as they relate to the study of the piano will go far in stimulating the broad musical interests of her pupil.

We haven't begun to realize the value of the tape recorder, both in the home and in the music studio, as another motivating factor. Hearing what one has played, the satisfaction in listening to one's achievement, the opportunity for evaluation and the stimulus this provides for improvement, make for tremendous support in the matter of effort. Playback is impersonal. It is not colored by anyone's approval or disapproval. Its complete objectivity as far as reproduction is concerned makes it more acceptable than the comments of another. Both procedures, however, are in order.

Influence of the Home

The kind of understanding and support that parents bring to their child's music lessons may well prove to be the deciding factor in his willingness to persist in his study of the piano or any other musical instrument. It is the nature of learning that progress has its ups and downs. Regular and consistent application to any task probably yields the best results for most of us, but blind adherence to routine for its own sake may produce only antagonism or boredom. At times, sympathetic interest may help a child over his hurdle; at other times it would be wise to allow for deviation from a regular plan. Short periods of practice of approximately fifteen minutes in length, one or two a day depending on the child, scheduled at a time when he is not deprived of playing with his friends, are usually more effective than spasmodic periods. Some children like to have their mothers close by and, at least, show interest. Others prefer to be independent. No child, however, wants to be independent of the family's interest in his music progress.

We must never overlook the incidental and unplanned opportunities that the very nature of flexible family living offer.

Colin McPhee gives a delightful description of his two Balinese house boys in pursuit of their musical education. His home in Bali presented many opportunities for the learning of music.

Two of them worked intermittently in the house, polishing knives and spoons, feeding the parrots, looking for leaves and roots the cook suddenly wanted for the daily curry, helping light the lamps at sundown. Between these occupations they would sit down and hammer away at one instrument or another that I always seemed to have standing about the house. They discovered for themselves that certain Balinese tunes could be played on the black keys of the piano, and they improvised astonishing duets. They had that quick, brief concentration one sees in small monkeys, doing one thing for five minutes, only to grow suddenly bored and dart to something else. But every now and then a musical phrase of extremely complicated rhythm would flash out from some metallophone on the verandah, hammered out with neat precision and quite unaccountable virtuosity.[8]

To be needed musically in the home, school, or church is probably the most effective kind of motivation in learning to

[8] From *Childhood in Contemporary Cultures,* edited by Margaret Mead and Martha Wolfenstein, Chicago: University of Chicago, p. 75.

play an instrument. The following recollections of a former student are a vivid example of this.

My grandfather was an old-fashioned fiddler who could play 250 old folk tunes and dances, some of which he "composed" himself (or thought he did.) As a young man he was considered "wild" because he played for "breakdowns" (old-fashioned square dances). My father was also a "fiddler" and all his brothers and cousins played instruments—banjos, guitars, harps. My mother saved butter and egg money and bought a parlor organ for me when I was a little child. I cannot remember when I learned to "chord" on the organ as my part in the family "musicales." My grandfather would say "Waltz time, Ethel," "key of—," and away we would go. If there was a change of key in the middle and I missed it he would look over his shoulder at me and say "D, Ethel." Imagine my surprise this year to find that the newest most modern series of books for children introduces "chording." When I was eleven, I went to live at my grandfather's in another county for a year in order to take piano lessons from an unmarried aunt, the only member of our tribe of musicians who knew one note from another. I practised two hours a day in an unheated parlor and loved it. This was all the formal training I had in music until I was grown. At 12, I began playing the organ for sunday school in our country church, learning a new hymn each week by myself. The sunday-school superintendent would say, "Well, little Ethel, which number did you learn this week?" and we would sing the song I had learned. *No modern child ever had a bigger incentive for practicing.* I was 18 when we bought a piano. At 20 I entered college as a music major. My lifework is teaching music in mission schools in the Far East. I have always envied the modern children and young people the opportunity they have to hear and know good music and I have wondered why so many of them seem to have no interest in music. Now I realize that my interest was awakened and nurtured in my own family of untrained but gifted musicians. No outside musical advantage could take the place of the home.[9]

[9] Used by permission of Ethel Bost.

Group Lessons

Good music instruction is a financial investment for the family. Even the younger child can be helped to be aware of this and the role he plays in assuming his responsibility in the investment. Group piano lessons have been promoted for some time in schools in an effort to acquaint a large number of children with the keyboard at minimum expense. The argument is that one teacher can reach more children at one time and, also, that learning together has its social values.

The usual way of teaching is through the use of dummy keyboards, one for each child. Either the teacher or a child who can play sits at the piano and, after instruction as to where to place the fingers, the entire group takes the position indicated on their boards at the time the person at the piano plays. There are, of course, variations in the way this plan is applied. There is bound to be, however, emphasis on the mechanical side of learning to play without the satisfaction of *personal* sound production that is the result of even the most mechanistic method at the piano keyboard. The elements of touch and sound which, together with hearing, constitute the making of music are missing in what ought to be a total musical experience.

Certainly we sympathize with any approach that will interest the maximum number of children in learning to play the piano. It is unfortunate that extravagant claims are too frequently made for any one of these "methods," and not only children but their families expect quick results and sustained interest. This kind of introductory piano lesson may reach some children and stimulate their interest, provided that a real piano is available for their use.

Group lessons are also predicated on the assumption that all the children in a given group need identical instruction and that individual differences are at a minimum. There may be economy as far as teaching is concerned. Whether there is *economy in learning* for each child is another matter and will have to be decided by those concerned. After all, what about the children who are already familiar, in varying degrees, with the keyboard?

It has long been a practice of some piano teachers to offer small-group experiences in music to their private pupils for a short period each week. The teacher knows each child as an individual, his strengths and his weaknesses, and can group three or four for some very worthwhile musical experiences. Children enjoy playing for each other and with each other.

Group lessons can never be a substitute for individual teaching. Small-group experiences in music can, however, supplement and extend the interests of pupils. We must be on guard against foolproof systems of teaching music. They are many and ingenious, and each carries the guarantee that *it is* the perfect system. It is logical . . . it is painless . . . it will amuse the child. Perhaps the most dangerous of these appeals is that of being "logical." Here, we are told, is a neatly worked-out plan that leads deliberately from one stage to another; it is infallible! To be sure, some teachers seem to be successful with these systems, but what is probably true is that the children learn in spite of them, for youngsters do have a way of weeding out nonessentials.

In learning to read and play music there is no one way that will fit all children, any more than there is in learning to read words. The secret of any teaching lies in timing it to the readiness of the child and making it fit his interest. To do this the teacher must lend himself to the child, must get under his skin, must see things his way, and above all have that rare ability to feel and hear his way. More often than not children are ahead of us. We have grown so accustomed to thinking in terms of age levels, or are so dependent on what some authority says, that we have lost faith in our own observations and intuitions.

Piano for Adults

Many of us adults who have studied piano, even for a considerable length of time, are unaware of the vast possibilities in sound-making that this instrument offers. We have spent our lives playing "written" music and have accepted the fact that creating music belongs to the composers. The inventive use of the keyboard is beyond limits and so we miss the joy and excitement that can accompany making our own music. No experience can be more exciting and rewarding than studying with a genuinely *musical* music teacher, one who is so at home with the theory and structure of music that it is an integral part of his teaching.

I should like to conclude this chapter with the following description of just such an experience. The writer is a very musical person who plays the flute. As a classroom teacher she felt she needed help in learning a more flexible use of the piano. Here is what happened to her musically: [10]

In experimenting with sounds and rhythms, it is often easier to be free and creative on the drum, or on the floor or chair than it is to be free on a piano. I suppose this is because we do not come to the drum or other exciting sound-making device with any set pattern of style or use. However, when we sit down at the piano, we expect to play notes in a certain rhythmic, predetermined pattern which results in a recognizable tune. This is necessary to a certain extent, but not to the point of limitation that often results. I was in this stage before I started taking lessons from *H*. I felt that, in order to use the piano in any way, I should be able to play the notes in front of me—and not always being successful with the notes, *I used the piano less and less.* This was the "before" stage. The "after" stage is quite exciting and now the piano beckons me to it rather than scaring me away. The following are some of the stages I experimented in to become freer and more creative in the use of the piano:

10 Used by permission of Verlene Parker Ota.

The first step of my experience was to be able to use the entire keyboard. When one is used to limitations, this can be hard. I would pick any interval I wanted and play it all over the keyboard. There were many to choose from—a seventh, a second, a third, a fourth. Soon I began experimenting with the many ways these could be played—both hands playing the interval together, playing the interval alternating left and right hand, playing the intervals close together—so close as to be almost on top of each other—then playing them far apart, alternating hands or together. This was the beginning stage. I did not use a mixture of intervals, nor was I trying to get a rhythm. I was only using *all* of the piano. However, one unconsciously falls into *rhythm* and it became my next area of concentration.

It is sometimes hard to "think" a rhythm and play it on the piano without actually hearing its beat on something else. Thus I would often like tapping the drum or bench first in order to feel the rhythm. Then I would play it on the piano, using one interval and differing it as mentioned before. This is the beginning practice of being able to feel a child's rhythm as he walks or runs and then pick it up on some instrument.

Another thing that was very beneficial in thinking of rhythms was to think of a spoken line, poem, or sentence. After verbal repetition, the rhythm would naturally flow from the phrase and this would also help in creating a mood. For example, "the rabbit goes hoppity, hoppity, hoppity." I would think of the sentence, clap it or tap it on the bench until the rhythm was established, and then play it on the piano using a chosen interval. In connection with this I learned the values of notes and how to put a rhythm down on paper so as to remember it.

In experimenting with these rhythmic patterns, I learned many more variations besides keeping the pattern on one interval and one tone: (1) I could take the rhythm in its interval up or down the scale; (2) I could use the rhythm in its interval at one place on the piano and then change to another place; (3) I could play part of it with the notes near each other, and then shoot one note up or down on the keyboard; (4) In playing the rhythmic interval I could use both hands close together or far apart or would even cross hands.

It was important to realize, as ideas and phrases ran through my head and I fingered them on the piano, that the *rhythm* or *touch* used in the notes was *much more important than the actual pitch*. For example, in trying to produce rain sounds, I would often feel that I would have to race down the piano. Actually one could sense rain much better by playing softly and lightly on high or low notes, using an interval and a rhythmic pattern. This was also true of a heavy walk. It need not always be in low pitch, but the important thing is to get a slow, heavy beat, with either high or low notes.

Even creative experimentation is more likely to be expressive if there is some kind of pattern to it. Thus I began to practice giving some kind of phrasing to my patterns. I would try to play a pattern and tune, giving it a phrase pause without ending it, go on playing, and then come to a stop. This gave some kind of balance to the rhythm which I felt helped me a lot. For example, one way of bringing form to the above rhythm would be

> *The rabbit goes hoppity—*
> *The rabbit goes hoppity—*
> *The rabbit goes hoppity, hoppity, hoppity.*

Playing with *only one interval* in my rhythms was easiest, but *using more than one interval was and is exciting*. To get away from my common and habitual thirds, I tried making rhythms using only seconds and sevenths. This is where I began to hit the black notes and it has been hard to keep away from them ever since. The same kind of experimenting with all sorts of variations went on here, too. Seconds and sevenths could be played alternating hands, together, in repetition, or up and down the scale. I was always trying to find new and different variations. I would also try to keep in mind the phrasing element, which was harder here because I was so busy using so many different ways of playing my rhythms. This can result in a hodgepodge of too much, yet it is important to keep on experimenting in different ways in the making of rhythm. The phrasing is more important when we come to tune-making, which should be simple for children and needs pauses and ends. In rhythms you can use more elaborate variations.

It is important to remember, in experimenting with rhythms

on the piano, that there are many places besides the keyboard. One of the most thrilling times of experimentation was the use of the strings of a grand piano. One usually uses the pedal in doing this, and can either use the hand or a drumstick with a hard or soft head. Also, it is easy to forget about one's own body sounds, voice, and the clapping of various parts of the body. I spent many moments trying to accompany *H*'s movement, using all these variations in a rhythmic pattern—moving from the piano keyboard to slapping its side, to hitting the inside strings. It gives genuine and pleasurable variation. Here again I began to realize that it wasn't necessary to use all of the many sound effects at one time, but just enough to give the composition unique and interesting variation. Two other interesting piano techniques are the use of the whole arm and the elbow, and the use of the pedal. The former can be very effective in rolling accompaniment or going up and down in some imaginative play. It is also fun to strike a chord heavily on the piano and keep the pedal on it as the child runs from one end of the room to the other. A succession of well-timed chords can provide interesting stimulation and support for movement.

At the same time that I was learning about rhythms, I began to study ways of accompanying a melody or tune. I was amazed to find out its simplicity when given just a few cues. One can simply use an octave in the bass of each beginning note in a measure or an octave in the third lower than each beginning note. If one wants to use a chord, look at the measure and determine two notes in the measure that make a chord and use it. This chord can be used in a variety of ways, in its inversions, or by breaking it up by playing one note on one beat and then the other two on other beats. I also learned the IV and V chords and like to use their beauty and solidity to make the accompaniment more solid.

Most recently we have been experimenting in rhythms and tune-making, using definite limits, as an octave or the three-chord notes. Using the two octave notes as a base, I would try to find various ways of alternating rhythms for accompaniment within it. This, too, was for the purpose of a structure we sometimes like to have. But where this structure is most important is in tune-making. I would try to think of some mood I wanted to create, a lullaby or spring song, and then improvise a tune using the notes of a certain chord octave. There are many variations here, too, even though one tries to stay in a limited range, that of a chord in a child's singing range. One could use only the single chord notes, or one could use repetition of some of the notes. I then moved on to the possibility of using passing tones or neighboring tones, bringing in the possibility of almost all the notes of the octave, yet keeping the chord the dominant tune. It is most important in melody improvisation to have some kind of phrasing or pattern. Thus, one would start out with one tune, change or vary it in the middle, and then go back to the beginning notes to end the melody.

I can not begin to describe the wonderful feeling I have about playing the piano now, in contrast to my former experiences. Both children and I find this approach stimulating, creative and flexible. I am more able to concentrate on their mood and changing rhythms rather than on notes with much turning of pages.

The above experience illustrates how a mature music student was helped to find and use the fundamentals of music through a direct approach to the piano keyboard. She had read notes skillfully and easily for many years. She played both piano and flute. To some extent she had experienced vicariously the fundamentals of music through the compositions of others. But she had not been able to "talk" on the keyboard with her own sounds. She could not say in music what was important to her except as her feelings were reflected in the compositions of others. She had never been awakened to her own potentialities for invention and creativity on the piano.

Notes, key signatures, note values are the symbols of music. They are a way of writing down the sounds and movement of sounds. And yet over and over these are taught as the fundamentals of music. According to the school system or the philosophy of the music consultant or supervisor, classroom teachers are instructed when and how to begin teaching notation. The latest mechanical teaching aids are handed out in an endeavor to make the teaching as easy as possible, and the classroom teacher laboriously goes to work teaching note reading. The real fundamentals of music—rhythm, melody, and harmony—are pushed aside to get children to recognize notes.[11] Reading notes becomes the music program.

I suggest that the basic task of teaching music in the elementary school is that of acquainting children with the *real* fundamentals of music, to be sure that they build pleasant associations with music, to whet their appetites so that they will have a constantly growing interest in it. For many this interest will be promoted by direct instruction in notation, but only when the child recognizes the need for it in learning to play an instrument or in singing in a choral group. For some this may come at any time in the primary grades; for others it may not become a necessity until the upper elementary grades or even later. When a child really wants to learn to read music he is ready for intelligent instruction. He does not need trick methods; he will learn directly. The usual methods of "systematic instruction" in notation applied in sequence from grade level to grade level miss the boat. Not all children feel the need for notation and time is wasted in "listening" but not learning.

The piano is a unique instrument in that it offers so many possibilities in helping the child discover the real fundamentals of music. There are many ports of entry in discovering these. Notation is one, but when it takes precedence over genuine firsthand personal acquaintance with the keyboard in ways that have real meaning to the learner, it too often obscures, rather than illuminates, the real fundamentals.

MUSIC SOURCES FOR THE BEGINNING PIANO STUDENT

Bartók, Béla, *For Children,* New York: Boosey and Hawkes.
———, *Mikrokosmar,* Vols. 1–6, New York: Boosey and Hawkes.
[11] James Mursell, *Music and the Classroom Teacher,* New York: Silver Burdett.

Burrows, Raymond (ed.), *The Horace Mann Piano Book,* Boston: Boston Music Co.

———— and Ella Ahearn, *Young America at the Piano,* New York: Willis Music Co.

———— and ————, *The Young Explorer at the Piano,* New York: Willis Music Co.

Frost, Berenice, *Companion Series for the Piano,* Books I and II, Boston: Boston Music Co.

Mason, Mary Bacon, *Folk Songs and Famous Pictures,* Boston: Ditson.

Mirovitch, Alfred (ed.), *Introduction to Piano Classics,* Books 1–3, New York: Schirmer.

Roseman, Floy Adele, *Keyboard Speech,* Evanston, Ill.: Summy-Birchard.

Schelling, Ernest, *Singing and Playing: The Beginning Book,* New York: Oxford. The primer in the Oxford piano course.

Chapter 7

DANCE

M OVEMENT IS the infant's first instinctive reaction to life. He is not consciously aware of it but, except during his sleep, he is getting constant experience in its use. In addition to his automatic reflex movements which give him pleasure and satisfaction, he soon begins to learn a measure of control over certain movements in order to achieve a goal. Is there anything more delightful for the observer than the experience of watching the infant's beginning explorations as he struggles to get his finger in his mouth—feels around in space and, finally, satisfactorily resolves a need?

Exploring Movement

Do we ever stop to think of the skill that is required for the toddler to balance himself on two feet, maintain his equilibrium, and walk? The acquirement of a similar feat of physical coordination is rarely equaled by the average adult in later life. Rolling and crawling, pushing and pulling, running and jumping, children are showing us constantly their delight and their "at-homeness" in movement; climbing and exploring, with leaps and bounds, they are all over the

144

place. To mother and dad, life seems to be just one catapult after another! Unhappy indeed is the home that does not provide unencumbered space for the baby, and unhappy is the baby if avoiding precious antiques and knickknacks calls for too much self-control.

"To prevent bodily weakness and infirmity, exercise is necessary: and one physician has said that he did not know what was most necessary to the human frame, *food* or *motion*." Over one hundred and fifty years have passed since this statement appeared in *Youthful Recreation*, a magazine published in Philadelphia. It would be interesting to know what this physician meant by "motion." Was he thinking of some prescribed form of exercise, or of games, or of dance, or of the usual normal activity of daily life? The demands of our early farm and village life went a long way toward satisfying the needs of physical development that in present-day life have to be artificially provided for. Whether or not our forefathers were conscious of the importance of "motion," it was of necessity a part of their very existence. It is unlikely that these forefathers were psychologically oriented to the therapeutic and physical values inherent in the movements necessary to carry on day-by-day living, but youth got on with "exercise" just the same!

In recent years, through our study of the child and how he grows, we have learned a great deal about the value of physical activity. Specialists in the field of child development have told us what children need, and manufacturers have produced a large variety of equipment to satisfy these needs. The home and the school have become increasingly conscious of the necessity of providing adequately for children's physical development. The slide has taken the place of the cellar door; the jungle gym, of trees. We have parks and playgrounds equipped with apparatus, and we see to it that children have an opportunity to use this equipment.

Too often, however, we think that when we have supplied certain equipment, we have taken care of all the child's exercising needs, and we are prone not only to overlook the value of his use of movement unrelated to equipment, but even to discourage it. Mothers, in their desire for cleanliness, urge their babies to walk rather than creep or confine them to a small place until they are able to walk. Yet physical-growth specialists tell us that children stop creeping too soon, and nursery schools encourage this way of moving about by providing low places to crawl through and under. With most children this is a natural movement unless it is denied them.

Schools are at fault as much as homes; building superintendents and administrators accept the fact that children in the nursery school use the floors, but kindergarten and primary teachers have a constant struggle (usually a losing one) with superintendents to have the floors kept clean enough so that older children may use them freely. Make no mistake about it: the fun of tumbling, rolling, and sliding does not belong exclusively to a nursery-school curriculum. If we watch any group of four-, five-, or six-year-olds we shall find that a large part of their time is spent on the floor, either in such activities as block building or just in the sheer physical enjoyment of tumbling around.

Boys and girls of elementary-school age find other ways of exploring movement since adults, both in the home and in school, are not usually sympathetic to the kind of activity acceptable in the younger child. They soon learn that tumbling and other similar uses of the floor are not what is expected of them, and they reserve their antics for times when adults are not around. But youngsters are resourceful and, even in the most formal schoolroom, they find ways and means of moving of which even they are unaware.

Have you ever really *seen* the many inventive and ingenious ways a boy has of getting out of his seat? Have you *seen* the ways he uses his legs and his torso while he is sitting in his seat, even when deeply interested in his work? Have you *seen* what happens in movement when excited and eager children raise their hands to reply to a question? Not long ago, after a college class in which we were trying to awaken and extend our perceptions in movement, an experienced teacher of ten- and eleven-year-old children saw for the first time the ways in which the children in her class raised their hands.

Here are a few of her observations: "holding arm straight out on a diagonal and sharply jiggling it back and forth; increasing the range by making their arms turn in a full circle about their heads; changing direction and level as they half stood up and rapidly changed the arm they were raising, at the same time there was a shift of body weight; changing focus and direction by crossing their arms in back of them and more or less hugging their heads; decreasing the range as arms were held taut and wrists were shaken." This teacher's observations made all of us *see* in a way we had never seen before and encouraged us to bring new eyes to the movements in day-by-day living with children.

How much more interesting to pick up papers around the wastebasket by squatting and hopping around the area than in the way a grownup would do it! Stairs are a chore to the adult; to the child they offer adventure—two steps at a time, backwards, sideways, eyes closed, reaching the top or bottom by two steps forward and one step backward. Two-and-a-half-year-old Johnny reached the bottom of the stairs ahead of his mother, then stopped and jumped from the second step. Mother's heart skipped a beat, and then she stood at the bottom and encouraged him to do it again. Over and over he jumped, and then learned to walk backwards up the lower steps. He had conquered the world.

Children are constantly talking to us in movement. They are showing us what is important to them; they talk with their hands, their heads, their eyes, their legs, their bodies. All of this is related to dance, for dance is composed of movement and rhythm. John Dewey reminds us that the esthetic arts are the "enhancements of the processes of every day life."[1] It is from living itself that the great dancers and the choreographers draw their "material." In a recent news interview with Clark Jones, who directed the telecast of the *Cinderella* ballet, he commented on the unique possibilities of choreography for television, for example, choreography for fingers and eyes combined into the whole fabric of a composition. What would a Clark Jones see in a class waving their hands in reply to a teacher's question? Perhaps not a dance composition, but he would surely see possibilities of which our dim eyes and kinesthetic perceptions are unaware.

Let us look at movement through the eyes of Thomas Bouchard, a photographer of dance, as reported by Walter Sorell.[2]

I am walking along 42d Street. It is ten o'clock. Suddenly I see a paper flying in the air. It is floating with graceful majesty without a single repetition in its movements down along the walls of this gigantic masonry. At the same time my eye catches sight of an old man trying to cross the street. Lifeworn, the incarnation of man's frailty. He steps down from the sidewalk. A jaywalker. A passing car at full speed just misses him. One jerk—he jumps backward onto the sidewalk. This backward movement, performed with unconscious intensity in fright and in his basic drive for self-preservation, is the muscular reaction of a split second. From head to toe complete coordination. The entire system unaware of its powers worn out by life, drained by age, suddenly concentrated in one little movement in one step in harmony with itself but also with the cacophonous world around him.

The paper. The old man. And also the girl.

While I see the paper glide down and the old man leap for his life—a girl is in the range of my vision. She comes toward me. She hurries. She must be late for her office. I see the movement of her body, the tender curves of her bosom, its hardly perceptible

1 *Art as Experience*, New York: Putnam's, 1934, p. 6.
2 Walter Sorell (ed.), *The Dance Has Many Faces*, Cleveland: World, 1951, pp. 62–63.

quiver under the tight blouse, her head slightly held sidewise. The image of natural perfection.

Thanks to my ocular perception, thanks to my two eyes, I can see the paper, the man and the girl—absorb their movements and be aware of the rhythmic flow of an inanimate thing, of muscular motion, of grace and beauty per se and be aware of all this at one moment.

Let us look at five-year-old Tom on his way to school as he goes the distance of a long block, weaving himself "scallop" fashion from one side of the sidewalk to the other, so as to touch the hood of each car parked along the curb. For Tom, walking that block each morning is an adventure in the exploration of space and a growing awareness of the possibilities of space. Tom, and the countless other Toms and Marys, are, *appropriate to their stage of development,* dealing with a very important aspect of dance—space—the increased awareness of it and its possibilities being one of the major contributions of Wigman to the dance.

Children are not dancers in the sense that years of study, devotion, insight, and training make the professional dancer, but they are constantly dealing with the stuff of which dance is made—movement and rhythm. They are unaware of what they do, they transcend the know-how and do the impossible because they will to do it. The dancer, aware of what he does and how he does it, can control and recapture a movement to express what he wishes to communicate.

A moving child, moving in a nonconformist way, can be a threat to a grownup within the home and in the school. We are afraid of what might happen, and so we tend to discourage movement experimentation except through regular channels such as games and the use of equipment. At the same time we talk a great deal about creative dance and rack our brains to motivate a group of youngsters to use movement creatively at dance time! Classroom teachers reach out for techniques, questions to ask, dramatic ideas to interpret, music that will evoke movement, hoping that the children will respond. Many of the children do, after a fashion, but there are usually one or two for whom this is sissy stuff. Yet these same youngsters, during free time, show remarkable skill in the way in which they use movement. But they do not know that these natural impulses to movement are the "raw material" of dance, and usually we do not know it either. It takes the kinesthetic sensitivity of a dancer, of a dance choreographer, of a dance photographer, to see the roots of dance in these basic movements.

What Dance Means to Us

Recreational Dance: Ballet

There are many kinds of dance, and tradition and association are important factors in determining what dance means to each one of us. Square dancing, folk dance, play party games, ballroom dance—each or all can mean social dancing. Ballet, for the most part, is what we see on the stage, television, or screen, and if we lend ourselves to it, lifts us out of the stream of daily living to emotional and imaginative heights. Perhaps we can identify so closely with the ballet that it becomes a vital vicarious experience. Fond mothers have visions of their children becoming great ballet dancers and, until the rigorous training of ballet has been experienced, these hopes are often shared by their children. To be sure, there are the exceptional few who have the potential talent and intensity of desire and the depth of inspiration that accept and transcend the long and arduous technical training which is necessary for this art.

Certainly we would agree that our children should be able to participate in and enjoy such forms of social or recreational dancing as ballroom, folk, and square dancing. The kind of dance that is the current vogue among their peers is something we do not have to teach. While we are going through any particular epidemic of these current manifestations of dance that are so important to the teen-ager, it is difficult to believe that they will pass. But they do. We do have a responsibility for teaching the more conventional types of dance. As a matter of fact, these are the dances which are usually taught in our elementary schools. Classroom teachers who, in the great majority of our schools, are responsible for dance instruction of their groups feel at home in these dances. The teacher is given many instructional materials related to this type of dance. Recordings of folk, square, and ballroom dancing are numerous. Books of singing games, in which dance is used, and books on folk and square dancing abound. Collections of music and careful directions have been compiled, suggesting ways to teach the dance.

Formally taught dances are good fun, provide good physical exercise, and are useful in teaching how to follow directions. But are they really creative? If the child can recapture in his mind the joy and excitement, for example, that inspired the folk dancing in celebration of a bountiful harvest, perhaps then he can re-create some of these feelings within himself. But do we approach folk dancing in this way? Do we ask children how they would feel after a long drought when rain finally comes and food is assured, and allow them to express their relief and joy? Or, if we do ask them, are their life experiences sufficiently similar so they can identify with the feelings of the people for whom this was a very vital emotional experience? Or do we teach them the dance as directed and tell them that this is what the dance is intended to celebrate? A measure of creativity, depending on the way it is taught, may be found, but too often it is not in evidence. These dances are fun and a part of the heritage of our children, but they are not essentially creative.

Creative Rhythms

But there is more to dance. We hear a great deal about "creative rhythms." Nursery schools, kindergartens, elementary grades have "creative-rhythm" programs. Music is played and children are urged to interpret it. There is a question, however, of how much real creativity is possible when music is the sole stimulus of dance.

Perhaps if we compare the art of movement with another art, painting, for example, we can see more clearly how we have unintentionally handicapped children in their use of movement as it relates to the dance. When we give paints to a child, we do not tell him what to paint; we encourage him to use his own initiative in experimenting with color and line. His first interest is in the art material itself and what he can do with it, and the teacher will not hurry this stage.

In movement, however, we play music for a child and ask him to listen to it and "do what it says!" In other words, we start out with a framework into which we expect the child to fit his idea. If we were to carry this method over into painting, we should say to the child: "Here are paints that you may use in painting a picture of a house." But someone will say: "Yes, we play music, but we tell the child to do what he likes to it." Carrying this analogy further, we should then say to the child who is painting: "You may paint any kind of house you wish, but you *must* paint a house!"

When music is played for children and they are asked to move to it, a pattern and a mood are set that limit the type of movement. Or we have the situation in which music is played, but the children do whatever they please, regardless of the accompaniment. In the first case, a child's creativeness is limited; in the second, music ceases to have any meaning as related to the movement.

Programs are built around animal rhythms, mechanical rhythms, transportation rhythms, and so on. Each set of rhythms has its own particular music, played either on records or on the piano. Depending upon the way in which the teacher works with boys and girls, a certain amount of invention and ingenuity may be encouraged. Dramatic ideas stimulate the use of the entire body in a way that is not possible with folk and square dancing. The sensitive teacher, working together with a group of children, can release imagination and make it possible for desirable skills to be developed. But what the child does must be apppropriate to the music.

Not a few, however, have gone beyond the bounds of the limitations of music and are working freely with children in the field of movement exploration itself. Even though one is not a dancer, a study of what movement means in modern dance can give us a truly exciting insight into the possibilities of dance with children. Gladys Andrews suggests many techniques intended to make both the teacher and the children more aware of the possibilities of the great variety of body movements.[3] The emphasis is first on movement itself and second on the interpretation of music.

Modern Dance

A consideration of the more liberal interpretation of "creative rhythms" leads us directly into an examination of "modern" dance and what its underlying philosophy has to offer those of us who work with boys and girls in the elementary school.

One of the greatest contributions made by modern dance has been its recognition of the independence of movement as an art medium. Music is used to support movement; it is part of the scenery; it is the handmaiden of the dance. Many times it is composed especially for the dance, since music that will clearly interpret the movement cannot always be found. Those of us who work with children have much to learn from

[3] *Creative Rhythmic Movement for Children,* Englewood Cliffs, N. J.: Prentice-Hall.

a study of modern dance if we are to be understanding guides of their use of movement. We have given children opportunity for unhampered physical activity on the playground during their free periods; but, as soon as a small group comes together for dancing, we have been too eager not only to tie their ideas immediately to music but also to use music as a stimulus. We forget that children's ideas and their urge to sheer physical activity are a much more powerful and vital stimulus than any music we can offer, and a far more rewarding one if we wish to capture their enthusiasm. We must therefore give them every opportunity to use their "material," the material of movement, and train ourselves in recognizing their natural functional movements as our most important asset in teaching. Their movements spring from feelings and needs that are strong within them. The expression of these in movement has vitality and, if we give it encouragement and support, its own unique form evolves.

It was her quest for the essence of dance that led Isadora Duncan to reject the prevailing dance forms of her day. Dance had become so crystallized and surrounded with so many sterile techniques that she could not find herself within its framework. She turned to the dances of the early Greeks, not because she wanted to dance as they did, but because she wanted to find out *why* they danced as they did. Duncan was responsible for the birth of what has come to be known as modern dance.

Wigman, who has been credited with "freeing" the dance from the domination of music, was also in search of the essence of dance.[4] Her idea for a dance sprang from within her, and she had the courage to allow this idea to find its own form without any preconceived pattern.

Great dancers such as Isadora Duncan and Mary Wigman threw aside the thwarting techniques of tradition and

---

[4] "Composition in Pure Movement," *Modern Dance*, Jan.–Feb. 1946. Reprinted in Brewster Ghiselin (ed.), *The Creative Process*, New York: New American Library, 1955.

recognized that the art vitality of their contribution lay in the development of techniques peculiar and unique to the individual and to the idea which they were creating. Should this knowledge not give us courage as we work with boys and girls? We are not trying to train professional dancers in our schools. We say, over and over again, that we want our children to have the joys and satisfactions that attend dance, and then, by our insistence on stressing *first* even the simple techniques of leaping, skipping, and keeping time to music, we unintentionally put obstacles in the way.

Take, for example, the concern of both the adult and the child because the child is a "one-footed" skipper. Such approaches as teaching the child to hop first on one foot and then on the other focus attention on technique, and he becomes self-conscious and more removed than ever from the goal. Skipping has to do with the feeling of lift in the body, reaching to the sky. If the adult focuses on this, and takes the child by the hand, skipping with him and taking attention away from his feet, it isn't long before he becomes a "two-footed" skipper. From the standpoint of the child, are we not trying to help him capture the "why" of skipping just as Duncan tried to find out why Greek dancers danced as they did?

Think of all of the other movements in which the "one-footed" skipper may be skilled, types of movements involving the entire body that are used so much by modern dance. But we do not recognize them in a "skipping, jumping, marching" program as being part of dance, and so undue emphasis is given to these *few* techniques. Many a dance teacher believes that the child cannot begin to create until he has learned and mastered these skills. The teacher may see no dance possibilities in the countless skilled uses of the body, floor movements of all kinds, the twistings and turnings and wigglings and squirmings (if you wish), the almost impossible (to adults) stunts and tricks, the ability to crawl into an idea and project the feelings that inspire it. These are skills that, to a degree, even the nursery-school child has and that, unfortunately, he too often learns are not respected even in kindergarten because we want him to express himself in our particular brand of movement.

For too long we have identified the means to the end with the goal. This has been pointed out to us innumerable times by such great thinkers as Alfred North Whitehead and Albert Einstein. We take on and give precedence to the techniques of an art rather than assiduously cultivating the essence of the art. The movement of modern dance exemplified this search for meanings and that is why, I believe, a study of it as conceived by the really great dancers in the field holds so much for us in our work with children. In recent years, it has lost its creative vitality, in some instances, through preoccupation with "systems" or "schools" of technique.

Writing on dance as a means of communication, John Martin gives us a clear and direct definition of modern dance: [5]

Indubitably no other art form has been so inaptly named as the "modern dance." Not only is the phrase non-descriptive, but it is markedly inaccurate, since there is absolutely nothing modern about modern dance. It is, as a matter of fact, virtually basic dance, the oldest of all dance forms. The modern dancer, instead of employing the cumulative resources of academic tradition, cuts through directly to the source of all dancing. He utilizes the principle that every emotional state tends to express itself in movement, and that the movements thus created spontaneously, though they are not representational, reflect accurately in each case the character of the particular emotional state. Because of the inherent contagion of bodily movement, which makes the onlooker feel sympathetically in his own musculature the exertions he sees in somebody else's musculature, the dancer is able to convey through movement the most intangible emotional experience. This is the prime purpose of the modern dance; it is not interested in spectacle, but in the communication of emo-

[5] *The Dance*, New York: Tudor, p. 105.

tional experiences—intuitive perceptions, elusive truths—which cannot be communicated in reasoned terms or reduced to mere statement of fact.

This principle is at least as old as man himself; primitive societies, as we have seen, have found it so potent that they have called it magic and based religious and social practices on it. But it had never been consciously utilized as the basis of art, so far as any record exists, until the turn of the present century when Isadora Duncan made it the very center and source of her practices, and the so-called modern dance was born.

In his lectures and writing, John Martin, the well-known dance critic of *The New York Times,* has pointed out two forces hostile to the development of modern dance (we shall continue to call it "modern dance" because that is the name used so generally; but we hope the reader will keep in mind Martin's concept of basic dance): first, the domination of music, and second, the literary mind.

The thoughtful consideration of these two obstacles, and relegating both music and the "literary" mind to their appropriate places in the art of dance, should give us a deeper understanding of movement as a creative medium in itself. A constantly growing increase in our knowledge of the scope and variety of movement, *attended especially* by a developing kinesthetic sensitivity to it, will promote this understanding. Some of the obstacles that get in our way and keep us from accepting and working with the movements that have deep meaning for children will be identified as we go along.

Increasing Our Understanding of Dance

We cannot teach something we do not know. We can, however, be "knowing" about that something—in this case, movement—in a way that will help us live with children so that we recognize and *see* with understanding eyes and feelings the dispositions and skills they already have. The following are a few of the ways in which we can learn more about dance and children.

Observing Children and Its Implications

Parents and teachers have long been encouraged to observe children to obtain a better understanding of how they grow and develop. The mental, emotional, social, and physical aspects of development have been the focuses of observations. While movement and rhythm are not unrelated to these, for the purpose of studying dance we shall focus directly on the movements of children. Our best laboratory here is found where the child is unsupervised: his free play on the streets, in the playground, in the backyard; the ways in which he goes about his chores at home and in school; his movements when he is "quiet," while he is reading, watching television, or listening; and the countless other situations in which he is unaware of his movements or times when he is consciously practicing skills in doing stunts.

What is happening when a seven-year-old walks backwards and zigzags up the stairs with his eyes closed? If he has been sent on an errand this may not be the time for "movement loitering," for it may take *three minutes* longer than if he dashed up the steps. We shall have to decide if the saving of three minutes is a matter of greater importance than his experience both movementwise and in relation to relaxation. Can we be "tolerant of trances" as "he feeds on time"? [6] Is it *time* that annoys us or the fact that he is using the stairs in an unconventional, though not antisocial, way?

To the imaginative child, and certainly to the dancer, the use of space is an adventure. The most interesting distance to a point is not a straight line! Have you ever watched the ways in which the dancer uses even a very limited space—the space possibilities he feels, horizontally and vertically, in the development of his dance idea?

[6] From the poem *Boy Dressing* by Mark Van Doren.

Can we allow for and utilize children's talent for space in our dance programs? Can we say to them, "This is what you do and you do it well, so we shall do more of it"? Can you recall the glow that you experienced when someone approved something you had been doing and how you bent every effort to do it better? Living with children in such a way offers the kind of soil for learning that cannot possibly be achieved with artificial motivation.

Let us put the idea of exploration of space to work in a typical school "rhythm" session where the group marches together. Usually the goal is keeping time to music. Once that has been achieved, the "march idea," with one or two possible variations such as tiptoe marching, has been exhausted! Children are trained to go in one direction, the teacher believing this necessary so that they will not bump into each other. The nonconformist youngster who starts to walk backwards or weave in and out, or go in the opposite direction, is promptly reminded that this isn't the way to march. He either conforms or he stays on the sidelines. The muscular impulse that he had toward variation and toward making a monotonous movement interesting is not recognized as a lead to a more advanced level of marching and certainly a more artistic one.

Why? Simply because we assume that children cannot walk in varying directions in a group without getting in each other's way. *But they can,* as the teacher of fours, of eights, and of twelves well knows who has encouraged this kind of exploration. "Find out as many different ways of marching as you can—*as long as you do not interfere with anyone else.*" Anyone who does not respect this can be removed from the group, and rarely will this happen more than once. For this is fun, this is adventure, and well worth accepting the restriction. As individual children in the group begin to explore space in interesting ways, the teacher can call attention to them one at a time, and everyone can try these variations out.

In other words, there are thirty possible teachers in a group rather than just one.

What fun for the mother in the home, and for the child, to open the door to dance for her three-year-old.[7] "Just as I noticed that Anne had noticed the squeak she made with wet fingers on her balloon, I also noticed the other day, when I was using the egg beater, that Anne was stamping her feet in a sort of Mexican dance in time to the rhythm the beater was making." After she stopped using the egg beater, Anne's mother played a game of "talking with her feet" with Anne. "Anne caught on immediately and she seems to use it not only as a game but as a test of whether I can recognize her stamps and also as a sort of transposed stamping that might be used in a temper tantrum!" Are we not all fascinated by the skillful "conversations with their feet" performed by groups of Spanish dancers such as José Greco's troupe?

From a student teacher who saw and accepted a child's way of hopping around the wastebasket while picking up bits of paper comes the following thoughtful understanding of her own increased awareness of children in the classroom.[8]

In watching children as they move about the room working, unaware that they are being observed, I have been amazed at the variety and complexity of the movements involved. It is impossible to discuss the free movement of the children without also discussing my change of attitude which has accompanied these observations. In the example of the child picking up the papers, my first impulse was to tell him to pick up the papers as quickly as possible without hopping around. However, I stopped myself in time. What difference did it make if it took a few extra seconds to pick up the papers?

I have found that the most interesting times to watch the children's movements are during the transition periods. After snack time we have a short session in which we clean up, turn one table on top of a second, and stack them against the wall. My

[7] Used by permission of Susan Ginsberg.
[8] Used by permission of Hannah Klein.

cooperating teacher and I turn the tables on top of each other, and two children push the tables to the wall. It is while they are waiting for the teachers to come and turn tables that all kinds of interesting movements take place. The table is often used in the same capacity as the bar in a ballet studio. Arms and legs go flying; bodies are twirling, bending and stretching. Here too, I have put the reins on myself. I once saw a boy doing some kind of arabesque with a beat (making the calves of his legs meet in mid-air) and was about to come out with some "schoolteacherish" comment to the effect of, "Is that the way to help?" when I caught myself just in time. It isn't that long ago that I stood at a bar in dancing school while the ballet master *laboriously tried to get us to master* just that step!

Children often approach me with new and interesting movements which they have thought up at home or have noticed themselves doing! They know that I am interested.

I have also tried to tie in movement with other things we are learning. We are trying to develop the concept of roundness. We have a science tray of things that roll and through experimentation have discovered that round things roll but square or straight things don't. Recently I read the children the story, *A Kiss Is Round*. We then found parts of ourselves that were round and things in the room that were round. Now I tried to fit in movement. "Can you make yourself round?" Immediately I had a group of round little balls on the floor. At my suggestion they were soon demonstrating the things they could do if they were round. We all tried the individual stunts of the various children, rolling, turning, rocking, and rolling just one leg or arm to mention a few. We stood up to see how we could go around while standing. Did we have to stand still to go round? "No!" They showed me how they could run *around* the room, skip *around* the room. We got into a circle and went around together. By this time everyone had had a grand time, had exercised his muscles, had used his body actively and creatively, and had increased his concept of round.

"They know that I am interested." This is the key with which this teacher is able to unlock the door for her children and for herself—in this case, the door to dance for five-year-olds.

An experienced teacher of elementary-school boys and girls has discovered the same magic key recently with his group of ten-year-olds.[9]

Whether we are parents, teachers, relatives, or friends of the child, the mere fact that we come to an awareness of movement and sound in *ourselves* is a giant step. It is contagious. Our next job is to allow this new awareness to develop and strike receptive chords within us. Then we must appreciate and encourage movement and sound in others; and finally, we must be willing to experiment and grow some more.

Until recently, there were limited things for me which dealt with motion:

1. Vehicles moved swiftly.

2. Athletes moved quickly and gracefully and skillfully.

3. Trees and fields of grass and grain swayed beautifully in the wind.

4. Dancers studied hard to express one of (or a combination of) the above.

But then, one day I began to observe closely a child who never sat in her chair in the "proper" way! ("Proper" is hereby defined as my once limited insight which led me to believe that proper was having the rear on the seat of a chair, feet on floor, back straight, and head bent slightly forward.) As soon as I assessed the situation and myself, I came to the conclusion that this was the *only* reason I was annoyed—limited insight. I began then to notice other most interesting movements: In the swimming pool, the shower, in the gymnasium, in preschool and postschool group gatherings, during activity and work periods, during, after, and before play-acting and singing times, and even during reading and painting sessions. Once I noticed and enjoyed them, I encouraged and appreciated "new" and more interesting ways of moving with the children in my room. Almost overnight, my classroom has become "radioactive" as each atom-child-in-motion

9 Used by permission of Charles Reasoner.

continues to set off chain reactions of movement in the others. But I had to be the one to begin—to release it all by way of reacting first so as to set the others free. I had to come out of my dark, soundproof cocoon. All of this loosened "energy-movement" may seem alarming to some who would have it harnessed. Indeed, teacher-harnessed movement would be void movement.

It does not run wastefully and dangerously amuck in my classroom. In fact, it *is* harnessed, but not by me! The faith I had in children paid off because they "harnessed" (perhaps controlled or limited would be better words) themselves. Because they have been free to experiment, because they have been encouraged at *appropriate* times, because they have been living in a democratic type of classroom—one that attempts to show that freedom *does not* mean lack of restriction but, instead, sets up regulations respecting others' rights—because of this, they *know*, without being told or reprimanded, that there are times when we move very little. (Fortunately these times are few in the course of a school day.) They know, too, that experimentation in movement is not permissible much of the time but, also, it is genuinely appreciated. They know and they do and they repeat and they try again.

And how good you feel inside (how you wish you were young again) when a child runs up to you and says: "Hey, Mr. Reasoner! Look! I've found another way of putting on my coat!" A smile from you and he places his coat on the floor, falls down, squirms into it, and runs home for lunch.

There are times, too, when we have to talk together about moving—when John bumps into Bill because he was walking backwards and wasn't looking and Bill decides to punch him back; when Sally uses two chairs to sit on and leaves Mary without one; when Alex says he can cross the street with his eyes closed; when Betty stands on another's desk (and books and papers) to spin and twirl, and so on. But here again we have a learning-teaching situation. Children learn to respect others and themselves; children learn that freedom to move does not mean moving without paying heed to safety rules, just as they learn that there is no freedom without restriction. Children learn this. Teachers, we hope, learn to have faith in children.

Through seeing children's movements with new eyes, and through feeling children's movements with increased kinesthetic sensitivity, our observations of children in everyday living can become a powerful force in our understanding of dance. The illustrations just used evidence a *readiness to accept variations* in children's ways of doing a routine thing (putting on a coat, going upstairs, picking up papers); a recognition of *change in attitude* in oneself; the ability *to see relationships* between a child's use of movement and dance; and a growing confidence in a moving child.

Vicarious Experiences

Movement in and of itself has a peculiar fascination for most of us. The incoming waves, the wind in the trees, rocking in a chair, watching the turntable of a record player, the revolving ferris wheel and carousel, horses racing, cars passing, and countless other similar experiences can contribute to our relaxation and sense of well-being if we allow ourselves to "tune in" with motion.

Sitting quietly in a seat at a dance concert can be a vital and tingling experience if we identify kinesthetically with the dancer. Many come away from an *Oklahoma,* or *Carousel,* or *The King and I,* either the screen or stage production, with a heightened awareness of movement and, for those who live closely with children, there is a quick realization of the similarities between the physical stunts and antics of youngsters in their unsupervised play and many of the body movements of the dancers. Children *are not* miniature dancers— the dancer has an acute awareness of every part of his body, and calls upon it at will to communicate his dance. But the freshness in the sure, pure use of the body that the child has captivates the attention of the observer who is movement-minded.

Mime is another art medium which can cultivate a greater sensitivity to movement. The very isolation of movement in this art makes for a greater impact on the observer. Do the gestures and almost imperceptible movements of children take on new meaning for us as our eyes have been opened to wider movement through the enjoyment of mime? I especially recommend the films of the French mime Marcel Marceau, such as *In the Park*.

Dance has come into our homes today on the television screen. Theatrical productions, religious programs, and even commercials call upon many forms of dance to convey their messages. I wonder if we are aware of the many ways movement itself is used by advertisers on television to accent their sales arguments! Turn down the speaker and watch. As a matter of fact, it is sometimes interesting to look at dance without sound.

How much do our children learn about movement from television? There is a feast of movement available for them, but we cannot possibly measure it, nor are we always aware of the meaning they take from any particular program. A mother recently reported that her two young children were fascinated with wrestling matches. After observing one herself, she saw no reason why this should prove to be so attractive until she discovered them zealously practicing the movements used by the wrestlers without any interest in wrestling *with* each other. A thoughtful study of dance on television and the screen, and in photographs of dancers, can contribute greatly to our knowledge of dance. One's movement sense cannot help but be quickened by the beautiful and artistic film, *The Works of Calder,* distributed by the Museum of Modern Art in New York. In this film, the viewer has a rare treat in color and motion as he watches the mobiles of Alexander Calder and movements in nature. The music accompaniment is by John Cage, in twelve-tone style, harp and Chinese gong used for the most part. (The longer edition of the film is recommended.) What a fascinating adventure can be ours as we read about dance in such autobiographies as those of Pavlova and Duncan and in the numerous books on dance written for the layman.

What does an old, low, sprawling apple tree mean to us? Of course it means apples, but to those of us who grew up in small towns or in the country *such a tree is an invitation to climb;* to swing from its branches directly or on a rope-suspended swing with its endless possibilities of knots and double-deckers, to twist and spin; to nestle snugly in the crotch of a branch on a summer's afternoon; to watch the patterns of moving leaves; to build our castle and dream. For many of us a fence was for climbing, a gate for swinging, a grassy hill for rolling, a wheat field for lying quietly and watching the waves of grain against the blue sky. And, if the home were fortunate enough to own a long mirror, this, too, became a rendezvous before which we secretly became great ballerinas performing for enthusiastic audiences which we knew were in the palm of our hands! Can we rediscover our childhood experiences in movement of all kinds, and can this rediscovery help us to discover more in children's movements? Recapturing the thrills and satisfactions of these experiences can be an important part of our dance education.

Direct Experience in Dance

There is no substitute for personal experience in dance. Fortunately, most parents and teachers have had some experience in one or more forms of recreational dancing. A few have studied modern dance in high school or college, but it is the exceptional teacher or parent who is a trained dancer.

Personal experience in modern dance can be a tremendous asset in working with children. If we have not had it, one is never too old to go in search of it, *provided* the right teacher is secured. My own first four "tries" in modern-dance classes proved to be not only exhausting but altogether concerned with techniques, the premise being that once the techniques were learned I could start to dance. Since my intention was not to become a dancer, but rather to become familiar with what is considered to be the essence of dance, I very soon decided that these classes did not meet my need, nor could I keep up with them! Perhaps fifteen or twenty years earlier they would have been more appropriate. I was fortunate, however, in finding a dancer who was interested in what I outlined to her as my needs, both for myself and in teaching children. She was one of those rare teachers who was able to identify with her pupil rather than teach a preconceived system. She, too, was interested in children, not as a "trainer," but as a learner. She visited my group a number of times and opened new horizons to me because of the significant movements she saw in children's spontaneous play.

I have known several classroom teachers trained in modern dance who were able to teach their children a few of the lesser techniques of dance, but whose focus was so technique-oriented that they saw no possibilities in children's spontaneous movements. Were they afraid of children? Did they not respect the use of their bodies, and did they not see skills in such use? Or was their way of living with children so limited that there was little opportunity for any kind of movement?

On the other hand, not long ago I observed a physically handicapped teacher so alive to the possibilities of dance in her class and so able to release her students's potentialities movementwise that an observer might have thought this class had been taught by a skilled dance teacher.

Skill in and knowledge of modern dance can be a rewarding experience for a classroom teacher providing she is able to cut through to the heart of dance rather than concern herself with the techniques. Not that techniques are not important—each child as he consciously and avidly practices a trick or stunt is using a technique, one that evolves directly out of the situation and has real meaning for him.

Our most important job in teaching dance to children is with ourselves. The foregoing discussion has been directed toward the encouragement of a constantly growing recognition of the vocabulary of movement. The more we see and feel for ourselves, the more we see in children. The philosopher Martin Buber reminds us of this power of awareness: "Nothing can be done without awareness. With it, anything is possible." The conscious pursuit of awareness in dance and the recognition of the "many faces" of dance are rewarding, not only in teaching children, but primarily in one's own growth. And it is in the minutiae of daily living where we can discover so much, as a student recently expressed so well: "While walking along the street, I have tried to think of, for instance, how my big toe *feels* at that particular moment, or to watch my hands doings various activities. A sensible amount of this mind training will, I think, help me in seeing more in children."

We can cultivate a consciousness of movement in its myriad forms—how a person walks, how he sits down, how he uses his hands, his shoulders, his eyebrows, how his body responds to the countless stimuli in daily living. The great dancer is aware of all of these and many more. We shall not be dancers in this sense, but at least we can enjoy a deepening understanding of the meaning of dance.

SUGGESTED READING

Dewey, John, *Art as Experience,* New York: Putnam's.
Driver, Ann, *Music and Movement,* London: Oxford.
Ghiselin, Brewster (ed.), *The Creative Process,* New York: New American Library.
Martin, John, *Introduction to the Dance,* New York: Norton.
Sachs, Curt, *World History of the Dance,* New York: Norton.
Sorell, Walter, *The Dance Has Many Faces,* Cleveland: World.
Terry, Walter, *The Dance in America,* New York: Harper.

Chapter 8

GUIDING MOVEMENT AND ACCOMPANIMENT

A̲ᴛᴛᴇɴᴛɪᴏɴ ʜᴀs ʙᴇᴇɴ ʙʀᴏᴜɢʜᴛ to the *individuality* of movement in the preceding chapter. Our physical make-up, our temperament, and our own peculiar responses to stimuli reveal this individuality. We have different rhythms of living. From those who move quickly and lightly to those whose approach to life is characterized by heavy and lethargic movements, there are countless variations in movement. Have you ever had the experience of walking with a friend and found that you walked (naturally, that is) either too quickly or too slowly? We all realize that some do a job quickly and efficiently; others do the same piece of work efficiently but at a more leisurely pace. In the rush of modern living it is very easy to get caught up into the habit of hurry. Yet this isn't such a new problem either. More than a half century ago, William James decried what he called the "great American nervous habit" of hurry, hurry, hurry. Perhaps there is more to this than habit.

Each one of us has his own rhythm but we have learned, in certain affairs, to conform to a common rhythm. In dance we keep time to the pulse of the music but, even in our

169

"timekeeping," there are variations in our total body response. The little child has not yet learned conformity either in rhythm or in many other matters. His whole life is centered on himself: what *he* can do to things and what they do *to him*. Frequently we hear a mother say, "My child has no rhythm. He can't keep time to music." But each child has his own rhythm, determined by such factors as his weight, height, and temperament. The rhythm of the light, dynamic child is different from that of the heavier, slowly moving child. His feeling for a rhythm apart from his own cannot be forced; it must wait on his development. If he is given encouragement in his own rhythm, he will proceed at his own rate. It is also true that this rate will be different for each child. He is growing in his ability to adapt to others. In the matter of rhythmic movement we can best facilitate this growth by adapting ourselves to his rhythm.

In Nursery School

What does the foregoing say to us in terms of working with groups of children? In nursery school much of children's rhythmic play will be individual. There are times, however, where several children will be able to accommodate themselves to a rhythm, one set by another child or an adult, but a group of this kind should be a flexible one, allowing children to come and go according to their interest. Children should be invited, but *never forced,* to come to dancing time; and, if they do come, they should be free to leave when their interest is satisfied. Individual children may show sustained interest, and with these we should go along as far as their interest carries them.

A word about the so-called "doctrine of interest" may not be amiss here, since it has recently come in for a great deal of discussion—sometimes for unfortunate misunderstanding. We hear considerable talk in nursery-school circles about "incidental" learnings. The environment is carefully

Teachers are learners too

Irene Strauss

Tricks and stunts are natural expressions of children's exuberance. Such movements are recognized as important by dance teachers.

Children respond with enthusiasm and surprising skill to encouragement in the use of the floor

The release of strong feelings and the fun of experimentation
take on unique dance forms

planned, children live in it and learn from it, and teachers do not hesitate to step in to guide them in their social development or in routine habits. Often, however, the teacher is extremely reluctant to introduce new experiences in content, as an extension of the child's interest; or else there is a tendency to go to the other extreme, especially in dance and music, to impose a program suitable to the social development of older children.

In the first case the teacher has not fully explored the possibilities of children's interests, and in the second she has not recognized the limitations of their physical and social development. There is a vast difference between being unaware of the existence of something and having it thrust upon one. Boredom can be overstimulating, too! We must not overshoot the mark, not mistake our interest for the child's; we *should* be sure that we reach for the child's maximum possibilities rather than rest content with his minimum.

As we work toward maximum possibilities in dance and music with the child in nursery school, we find, because of his stage of social development, that we shall do much of our work with the individual or with small groups. The nursery-school teacher and her coworker are accustomed to this. In a growing number of states the staffing of nursery schools is regulated by the state, requiring two adults for each group of nursery-age children as a safety measure and also to better meet individual needs.

The adults in a nursery group need to plan carefully for the support and encouragement of the children who are ready for stimulation in dance and for trying out ideas together. This cannot be done in a room where other activities dominate and distract attention. The children who are interested need protection from those whose interests lie in different areas. This is the responsibility of the teachers, and consistent, day-by-day opportunity for dance and music, free from interruption and encouraged by adult guidance and support, should be available to those who are ready for it, in addition to the many incidental music and dance experiences that are a part of the regular program.

The person best able to provide and guide a program in dance for children in nursery school is the teacher who works with the group. She knows the children; she is with them all day when they are exploring sound and movement in various and ingenious ways. She is there to recognize and encourage and see possibilities. Much of her guidance will come during the day in her work with individuals. Out of her sensitivity to what she sees and feels will come ideas for small-group work. No matter how great the skill of a visiting music or dance teacher, it cannot compensate for the classroom teacher's awareness of movement that goes on all day. It is true that some special teachers have great skill in "tuning in" with a group and we have seen this evidenced to advantage with nursery-school children, but these special teachers also spend much time during the regular program with children, getting to know them and their interests, and then working with them in small interested groups.

The regular classroom teacher may feel insecure. She cannot play the piano, or perhaps there is no piano, and she feels that she cannot help children in music. What she needs is not skill in performance so much as skill in "feeling" and understanding. If she can rediscover in herself that curiosity in sound and movement with which children are endowed, her guidance of their musical interests may well surpass that of a concert artist.

Recently we visited a nursery school directed by a young woman who had had no musical training. She had, however, a genuine love of music and was keenly alert to the ways in which children use movement and sound. She learned and "felt" with them, and this little group had, without exception, the richest musical environment of any group we have observed. Experiences in music and dance in this nursery school were "incidental plus," not accidental. The children were alive to the joy of these arts, and their teacher became so interested that she enrolled in a modern-dance class in order to learn more about movement.

The dance or music teacher who enters any classroom and, because of her skill and personality, puts over a program that captivates children is a threat to the classroom teacher who, deprecating her own ability, withdraws completely from the teaching of music and dance. The skilled special teacher, however, who joins a group and whose primary purpose is to see and feel together *with* the classroom teacher, can be a wellspring of encouragement so that the regular teacher finds herself doing what she thought she could not do. The dance and music specialist in such a setting can contribute her technical skills to enrich a program and, at the same time, can stimulate the daily interests of both children and teacher.

Skill in an art is no handicap. Indeed, it should be a tremendous asset, since the more we know about an art, the more possibilities we see in it, and the richer the experiences we can bring to children—provided we have not lost our "at-homeness" with the soul and body of the art.

Kindergarten and Elementary School

The problem of working with children of varying ages in schools is primarily concerned with the degree of social organization in any particular group and the degree of skill in body movements, for we are concerned here with dance. For too long we have put ourselves and children in boxes or on shelves. "Authorities" have said that this is what a three-year-old, a seven-year-old, a twelve-year-old is like and, therefore, these are his particular interests. Thinking about children in terms of layer upon layer, age level upon age level, each with its particular ceiling, has blinded us to the development of, and has weakened our confidence in, our own perceptions.

These generalizations, unfortunately, become substitutes for thinking for ourselves. Can we really say there are kindergarten rhythms, third-grade rhythms, fifth-grade rhythms? There is movement—all children are interested in it, all explore it, if we allow them. The nursery-school child, as he propels himself across the floor, rolling, swimming, crawling, is using not only his arms and legs but, more especially, his torso. The difference between his use of these floor movements and that of the older child and of the trained dancer is one of purpose and skill.

This seems a good time to note that we should not overlook the contribution of these floor movements to the development of good posture and to recognize their therapeutic value as an outlet for children's feelings. The psychological importance of these primitive reactions is stressed by Bender and Boas: "The whole system of postures is fundamentally different when an individual is lying on the ground. . . . The usual dances keep the individual in the upright position. They restrict the possible varieties of postural experiences. The whole muscle tone is different when standing." [1]

These more primitive movements, being full of vigor and strength, appeal especially to boys, though boys have no priority rights in them! "Stunt" time should be a part of any dance period, and it will be if the children have anything to say and if the teacher is aware of the many dance "leads" that are offered by the group through this kind of activity.

A good vigorous workout virtually massages the body, and, when it is over, the children are only too ready to "let go" and lie flat on the floor for a short rest. Full relaxation, the kind achieved by reaction from its opposite, comes through a feeling in the muscles themselves and not through any outside stimulus or device. Children are ready to rest because their bodies feel the need of change.

It is essential, especially when children live in groups, to

---

1 Lauretta Bender and Francisca Boas, "Creative Dance in Therapy," *American Journal of Orthopsychiatry*, April 1941.

give them opportunity for vigorous play in order to relieve tensions. What really makes for overstimulatior is the program that stresses inactivity and quietness, and obtains these by "busy work!" This holds true both in the home and in the school.

To get back to children's social development and its relation to movement. The very young child is interested in his own body and what he can do with it. He has big feelings which are evidenced in, what are for him, strong movements. It is *out of the use of his strength* that control comes. He has to achieve self-satisfaction before he begins to be interested in others. This is true also with youngsters all through elementary school, but they become increasingly conscious of the satisfactions in doing things with others and in learning from others. They have become group conscious. If we are not careful, we can easily take advantage of this "groupness" and pay less and less attention to the individual and his creative possibilities in dance. The older child, as well as the younger, needs time, encouragement, and respect from us as a "moving" individual. He and his friends also need the protection of the most encouraging environment possible to promote the development of their ideas. And they need guidance, the kind of guidance that opens new vistas as well as supplementing present ones, the kind of guidance that helps to develop the ideas of others rather than uses these ideas as invitations for the teacher to take over and promote his own ideas.

Analysis of Movement

A knowledge of, or at least an acquaintance with, the types of movement recognized by the dancer is helpful in our work with boys and girls. Movement falls into two general types: *locomotor* movement, which has to do with getting from one place to another, and *nonlocomotor* or *axial* movement, in which the body is the axis and movement takes place in relation to it. Typical locomotor movements are walking, running, rolling, skipping, galloping, sliding, hopping. Typical nonlocomotor movements are spinning, stretching, bending, twisting, reaching, turning.

Any movement, even the wiggling of one's little finger, has three basic characteristics: *timing, space,* and *dynamics.* Take a single child or a group of children walking or marching. Is their movement fast, medium, or slow; are they going in a straight line or exploring space either horizontally or vertically (high, low, or medium); what dynamics are in use? Even if every child is conforming to the same time and space pattern, are there differences in the degree of intensity with which they move?

Learning from Each Other

Guidance comes from our awareness of the possibilities that even the simplest movement of a child offers. Making children aware of what they are doing is an important part of this. In Chapter 7, we mentioned the possibilities in exploring space, which involves low, high, large, small, forward, and backward movements. Dynamics refers to the degree of force or intensity involved in movement. For example, such comments as, "Mary walks as if it were very important for her to get somewhere, while Jerry walks just as fast as Mary but as if he doesn't care where he is going," or, "Jim walks with jerkiness and Sally walks smoothly; Bobby bounces when he walks," call attention to the variations in dynamics of movement. The feeling for fast and slow qualities of timing are readily apparent.

As we work with children and call attention to their variations in basic movements, we can make it possible for them to experience these variations. When children are ready and eager to learn from each other, we can suggest that the group try Mary's way of walking, or Jim's way, or Jerry's way, or

Sally's way. Likewise we can focus on variations in timing, or in moving in space. Do not these possibilities open the door to guidance of movement, any movement at all—running, skipping, marching, rolling, swinging, spinning, jumping, and so on?

The Teacher Stimulates a Group

The basic assumption implied here is that the teacher works *with* the children, not necessarily moving with the group, but alert to everything that goes on. If she is busily engaged in following notes on the piano, she will see little. If she expects certain results from a recorded piece of music, she will see little. If she plays the piano by ear, but also expects certain interpretations, she will see little.

In order to work really creatively we must free ourselves of these controls. Not that music isn't important to the dance. *Music is important to all dance, but in different ways.* In the usual types of recreational dance it serves as a control and a stimulation. Its basic function in modern dance is that of a companion to the dance, an accompaniment. Choreographers work in different ways with dance and music. They may create the dance and commission a composer to write music for it. They may see dance and music evolving together where the dancer's movement suggests the sound, or they may get their initial stimulus from a composition of music.

Since the practice of having children dance to music is so deeply established in our teaching, we have come to depend on it. We feel insecure without music. It affords a beginning and an end. By building up certain associations with certain sounds from the piano the group responds, and what might seem to be the spark of an "out-of-hand" idea or a really creative impulse is brought under control. Teaching cannot go on without group control by the teacher, but there are different ways of achieving and exercising this control. We find other ways of group control when we go on an excursion or engage in a discussion of ideas with children. Can we not work with children in the realm of movement ideas and expect similar respect for control? *Gradually* breaching the gap between our dependence on music as a control and working with movement in and of itself will help us hold on to our security. Of course, we have to be willing to be a bit uncomfortable and take chances, now and then, in trying out the steps beyond. The following account of a student teacher's growth in working with children in a second grade reveals her step-by-step approach, her insecurities, and also her rewards. She was fortunate in being able to work with a very understanding cooperating teacher.[2]

The program was rather formalized and rigid, and the principal placed great emphasis on discipline. Consequently, no talking or running was permitted in the halls, and it was expected that there be a minimum of unnecessary noise within the classrooms. Technically then, the children were allowed to express themselves through bodily movement (aside from the movement which is a natural part of free play time) only during the specified dance period. These circumstances naturally played a large part in the initial responses I received from the children in attempting "creative rhythms" with them. However, the teacher with whom I was working was extremely cooperative and helpful and let me try out many ideas, encouraging me when many things I attempted proved unsuccessful. Often she left me alone with the children during dance time, realizing that I would be less self-conscious then in dealing with the youngsters.

I finally came to the conclusion that my experienced friends who followed the traditional pattern of playing music and having the children do the appropriate actions had been using an incorrect approach and technique and that, after all, it would be a simple matter to get the children to participate enthusiastically in expressing their own individual selves through creative movement! So, armed with a variety of ideas and an overdose of optimism, I set out to "reform" the dancing period!

I called the youngsters together in a group, told them I was

2 Used by permission.

going to play something "special" on the piano, and that they were to do whatever they wanted to do after they had listened to the music for a while. With great confidence I then proceeded to play the pulsating and exciting tango *Olé Guapa* (believing that since the majority of children were Puerto Ricans this was just the right type of music to stimulate them to all sorts of beautiful dancing). The response that I got from the youngsters was quite unexpected, not at all what I had anticipated or imagined. The boys and girls simply stared at me in utter bewilderment and didn't even move a muscle! And with that, my optimism vanished. However, I did try a number of other selections on the piano—ranging from a Chopin *Valse* to a toned-down version of boogie. The reaction of the children was the same each time, but I managed, nevertheless, to survive the half hour! The lesson seemed to me to have been a complete and dismal failure. However, even if the children derived nothing from it, it proved to be a very valuable learning experience for me. At the moment, I was too discouraged to think the matter through rationally. Later, however, in verbalizing the experience, I realized what an important lesson this had been for me: before any form of free expression in dancing can take place in the classroom, the teacher must help free the children of their inhibitions (and it's truly unbelievable how inhibited many children already are at the age of seven). This is a gradual process, in which the teacher must show patience, understanding, and, above all, sensitivity. This is definitely not to be accomplished in "one easy lesson" as I had so naively believed.

My reaction to this first attempt at free rhythms and its failure was a perfectly natural one, I assume. For the next three or four days I reverted to playing specific selections for jumping, skipping, and so forth, and regained a bit of security, feeling that the situation was well under control. However, after a while I became adventurous again and decided to try out some other ideas. My cooperating teacher and I discussed the matter and determined to attempt to interest the children in "nonregimented" dancing by means of Greek records. This time I was prepared for any kind of reaction from the youngsters! I introduced the music briefly, asked the children to sit down, and to get up and dance when they felt like it. As was to be expected, the youngsters were rather hesitant; gradually a few got up and skipped around. Impulsively, my teacher and I stepped in and danced with the children. The boys and girls thought this was very funny indeed (and frankly we both felt a bit self-conscious and hoped that no one would look into the classroom just at that moment). On this particular occasion and on succeeding days we did get the children to join in with somewhat more enthusiasm, although it was obvious that most of them were imitating our movements. This was not exactly desirable, I felt, but this imitation at first might serve the purpose of helping the youngsters become less inhibited. Above all, it seemed to me of greatest importance that the children were gradually beginning to show enjoyment; in time they would become less imitative and more creative in their movements. At this point I learned my second lesson regarding "creative" dancing: the teacher can help stimulate the children by *her own active participation,* by *her enthusiasm,* and by *her adventurous attitude.*

As I mentioned previously, discipline was greatly stressed in this school, and consequently the children were discouraged from unnecessary "exploration of movement" outside of the specified dance period. However, while working with the children in rhythms directly, I *simultaneously became more conscious and observant of their rhythmic bodily expressions during other times.* I was surprised that under the relatively rigid circumstances the youngsters actually were exploring movement in a great variety of ways. At first this was not very obvious to me, but as I began to "look" closer, I started to "see" more. I saw children engaged in activities seemingly completely unrelated to dance suddenly evolve a graceful pattern of movements. One morning a little boy was at the painting easel working on a spring landscape; he picked up two brushes and began to paint simultaneously with both, coordinating his movements rhythmically till this developed into a beautiful pattern, which he varied from time to time; for five or six minutes his attention was concentrated on this activity and he completely forgot about the landscape! Had I had sufficient insight at the time, I might have taken advantage of this completely spontaneous occurrence—I could have referred to it immediately or later during dance time—and given recognition and encouragement to the boy, perhaps even have used this lovely arm and hand movement as a basis for some of our rhythms.

Several times I observed what might be termed "group dancing" originate spontaneously from a number of youngsters during "play period." On one occasion, three children sitting on adjoining chairs started to lean backwards and forwards, lifting and setting down their feet, while chanting "see-saw, see-saw." This engaged the attention of the youngsters for quite a long time, and they really developed a lovely, coordinated pattern of movement. The chanting proved to be excellent accompaniment for this particular activity, and on later occasions during dance time I let one group chant while the other group danced, thereby eliminating the piano as accompaniment. The children enjoyed this variation tremendously.

A favorite diversion of the girls in this class was to spin around as rapidly as possible so that their skirts would billow out around their bodies. It was truly amazing how differently each child performed this basically simple action; one would give herself impetus by swinging her arms about; she would balance on one foot and not lift that foot from the ground. Another would spin around by lifting one foot after the other without using her arms at all.

I found that these observations during free-play period were of great benefit to me in developing my thinking about creative rhythms. I began to see how varied and individualistic the basic movements of children in an "uncontrolled" situation are. If only this spontaneity and creativity would be maintained and encouraged rather than stifled during actual dancing periods!

The first tiny bit of success I achieved in working with the children was, as previously mentioned, by means of records and teacher participation. Very gradually the youngsters began to accept the fact that dancing need not be "formalized"; some children reached this stage of development more rapidly than others. Many were still quite reticent and continued to imitate their peers; I did not discourage this imitation, because I felt that for these particular children even "copying" revealed growth—at least these boys and girls were participating with more enjoyment than had been true on previous occasions. However, I was somewhat disturbed about one little girl, who was studying ballet, and who revealed much creativity in movement during free-play periods; amazingly enough, during dance time, she was quite "stiff" and "conventional." At first, thinking in terms of her background, I tended to single her out and, subconsciously at least, expected her to perform outstanding feats. Later, I realized I was using the wrong approach and therefore I let her dance with the group without drawing special notice to her. When I left this student-teaching situation, the youngster seemed to me to be less inhibited, although there still must be much work done before she becomes truly "free" enough in these circumstances to express herself rhythmically with ease and confidence. With other youngsters, whom I had given up as being completely "un-musical" and "unrhythmical," I noticed that all at once they seemed to develop great feeling for these activities: it was really a joy one day to see Sarah, who for weeks had been shy and seemingly "uncooperative" during dance time, abruptly join in with enthusiasm and move about with unexpected gracefulness.

Toward the end of these ten weeks, I began to use the guitar as a form of accompaniment. I found somehow that through this instrument the atmosphere became more cozy and informal; a group of children would sit around me and hum calypso num-bers, while others danced. The youngsters did not seem to have the feeling that I was scrutinizing their every movement as they danced about; I imagine that this helped them feel free in their rhythmic expression.

At the conclusion of my student-teaching experience, then, I felt very pleased with the accomplishments of the children, al-though to most people I imagine these "successes" would seem rather minute and unimportant. Admittedly, nothing truly spectacular had occurred during this time. Many of the boys and girls still were not relaxed and spontaneous in their movements. Certainly, I had failed to take advantage of many situations that arose in class. Nevertheless, I now feel much more confident in this area of creative movement, for even from the lessons that proved unsuccessful I think I learned very much. Above all, I realize, now, that it *is* possible for a person, completely untrained in formal dancing, to work with children in creative movement and achieve definite results, even if these results are relatively small! One of the greatest satisfactions for me, before I left this school, came when I once more played the tango *Olé Guapa* for the children; their response to this when I first started working with them had been a source of discouragement to me. This time, however, the youngsters responded spontaneously and enthusiastically, and thereby gave me the greatest possible reward!

I have chosen the foregoing illustration because it seems to me that most of us can identify with the "adventuring" of this student teacher, and, I hope, we find encouragement for more and more adventuring. Her guidance of children (and of herself) is apparent throughout.

Another factor that can operate against creativity is our impatience to get results we can see quickly. Not only in music and dance does our rush to the future keep us from savoring the qualities and the possibilities of ideas and experiences. The old quip that in our hurry "we miss more than we catch up with" is true enough to be disconcerting. We need to cultivate "loitering in movement" with children as an ingredient in the process of living creatively. Organization grows out of taking time to explore ideas. The organization should fit the idea rather than the idea being manipulated to fit the organization.

I suppose that one of the hardest tasks teachers face is learning to take time—time to wait, to listen, to see. I well remember one of my most uncomfortable moments of teaching when a class of students from a nearby teachers' college visited my group of six-year-olds. The music period had just started when Sally asked to play "birthday cake." We had not played "birthday cake" before, so I agreed, thinking this would be a good opportunity for the visitors to see an idea develop. Since the children were accustomed to putting their ideas into immediate action rather than talking about them, all thirty rushed out on the floor. Taking their cue from Sally, each lay on his or her back with legs and arms in a perpendicular position. There they lay—*not a sound!* I sat quietly for as long as I could, and then asked them to come back and sit beside me. They responded, but had no more

returned then they said, "Let's play birthday cake again."
This happened three times before *I* understood.

When birthday cake was mentioned, my thinking had
jumped to the possibilities of a composition, for this group
had considerable inventiveness in working with an idea. But
the children were "listening to the beating of another
drum" [3]—candles on a cake! Of course, everyone knew but
the teacher. With one big "blow," I blew out the candles.
The "play" was finished with no comments and everyone
eager for floor stunts. The music period proceeded and I
gradually became comfortable again when things began to
happen.

But something had been happening all along. An idea,
perhaps even a trifling one, had been spontaneously put into
movement form. This idea came full blown; it was expressed
and finished. We never played birthday cake again, nor did I
hear it mentioned until thirteen years later when a college
student who had been one of the six-year-olds recalled it for
me! This example illustrates one of the many ways in which
children use a vocabulary of movement if we give them time.
Their ideas vary in relative importance, but the habit of
turning to movement behavior is of great importance; and it
is not easy for us to take time to let this happen.

Here is another very recent experience illustrating the
movement behavior of a group of twelve-year-olds who came
into a college class to work with students in movement and
sound. They lived in a classroom where freedom to think
and do, together with responsibility for their actions, was the
way of living. I explained to them some of the ways in which
we were learning about sound and movement, and that the
college students had asked if we could have a visit from some
older boys and girls to give us more enlightenment. We were
putting this up to them. How they would go about it was for
them to decide, and we would give them as much time as
needed.

3 Thoreau.

Immediately they separated into two groups, one of boys and one of girls. The girls arrived at their contribution first: two double circles, the inner one squatting, the outer on their knees. At a signal, those on the inner circle slapped the floor. As soon as a rhythm was established, those on the outer circle played against it by alternately slapping hands high in the air and cupping one hand in a chest slap which gave a hollow sound. It was a beautiful little composition in sound and movement ending in a "shout" climax. The boys' group played a ball game in pantomime. The only sound used was the "catching of the ball." After a minute or so, the synchronization and rhythm became so established and so "catching" that everyone in the room had a truly vital vicarious experience.

In discussing this experience later with the class, their teacher said they had not done these two "compositions" before but that, in the last two months, she had been encouraging them in both movement and sound exploration with the result that she was constantly amazed with their inventions. This was a group of average children, if any children are average! They were not what is usually classified as a superior group. All children can amaze us if we give them a chance! Because this teacher believed in the importance of this type of creative experience in music and movement, she had provided *time* in the program and a *place,* and *encouragement.* She had confidence in their ability to organize in relation to ideas that had meaning for them. In addition, she had opened doors for them several months earlier because of her own growth. This is guidance.

It is hoped that the illustrations just used helped to make the reader more aware of the fact that children's organization of an idea in movement is possible. It takes time, the outcome is unpredictable, and most adults have feelings of uncertainty and insecurity as they stand by. If the reader will recall, we were discussing the ways of guiding walking movements through our increased knowledge of the characteristics of any movement. Because of my long experience as a class-room teacher, working with large groups of children (too large, in fact), I find myself identifying with the classroom teacher and the problems she faces in working with groups. So it seemed a good time to take a look at working with a group through illustrations. Problems are real, *very real*, and it is easy for the classroom teacher to feel that she cannot try out ideas because her situation is not the kind in which these ideas would work. Sometimes, in fact many times, the problems recede in proportion to the expansion of an idea. Many times, too, the problems we think will attend any new experiment do not materialize.

The examples used are in no way intended to illustrate a method. It is hoped that through them, however, we can *see an idea* more clearly. Of importance, too, is the reassurance that we all take from each other's adventures with children in movement.

Movement Stimulated by Ideas

Now let us return to our discussion of walking. The suggestions made to encourage variations in time, space, and dynamics were for the sake of variations themselves. Ideas, too, can be an important stimulus. For example, how do you walk in the rain, in the wind, in the cold, in the snow, when it is very hot? Walk barefoot on the sand, on grass, on pebbles, on a hot pavement, in cold water. How do you walk in the dark, when you are going somewhere special, when you are going somewhere you do not care to go to, and so on. Follow your hand as you walk, lead with your shoulder, with your ear, with your eye. These suggestions are applicable to other movements such as running and marching. Children themselves can think up dozens of ideas.

Sometimes we have a group of children who have been conditioned ever since they have been in school to a formalized rhythm program and whose own ideas have not been recognized and encouraged. These children have learned to respond only to directions and so seem lacking in any kind of creativity. Playing games with movement offer many possibilities. How many ways can you find to go from one end of the room to the other? How can you go using only one foot? How can you go using no feet? It isn't long until the children start setting up the hurdles. Or play a familiar piece of music on the piano or on a record, or sing a familiar song, and ask the children to start moving when you start and reach a designated goal at the *exact moment* when the music stops.

Of the many responses that come from such a game one can always spot several significant or unusual ones. Call attention to them and ask the entire group to try them. These leads may have dance significance, or a variation may have only slight significance but it may be very important to call attention to the contribution because of the child involved.

All of us are familiar with the old game of "follow the leader." This can be played in groups of two or more where one child leads and the others follow. This can be a game of imitation and blind following. Or the leader can be the strong force and *through movement alone* control the group. He can push, pull, coax, cajole—in fact, do anything he can movementwise with his entire body to get the group to do as he wishes. Movement is his language; he cannot talk or make a sound, he cannot touch anyone. This game can be varied by using two groups, a strong group and a weak group. The strong group needs to coordinate so that they will all "push" or "pull" at the same time. A class of one hundred college students played this game. They divided into four groups, each with a volunteer leader, whose job it was to get his group of twenty-five from one end of the room to the other in a given time. Cooperation was expected of the twenty-five but not identity of response. The four leaders revealed extraordinary individuality in the ways in which they managed their groups. They "talked" with every part of them, their characteristic gestures were highlighted, and the members of the cooperating groups revealed a similarly tremendous amount of individuality in their various responses to the leader.

We referred earlier in this chapter to the use of the torso and floor movements, and their importance in modern dance. In the Bender and Boas study (see the footnote on p. 174) the authors point out that older boys and girls have become inhibited in the use of floor movements and have to be encouraged through suggestion and stimulation. This study was made before the days of television. Certainly there are still inhibitions in older boys and girls in relation to this type of movement. Anyone who watches the great variety of dance programs on television sees ample evidence of the use of floor movements by men as well as women dancers. The discussion of these programs could be of help in freeing children, but it is the gradual day-by-day concern for movement in any of its forms that will gradually eliminate the dividing line between movement relating to upright posture and "horizontal" type of movement.

A child's flop on the floor can be an intrusion and dealt with as a problem, or it can open the door to the possibilities in movement when one is lying on the floor. A suggestion to find a spot on the floor where you can move your arms and legs without interfering with anyone can be an invitation to find out what you can do with your legs, or arms, or torso, or head, or hands, or fingers, or combinations of two or more limbs. Can you use the middle part of you without moving shoulders or legs? (This is a very important technique in dancing.) What are the possibilities when sitting on the floor in one spot—spinning, bending, swaying, rocking? Sit in a small circle, take a walk with your fingers to the center.

There is nothing original about the suggestions for movement just mentioned. They, and many more, are part of the usual class in modern dancing. They all contribute to an awareness of the possibilities of movement in every part of the body which is basic to dance. As classroom teachers we do not aim to develop professional dancers, but we can do a great deal more in helping each child to "tune in with dance" than we are now doing and have a lot of fun along the way.

With several exceptions, I have only discussed movement motivated by the joy of sheer physical activity—"muscular imagination" as it is called by a dance teacher. Stunts, tricks, movement for movement's sake, go on much of the time without any association of dramatic ideas. But there is, also, a great deal of movement in which imagination is the motivating force. For example, two five-year-olds were each walking on "all fours" with their faces toward the ceiling. One was a dinosaur and the other was a walking table! As the walking table was an especially good idea, it was not long before the room was full of walking tables—with "chairs" under some of them. This was a fine game and, after several days, we accompanied the walking chairs and tables by reciting *The Table and the Chair* by Edward Lear.

One day a four-year-old all curled up in a huddle propelled himself across the playground with an irregular humping movement, telling us that he was a cake of ice running away from the refrigerator. "Snakes," another favorite dramatization, requires a good deal of active wriggling of the torso.

All children play airplanes, trains, and boats. Here again, such activities are accepted at face value during free play, but in a dancing group the teacher hesitates to work from the idea itself, and, instead, immediately plays, for example, airplane music, usually becoming so preoccupied with reading and playing the music that she loses sight of the children!

The dance is more nearly related to drama than to music. This one exception is that of time—rhythm. Dance and drama are internally related! They are of the same essential stuff; one works in the medium of movement, the other of action which are prac-

tically inseparable. The dance and music are only externally related to the extent that both make formal patterns in the one
common dimension of time.[4]

The natural accompaniment of airplanes, at least for the
young child, is the rhythm of his own motor, and we do not
need sharp ears to hear its rhythmic flow. The sustained
sound of the child's accompaniment fits the uninterrupted
rhythmic movement of the airplane much better than any
piano accompaniment can do.

This type of dramatic play should be developed by introducing added content (usually the children know more about
airplanes than their elders do), by discussing it and by helping the children to become aware of the motor's rhythm and
its natural rise and fall in intensity. There may be times
when a piano can be used advantageously, but in our experience the piano has usually reduced the emotional tone of
the play.

The traditional way of playing trains is another example
of how our preconceptions can handicap the child's use of an
idea. One morning, while a few children were sitting on the
floor waiting for the rest of the group to change their shoes,
they began to shuffle their feet back and forth because they
liked the sound of their chamois dancing shoes on the floor.
Almost at once the shuffling took on a definite rhythmic pattern. Soon the children were accompanying these "trains" by
saying *choo-choo,* and we supported their rhythm by slapping
a large drum with one hand and swishing back and forth over
a second drum with the other hand.

These trains, however, were not active enough to keep
their attention for long. One child wanted to play train in
the good old-fashioned way, and of course *she* wanted to be
the engine. But so did twenty-five others! Obviously, taking
turns would not solve this problem, because there would
have to be too many turns. Since engines are the most dra-

4 John Martin, *The Modern Dance,* New York: Barnes.

matic part of trains to youngsters, we suggested that each one be an engine, and then he could haul any kind of train that pleased him. The engines took various forms—some shuffling ahead on their feet, some moving on all fours, some sitting down and shoving along; one child, swinging one arm in a wide, revolving movement, showed that it was the engine wheels that loomed largest in his experience.

In connection with little children's dramatic play, it is important to remember that they are not interested in "composing" a train, for example, according to any picture we may have in our minds. They seize upon what is to them the most outstanding aspect of an idea, and they dramatize that. Nor is this a mere process of "imitation." They jump right into the heart of the idea. They are not like an engine: they *are* an engine!

As children grow older, they become more interested in the picture of the whole, and take the initiative in planning its various parts and in choosing each other to dramatize these parts. Unfortunately, this later stage of development is too often thrust upon younger children by an unimaginative adult who wants to see results as *she* pictures them. But when we are able to retain the children's enthusiasm by utilizing their ideas and helping them develop these ideas along the lines of their own thinking, we get results that are vital and truly creative.

Reflections

I believe that the more we know about movement, the more willing we are to let movement happen. From the natural movement impulses of children of any age we can find the roots of dance. Children are at home with this material. We can identify it and help them identify what they are doing. Together with them we can assemble and reassemble what they already know in a new framework. Because they know that we have respect for what they can do, they will be eager for opportunities to extend their knowledge and skill through appropriate new experiences that we can bring.

Each group of children is unique, with its own way of life determined by the interaction of children and teacher. The really important factor is the *quality of the relationship* between them. Materials, space, equipment, size of groups, are of lesser importance, although continuing effort should be made in any situation to improve working conditions. The recognition by a teacher of a child's squirming or wiggling in a crowded classroom to compensate for lack of space can be treated as a sign of nonconformity or welcomed as an opportunity for everyone to wiggle or squirm to relieve tension. Children can be tremendously resourceful in the use of even the smallest space. Not that cramped space is beneficial, but it is amazing how many possibilities a child can invest it with! The therapeutic value in such a use of movement certainly takes priority over its dance aspect.

It would be most unfortunate if the suggestions on variety of movements were to be thought of as a series of activities "to be taught." They are intended essentially to alert us to possibilities so that our understanding will make us more knowing and more accepting of movement. This is a progressive faculty—the more we see, *the more we see*.

Resources for Accompaniment

From the foregoing discussion on creative movement, it is obvious that accompaniment must be varied and flexible if we wish to work *from* movement rather than *from* music. Flexibility in thinking, on the part of all concerned, is an absolute essential underlying the whole process. What type of music, or what kind of sound, or what sound-making instrument will best supplement, heighten, and accompany a particular movement?

The accompanist will not only have to be flexible in her choice of sound; often she will have to improvise. Yet even the untrained musician need not feel discouraged since there are many possibilities for the amateur, and especially for those grownups and children favorably disposed to adventure in sound-making. The reader may want to refresh his mind on the possibilities for the use of sound suggested in Chapters 1–6, at the same time keeping in mind their appropriateness for movement.

Percussive Body Sounds

Sounds made by using various parts of the body have long been used as a part of dance. Sound patterns of the dancer's feet are recognized by everyone. In many of the colorful Spanish dances, the hands are used percussively, not only by the dancer, but, more important, by his group of accompanists. One of the most ear-opening experiences my college classes and I have ever had happened recently when a member of our class guided us on a "tour of hand clapping." She had spent more than a year in Spain, studying voice, and was especially interested in opera. To this end she had studied with Spain's leading castanet teacher.

The first six weeks of her training consisted of developing and strengthening the use of her *hands only* as percussive instruments. In a short time, even without our having "trained hands," she had us experimenting with a truly amazing number of sound qualities. Cupping of the hands and clapping contrasted with *flat-hand* clapping; tips of the fingers of one hand playing on *different* parts of the other hand; tips of two fingers; the tips of one finger only; a great variety of snapping fingers, which I am sure children are more skilled in than we are. While some of the less distinct or softer sounds seemed barely distinguishable from other sounds, often when everyone in the group made the same sound together its sound differences were accentuated and there was a real contrast.

What fun children can have in accompanying part of their group as they learn to use these various sounds! We all know that regular clapping can soon be monotonous because of the lack of variation in sound.

The slapping of different parts of the body—chest, cheek, arms, thigh—all have their special sound and, if we listen carefully, the contrast is easily observed. The feet, too—tapping toes, heels, sides, shuffling, scraping, sliding—offer a great variety of sound effects.

Things in the Environment

Then there are the sounds that are made by using what we have in our environment: tapping on a table, seat, or desk with a pencil or fingers; tapping on a radiator; the closing of a door; the kinds of sounds that youngsters in a group so often use to annoy adults or each other. A teacher in a crowded classroom which was furnished with stationary desks told us about one of the ways her class experienced movement. Part of the group used the aisles around the sides of the room while the remainder stayed at their desks and supplied the accompaniment. The teacher's job was to help them organize the variety of sounds so there would be contrasts and a feeling for form. One day the group on the floor seemed to be marching a long, long time and the accompaniment was monotonous. One youngster at his seat near the door was impatient and stood up by the open door. Suddenly, at the end of a phrase, he closed the door right on the dot and with finality. The closing was exactly on the accent and everyone stopped and laughed. It was a fitting climax.

It is surprising how long one can live in a place and be unaware of some of its obvious possibilities for creative sound-making. A short time ago a group of boys and girls visited our class to get acquainted with the variety of instruments we had. One boy became so intrigued with a two-toned Indian bell that he could not let it go, and his interest in it was contagious. Instruments that produced ringing sounds became the focus of attention. At the end of the session I suggested that the class look around at home and bring in objects that had a ringing sound. I would do the same in my office and home.

Shortly before the next class I suddenly remembered my promise and looked around desperately for something to ring. All I could see was a metal book end. I put a loop of string through it and then tapped it with a hard rubber stick. It produced a truly beautiful sound, like a church bell far away. My assistant had more foresight than I and had discovered in her kitchen a metal tea strainer that produced two different tones.

We wondered what the children would bring. Three of them had found small bells which had different sounds; the others brought nothing. We tried all of our "ringers" together and then separately, and then we asked the students to contribute anything that would ring. Pockets and pocketbooks were explored. We put the "key-ring" ringers in one group, and the "jingling-coins" people in another, and then we experimented, at my suggestion, with words and voice sounds that had ringing qualities. Out of it all, step by step, came a song about ringing bells, a song whose form was harmonic, the play of contrasting words and sounds simultaneously.

I have used this illustration to point up the possibilities of the very simple things in our environment. In this particular case, these sounds were not associated with any movement, but this experience made all of us more aware of the potentialities of sound-making. Furthermore, I have never experienced such sensitive and thoughtful listening in any group of children or adults, and for such a sustained period of time.

Voice Sounds

Many voice sounds can be fitting accompaniments to movements. Certain sounds, such as sighs or groans, may be the result of physical movement or may serve to stimulate action. The slow, steady repetition of *letters,* such as *T* and *P,* have an explosive quality. The *vowels A E I O U* can be endlessly varied in form and rhythm. *Nonsense* rhymes or jingles also have a rhythmic impact on the ear. *Poetry* used responsively in choral groups can either support or stimulate movement. *Words* themselves, whether dramatic or even abstract, can be used very effectively. A phrase can evolve into a powerful dramatic chorus. One teacher improvised such a phrase to accompany thirty-one nine-year-old children playing "bears," inspired by one of their group who had seen a real bear in the mountains where he was camping. They repeated "Thirty-one bears prowling in the woods" slowly and rhythmically four times, followed it by "walking and prowling" four times, and then they reverted to the first phrase as a finale. These improvised voice sounds are so "simple" that many grownups find it difficult to use them effectively. We have become inhibited and feel foolish in this kind of pattern. It takes considerable relaxation and courage to experiment with what comes naturally to the dance accompanist and the dancer.

We all feel more comfortable in the use of *songs* for accompaniment—folk songs, nursery songs, ballads, or any other that seems to catch the rhythm and spirit of the movement. We can sing them with or without an instrument, or we can turn to a recording.

Musical Instruments

Musical instruments are our most important resource for dance accompaniment. Percussion instruments of all kinds—drums, gongs, temple bells, Ghana marimba—have many possibilities for both the amateur and the trained musician. They offer a variety of sounds and lend themselves to the grownup's experimental impulses as well as to the child's. A child can easily learn to accompany the movement of another child; and, in a group, several children can work independently while the teacher is busy with other things.

The large gong is a very dramatic instrument whose climactic effect thrills the children. To be used to best advantage it should be suspended from a stand. Children should be introduced to it out-of-doors, first, rather than indoors, for it is capable of giving out "big" sounds, and children's early experimentation is none too controlled! When played in a steady, low tremolo, it will induce relaxation. It can be used to great advantage in accompanying a sustained, flowing movement.

All too frequently we fail to realize how important climaxes are to children, and in working with a group we do everything possible to avoid these lest the group get out of control. But children who are given a chance to "explode" once in a while are much less likely to get out of hand than they are if the lid is kept clamped on tight. How often we have seen a child running faster and faster, "louder and louder," working up to an intensity that reaches its climax with a shout, a leap into the air, and then a dive to the floor! And how often we have seen that youngster penalized by being asked to sit on the sidelines until he thinks he can run without falling down! This robs him of the high spot of his enjoyment—the climax, making impossible the development of his play into an art form.

What we should do in a situation of this kind is to help the child learn how to take his climaxes and then to return to an even keel. We need to help him to a better and more artistic use of that form. If his running, for example, is accompanied by playing on drums, his climax can be accented by a corresponding climax on the drums, or perhaps by a crash of the gong. Among the many varieties of such play are different ways of falling and of getting up again, the use of the time when lying down as a part of the whole activity, the crescendo and decrescendo of movement, and the use of the voice.

The possibilities as well as the limitations of percussion instruments are discussed by Harriett Graham, who points out that they should not be used exclusively because they do not furnish a fitting accompaniment to certain types of dance.[5] It is true that continued use of them can become monotonous since they deal largely in the rhythmic element of music. We can, however, vary our use somewhat by adding different kinds of percussion instruments, or by the way we combine those we have. A keen ear will discover many variations in sound, depending on the way the instruments are played. Since there will be times when a piano is not available, or the grownup does not know how to play, a thoughtful use of percussion can add greatly to the musical and dance development of children. The outdoors is an ideal place for rhythmic play for little children, and these instruments offer an accompaniment that can be *taken to* children.

Skill in playing drums can, as we know, be developed to a high degree. Though this is not the place to discuss technique, certain fundamentals may be mentioned. In order to obtain an easy, relaxed rhythm, we must first feel the rhythm of the movement in our bodies. The rhythm on the drum should be the product of this feeling, and not the result of merely tapping out the time beat.

A sensitive player can obtain good results in the quality of tone produced by remembering to "pull the sound out" of the drum rather than beat it in. There are many ways of playing: slapping or using the hollow hand, the fingers, or a wire brush. The sides yield various sounds, as do different parts of the drumhead. Regular timpani sticks are best, and

[5] "A Study of the Use of Percussion Instruments as Accompaniment in the Dance," *Research Quarterly of the American Physical Education Association,* March 1934.

here again there are various ways to use them, such as playing with the hard end or with the padded end.

For most of us, improvising on drums is much easier than improvising on a piano. Yet a working knowledge of the basic elements of musical structure need be no formidable hurdle to jump. Most of us are not among the lucky few who can sit down at a piano and improvise without any knowledge of the symbols of music; such people are fortunate in being more experimental and sound-minded than we. But if our piano teachers had had the imagination and courage to teach us first through the "raw materials" of music, sound and rhythm, we might from the beginning have established that feeling of at-homeness with the keyboard and that feeling of security which no amount of "playing pieces" can give. Some teachers are working in this direction with children, but too few use the same approach with older people. One does not need to be a creative genius to improvise, for improvisation is largely pure invention, and an immediate acquaintance with the theory of music gives us a considerable foundation on which to build.

In using the piano as accompaniment, we are able to bring to movement the added elements of harmony and melody that are not possible with drums. A few simple chords may be just what is needed to add substance to a group of four-year-old "tugboats." Occasions will arise, however, when improvising is far from adequate, and when even the person with a fairly extensive repertory cannot summon just the right music to fit the child's movement, though she knows that to round it out music must play a more important role. When this happens, she will (even though she may improvise temporarily rather than lose the spirit and enthusiasm of the child's idea) at the earliest possible moment search for music that will add more meaning to the child's experience.

It is not difficult to find music to accompany activity of a purely rhythmic character, that is, movement not tied up with content or idea. Our richest source is the field of folk music. The music of simple folk games, songs, and dances makes excellent accompaniment for such activities as running, jumping, skipping, galloping, marching, and swinging. It is simple, well accented, and, best of all, easy to play. It responds to the child and the child instinctively responds to it.

A number of the world's greatest composers have written some compositions that are similarly rhythmical. For the accompanist's use, several collections of these have been made, the compilers having carefully edited and sometimes skillfully simplified the music so that it is not beyond the ability of the average pianist. Generally speaking, the simpler the musical accompaniment, the easier it is for the child to respond, and the more likely it is that the music will be well played. Music for accompaniment must be played clearly and evenly, and must be well accented, especially for the longer line of its phrasing; it is always of prime importance that the accompanist be keenly sensitive to the tempo and mood of the child or the group, and adjust her playing to that tempo and mood.

Recordings

A great variety of recordings have been produced, intended to stimulate dance. Many of them, for the very young child, make such a point of dramatic interpretation, and change so rapidly from one activity to another, that the child who tries to follow the music no more than tunes in physically until the "music tells" him to do something else! This is very unsatisfactory from the standpoint of movement. Our best source for recorded music for the younger child is that intended for older children and for adults. Much of this is nondramatic, but has a well-accented rhythmic pulse and makes for a variety of responses (see Chapter 9 on Records). Music of a purely rhythmic character, such as folk music, can accompany children's dancing to great advantage after they have had considerable free experimentation and are ready to conform to a group rhythm.

In this discussion on accompaniment we have suggested five general sources as possibilities in providing significant and appropriate sound or music for movement. If we, together with boys and girls, can free ourselves from our conventional practices (and some of them are good), we can have an exciting and truly creative experience in dance. Even young children can begin to get the feeling of accompanying others. Older ones, working in groups, can surprise us with their resourcefulness. Recently I observed a group of seven girls in sixth grade compose a dance, show it to the class, and ask for accompaniment. The class divided into five groups and each group worked on what they thought would be appropriate. After trying them all, the dance group chose one which seemed best fitted to express their idea.

We have considered the relation of sound-making to movement, the possibilities of sound-making within ourselves, the material things that surround us with which we can make sounds, and the use of a variety of instruments. We have also considered music compositions and recorded music.

The challenge is what inventiveness we can bring to these resources. How can we improvise on or with anything that will provide a fitting accompaniment for creative movement? Are we eager to go in search of more and better "sound companions" to dance?

Picking Up the Rhythm of Movement

Any group movement, except that of the very youngest children, tends to take on a common rhythm if given time for repetition. Can we relax and wait for this to happen? If we can, we can tune in physically to this movement and catch the strong accent or pulse. Once we *feel* this, we can accompany the run, for example, by an even tap on a drum by listening to the feet of the runners. We soon discover that if the tap on the drum comes just a fraction of a second before the sound of the feet, it not only supports the running but gives it a certain impetus. This is the simplest way of accompanying running, but it soon becomes monotonous. Using several drums or other percussion instruments that have different tone color can add variety—one instrument playing only the accent and the other playing the "in-between" part. If one can let himself "go," he will soon begin improvising a variety of interesting beats, yet he can give enough support to the pulse of the movement so that the runners have something to hold on to.

Silence in accompaniment is very effective, as a friend from whom I am learning much about accompaniment, pointed out. To illustrate piano accompaniment for running, I was contrasting a piece of music in which the emphasis was on a note to each step, the total effect being a picayune step-by-step affair, with an old Russian folk piece in which there was an over-all feeling of swiftness and excitement, and in which one felt the rhythm not as a pitter-patter but as a cycle of upsurge and fall. My friend suggested, however, a crashing chord on the piano as a blowing-off sound, allowing the runner to run on the overtones, and then catching the end of the cycle with another chord, and so on. This use of "silence" requires that the accompanist be perfectly attuned to the movements of the dancing group.

As we respond kinesthetically to the trained dancer as he runs across the stage, we are aware of the excitement and swiftness of his motion and not of the tap of his feet. This means running also to children, until we concentrate on "stepping by note" and so often inhibit the impulse to movement itself. There are always, thank goodness, some youngsters whose creativity will not be drowned by us. Ethel Crowninshield, who has written many songs for younger children, tells the story of a six-year-old who was running fast and furiously around the room during rhythmic play. A little girl called, "Don't you hear the music?" "Yes," he yelled, "but it don't bother me none!" He was running for the fun of running.

Once our accompaniment is tuned in to the essence of children's running, their feet, in turn, tune in to the underlying beat. If this happens often enough, the children then enjoy keeping time to the music and do it with no effort at all, responding to any change in tempo set by the accompanist.

Sometimes we can help ourselves provide varieties in accompaniment on percussion instruments by thinking of the melody line of a piece of music such as a Schubert country dance or his *Eccossaise* or Schumann's *Soldier's March,* and tapping it out; or a song with rhythm that seems to catch the feeling of the movement. We can begin to get a feeling for form in our use of instruments, even the simplest ABA form, a feeling for beginning, middle, and end. There are so many ways of elaborating on a single beat in terms of pause, dynamics, off beat, double or triple beat, and so on, that lend variety to sound.

Response to Music

What about interpretation of music? Does one never play music first, and ask the child to listen and then respond to it? Certainly response to music is an important part of any dance program for children. Since this has been the *only* approach to dance for so long, we have stressed instead the response of music to movement. In considering the response to music, the dancer's interpretation of the mood and spirit of music definitely constitutes a part of dance that cannot be neglected. Because so frequently it results in sterile ideas and artificial form is no reason for not revitalizing it. We believe that one of the most promising ways to do just this is to build with the child through a two-way process, that is, working from movement to music as well as from music to movement, an association with music as an accompaniment that has real meaning to the child.

"Do what the music tells you to do," unfortunately, to many a teacher means "do what *I think* the music tells you to do." If we use this approach to interpret the *content* of music, we must make sure of letting the child be the judge of what the music means *to him*. The same music means different things to different people, and we are on dangerous ground when we try to interpret it for others. Different composers frequently treat the same idea, but their musical interpretations of that idea are widely different. If we want a particular response to a piece of music, let us be forthright and ask the children for it. A teacher is the leader of a group. If she feels her group would benefit by a certain kind of dancing, and if the music that she plays means such a dance to her, then let us ask for it. This is part of teaching. An indirect suggestion in asking the child to do what he feels in relation to a stimulus and then, if it is not acceptable, to maneuver the child and situation to conform to what the teacher wants, is not an honest way of dealing with children.

A teacher from the Northwest tells an amusing incident illustrating a child's interpretation of music. She had played music from Mendelssohn's *Midsummer Night's Dream* to accompany fairy dancing, and the groups had responded like fairies, all but one little boy who had recently moved into the community from Florida. Every time the music was played he sat in a stiff huddle in the middle of the room, and no amount of talking about the way the music sounded had any effect on him. Finally the teacher asked: "But if the music does not make you want to be a fairy, what *are* you?" "I'm a frozen milk bottle. The music makes me think of *that!*" said the four-year-old from the Deep South. He had been intrigued, day after day, by the bottle of milk left on his kitchen doorstep, which was always frozen when it was taken in; and for some reason the "fairy" music had stimulated him to dramatize a frozen milk bottle! A musical experience, or any other for that matter, can have many meanings, depending upon the individual.

Collections of dramatic music published for use with children can be very helpful if chosen judiciously. For instance, a composer or an editor has named a piece of music *Airplanes*, and it has been used successfully by some child or group to support their play, but this does not guarantee that the piece will fit other children's airplane play. (Why is it that most "airplane pieces" are composed for the upper range of the piano when the sound of a flying plane is anything but "high and light"?) If the teacher feels that a given child needs music of a dramatic character, she should first find out from him what kind he wants, and then play several selections for him that seem to her to fit his play, and let him be the judge of what he wants to use. If a child chooses to interpret "elephant" music by rolling over and over to the rhythmic flow of the music, we should encourage his interpretation rather than insist on his "being an elephant" by walking on all fours or swinging his trunk.

When we give the children a chance to hear a variety of good music from which they can choose what seems to them most fitting for their play, we make them conscious of the music itself and more discriminating in their choices. It is then that we are really encouraging *good listening*.

The Classroom Teacher

In the great majority of our schools, the classroom teacher is responsible for whatever dance program goes on in her class. In schools that have a special dance teacher who works directly with boys and girls, an accompanist is provided or, at least, the dance teacher has the help of the classroom teacher.

But this situation, unfortunately, is rare. And so the class-room teacher, who is the only guide of her group's dance experiences, has a unique problem. She is pushed into work-ing with groups that are too large, her space is limited, and she must provide her own accompaniment. She also has to be skilled in the techniques of group management which are closely related to the age of the children with whom she works. All of this is no mean assignment, and it is one that would confound the specialist were she faced with a "solo" job.

All through this discussion on movement I have tried to identify with the problems faced by the classroom teacher. They are many, but it is my honest conviction that the oppor-tunities presented in living day-by-day with children, in recognizing movement, in encouraging it, and in helping children recall at a dance time some of the significant move-ments that happen spontaneously all during the day far out-weigh the limitations.

General Experiences in Movement

We have been concerned with general experiences in the whole area of movement rather than with steps or specific patterns. These cannot help but follow naturally when move-ment takes priority. Practicing such skills then takes on real meaning. If we can help children to set dance processes in motion, to give congruous expression to their strong emo-tions through dance, if we can help them to find in dance a bridge between strenuous exercise and imagination, then movement will be a really satisfying and creative art medium in their lives.

There is no one method, no one system, that will accom-plish this. We must have broad vision, must use our imagina-tion along with that of the child, and recognize the *educative value of progressive growth in an art rather than the final product.* Our most important contribution to this whole process is our attitude toward the art of dance. We are responsible for building the environment in which we work and live with children, an environment that will foster a genuine respect not only for the art of movement but for all the arts.

Here are a few suggestions to increase awareness of movement.

1. Do you find yourself looking more closely at movement in children, in adults, in things? When and where?

2. In what way do the home and school encourage, allow for, or discourage movement?

3. Do you "feel" movement as well as see it?

4. Observe people's movement behavior, for example, the shape of the hand in reaching for a rock or balloon.

5. Do you find yourself "tuning in" with a child's interest in, for example, the movement of a mobile?

6. Take pictures of children in movement.

REFERENCES

Andrews, Gladys, *Creative Rhythmic Movement for Children,* Englewood Cliffs, N. J.: Prentice-Hall.
Kraus, Richard, *Square Dance of Today,* New York: Ronald.
La Salle, Dorothy, *Rhythms and Dances for Elementary Schools,* New York: Barnes.
Murray, Ruth, *Dance in Elementary Education,* New York: Harper.

MUSIC SOURCES

Hughes, Edwin (ed.), *Master Series for the Young,* New York: Schirmer. Selections from Bach, Beethoven, Mozart, Schuman, and Schubert.
MacCartney, E. P., *Songs for the Nursery School,* New York: Willis Music Co.
Pinto, Octavio, *Scenas Infantis,* New York: Schirmer.
Rebikov, Vladimir, *Silhouettes,* New York: Schirmer.

Robinson, E., *School Rhythms,* Evanston, Ill.: Summy-Birchard.

Seeger, Ruth Crawford, *American Folk Songs for Children,* New York: Doubleday.

Waterman, Elizabeth, *A B C of Rhythmic Training,* Evanston, Ill.: Summy-Birchard.

Whitlock, V., *Come and Caper,* Boston: Ginn.

World of Music, *Play a Tune,* Boston: Ginn.

Chapter 9

PHONOGRAPH RECORDS, RADIO, TELEVISION

$$\approx\approx\approx\approx\approx\approx\approx\approx\approx\approx\approx\approx\approx\approx\approx$$

THE LAST DOZEN YEARS have signified an auditory-sensory revolution for millions of people. The long playing record with its advantages of uninterrupted sound and relative economy, the development of high-fidelity systems and their reproduction of realistic sound, and now the era of stereophonic sound have literally thrust a nation not only into a new sound awareness but a continually expanding one. Never before have so many people been exposed to so many opportunities to know and enjoy music. Girls and boys of all ages come to school with a vastly different "sound" background than ever before.

In many homes playing records is a family experience, each member of the group taking from a given recording what has meaning to him. Teachers frequently come upon interesting and amusing bits of evidence that show pretty clearly what is of most interest to a youngster. Four-year-old Altha, whose family were record enthusiasts, had her own form of records in kindergarten.[1]

[1] Used by permission of Marjorie Feldman.

She took several blocks of wood, with holes in the center, putting a long thin stick through them, revolving these blocks with her finger, and singing her impressions of songs or, more accurately, her impressions of recorded songs. She had a different song for each record. The thick square block was a wailing, slow blues, and each time she put on that thick square block a similar wail came forth. A round thin block was a fast, nonsense song; another was an activity song; and, turning the record with one hand, she would go through appropriate motions with the other, all the while beating her knees together. She ended with something low and crooning, putting her baby doll to sleep.

The second day she discovered that the blocks could be turned over on her phonograph, so she would start playing one side and immediately turn it over. She kept this up for over half an hour. The next day she kept singing the same phrase over and over again. When the teacher asked her why she kept singing the same phrase, she indignantly shouted out that she was not singing; that the record was broken; and that was why the voice on the record was singing the same thing again and again.

Six-year-old Janet had a different kind of interest in records. On her own phonograph she played a discarded opera record until her family were convinced that her musical perceptions in the classics were at a high level, only to discover that it was the crack on the disc and its rhythmic recurrence that intrigued her. For both Altha and Janet, the responses were unconventional, yes, but certainly not devoid of musical overtones.

We respond to certain musical selections because of the associations connected with them, both musical and social. And we may find that a particular piece of music or the narration of the spoken word has the power to stretch our imagination and sense of discovery. Our response is essentially individualistic. This is also true of children and should give us a warning too often overlooked in our usual music-appreciation classes, where the teacher's expectations tolerate little nonconformity of response.

Independence in Learning

Music encompasses such a tremendous field of possible experiences that no one person, family, or school can meet the variety and amount for which many children are eagerly reaching out. Also, adults have other things to do, and even though they may be very competent musically, people cannot possibly "turn on" these experiences every time a child is ready for them.

We should, therefore, welcome any *additional* ways in which children can pursue their musical interests without benefit of adults. Records can give a child an opportunity to go ahead on his own momentum, and where this momentum will take him is many times unpredictable. He will upset our finely spun theories of what is just the right music for the three-year-old or for a ten-year-old. He refuses to be packaged in neat compartments. Many records not intended for the juvenile trade find a responsive chord in a child's heart. Snatches of the classics, ballads, and popular and folk music that are favorites of adults or teen-agers will filter down to the smaller child, and the process of discarding or taking what he likes from what he hears goes on from day to day. He may even go off the deep end for a while, and we may deplore his taste. But if he grows up in a home and school where there is a large variety of good records, his chances of developing reliable and discriminating tastes are quite good.

An effective teacher is one who finds out what a child already knows so that she may do a better job of helping him learn more. But, when there are thirty youngsters in a classroom, this is not an easy matter. A skillful person, however, can work with children in such a way that they can be independent, and she can give them many choices and opportunities. In other words, a third-grade teacher can take away the "third-grade" ceiling laid down by tradition, the music course of study, or her own limitations, and allow children to learn what they are ready to learn. We cannot force certain music experiences on them if they are not receptive. What the clever child learns from such an experience is a technique of avoidance while giving the appearance of listening. He is learning how to pretend he is listening when he is not. How can we decide for any one group just what music should be learned or "appreciated" in a given year without knowing something about their musical capacities and tastes? This is where free choice in the school's collection of records can pay untold dividends: the greater the variety of recordings to choose from, the luckier the child in that school.

If children in a nursery school can operate their record player individually and independently (and they can), most certainly older boys and girls can do the same. Yet this opportunity is frequently denied them, not because they are not responsible enough to manage the player, but because playing records disturbs other children at work or because the only player in the school is a handsome large console model, either in the music room or in the assembly hall, and is used only for group listening. Schools need portable record players that can easily be moved from room to room. If the sound disturbs others (often it is the teacher who is most disturbed), children can be helped to keep the volume turned low or ear phones may be attached so that they may use this resource for learning. I do not intend to suggest that all of the children's record experiences should be on an individual or small-group basis. Certainly, there are many times when teachers and children, too, will want an entire group to have an experience together. If the discussion has seemed weighted on the side of individual use, it is because this has been sadly neglected and also because it can yield so much. Perhaps, too, it is a reaction against the "music appreciation" period where emphasis is placed on identification of selection played on a phonograph, followed by a music test where the ability to name the piece and composer determine the pupil's musical rating. If test we must, why can we not have a test built on interest and pleasant associations?

One more comment on this matter of the individual pursuit of learning, not only in music, but in many aspects of the curriculum. Today we are going through a period of experimentation in various methods of mass education. Some of this is thoughtfully directed; but some of it reflects an alarming disregard of individual differences in learning. Unless the measures taken to meet the financial crisis in education are more realistic than they have been, oversized classes and the mass-education approach will be continued. Out of this experimentation, I am sure, help will eventually come. I cannot but wish, however, that this problem might also be approached from another angle. We hear little of experimentation in setting up our schools and classrooms as *self-service* centers in education, in providing so many "invitations to learning" with self selection the key to their use that every child would find a beginning place unique to him. Children's independence would be recognized, cultivated, and supported. Learning would be relevant to them, and, make no mistake about it, every youngster wants to learn and he is eager to do hard things.

Variety in Records

The scope and variety of sound experiences on records is incredible. Speaking only of music, Aldous Huxley contrasts the "musical ocean" on records with the "repertory pond" available to concert audiences. Music of all kinds and from all ages and from all over the world has been recorded. The esoteric and the conventional are there for the taking. In the following groupings we shall consider some of the representative sound reservoirs.

Environmental Sounds

Reference has already been made in Chapters 1 and 3 to recordings of environmental sounds. In the early days of this type of recording, the material was produced to serve a utilitarian purpose such as sound effects for movies, television, radio, and theater. The medical profession recorded varied types of heartbeats, for example. Today there is great demand from a small but eager group of sound enthusiasts for sounds of nature, industry, transportation, the city, the country, and so on. A friend who is a highly talented pianist goes into ecstasy over Cook's *Voices of the Ocean*. Sounds of the jungle, of rain, of birds; sounds of fireboats, of airplanes, of ocean liners—these and many others have been and are being recorded. Columbia has recorded the latter group in a series for the young child. Children respond to these sounds with their quick imaginations, and each in his own way supplies the associations and content that are unique to him. Surely, in encouraging a child's natural disposition to environmental sounds, their differences and unique qualities, we are increasing his aural perceptions. Is not this a source for ear training that has real potentialities?

Documentary Records

I cannot imagine a better approach to the sociological study of the complexities of New York City than careful listening to *Nueva York* (Folkways), on which Tony Schwartz, a keen student of his environment, recorded the comments of people on the streets which reveal their feelings about "newcomers." Columbia has recorded for those interested in sounds of history *The Union: The Sounds and Music of the Civil War*. There are also a number of Columbia's excellent *I Can Hear It Now* recordings available. Ward Botsford captured the penetration of the sound barrier on *The United States Air Force, A Portrait in Sound* (Vox). Enrichment Records uses materials from the Landmark series of books to produce social-studies records for children in the elementary school. Folkways is a prolific source for documentary material from all over the world in story, song, and music. Kaydan's *The Living Constitution* and Tribune's *This Is the UN* are unusually rewarding experiences for older children and adults.

The Spoken Word

Many exciting things are happening in the field of recorded stories and dramatic readings. What a boon to the overworked mother and teacher on whom there are so many demands for "just one more story!" *Records never should take the place, either in home or in school, of the told or read story,* but, when a child can turn to a record and hear over and over again a well-told story, he has at his command a truly wonderful resource for education. In choosing story records for children, we should demand honesty of approach, directness, and a voice that is not patronizing and free from cuteness and studio overtones. Nor do good stories need to be dressed up with exaggerated sound effects to interest children. An excellent record illustrating the simple, direct approach is *But Muffin Can Hear* (Young People's) for the nursery- and kindergarten-age child. The narration is intimate, unhurried, and natural. Among the many good records for the younger elementary age are *Lentil* (Young People's), *Just So Stories* (Caedmon), *Horton Hatches the Egg* (MGM), and *Many Moons* (Columbia). For the older children, we have *Sinbad the Sailor, Three Musketeers,* and *Peter Pan* (all Columbia), *The Wheel on the School* (Newbery), and *Grimm's Fairy Tales* (Caedmon). Among numerous readings of Bible stories are those produced by Folkways and Judson. No school or town library of recordings should miss the complete *Alice in Wonderland* (Riverside), accompanied by a facsimile of Lewis Carroll's original edition of this all-time classic. I cannot imagine a finer literary experience than Cyril Ritchard's superb, unaccompanied reading supplemented by Alec Wilder's appropriate and sensitive musical introduction to each chapter. The American Library Association has done some outstanding work in records. Here we have straight storytelling without sound effects or music, and there is no question that such stories as *A Paul Bunyan Yarn* and *A Pecos Bill Tale* hold children's interests. In some sections of the country bookmobiles which serve rural areas are equipped with a loudspeaker, and, when they stop at a school, they broadcast a record which stimulates a great demand for this story in book form.

The child can turn not only to music, then, but also great literature and fine storytelling on his own volition, and here again he may break down our notions of what we think will interest him. A twelve-year-old was listening to a recording of *Treasure Island* (Columbia). Her six-year-old brother was apparently absorbed in his own play. At the end of the story, however, he asked his sister for an explanation of certain parts that he did not understand. This album is now one of his favorites. One would not be likely to suggest buying this record for a six-year-old, and yet here was an experience from which this youngster took his own measure. At the same time a great favorite of his is a story about a little dog which is intended for the preschool child.

Records of the spoken word offer rich variety in speech, voices from other countries, voices that reflect regional speech patterns of our own country, and the unique and distinctive voices of authors such as Carl Sandburg, Robert Frost, and Dylan Thomas, as they read their own works. Listening to the *sound* of words as well as to their meaning can be a beautiful experience.

Music and Story

During the last ten years there has been steady improvement in the production of this, the largest group of records made especially for children. One still needs to listen before buying, for an occasional producer has not yet learned that good taste is equally important to both young and older listeners. The classic fairy, nursery, and folk tales have been adapted, modified, and changed with varying degrees of success depending upon the adult's music and literary standards. But, in general, there has been progress.

In this group we have a wide range in type of production, from the simple and delightful *Walk in the Forest* (Young People's) for the preschool child to such outstanding musical plays taken from original productions as *Peter Pan,* with Jean Arthur and Boris Karloff (Columbia). Children's Record Guild and Young People's Records have a catalog of musical plays for children from about five to ten years of age. Included are *The Emperor's New Clothes, Midsummer Night's Dream,* and *Sleeping Beauty.* Good music and respect for children are evidenced in these presentations. One of the best-known musical plays is Prokofieff's *Peter and the Wolf.* Records of the entire story as narrated by Alec Guinness (Victor) and Cyril Ritchard (Columbia) are excellent.

The Walt Disney moving-picture productions of many of our classic stories offer a vast source of stories and music for records. Some of us adults who grew up with the original stories may not welcome some of the Disney versions, but many of the Disney songs have become a part of our musical storehouse of songs that will live for a long time. A few delightful Disney stories have been released in combination with a picture story book. Representative of these are *Robin Hood* (Capitol), *Pinocchio* (Victor), and *Lady and the Tramp* (Capitol). This combination of book and record showed exceptional promise a few years ago during the days of the 78 rpm records. The child can follow the story in the book while the record plays. If he cannot read, he can follow just the pictures, and the child who can read, or who is learning to read, can follow the words. As for the nonreader, how can we tell when he begins to pick up a word here and there?

Many children react favorably to these books, and quite a few teachers have found them helpful. I am not suggesting this as a "reading system" but we should not disregard one way in which a child may be independent in helping himself learn to read. Little Golden Records has released some of their Little Golden Books, such as *The Saggy Baggy Elephant,* in combination with records in which the narrator follows exactly what is written in the book. Perhaps the best-known example of the record story-book album is Capitol's delightful *Bozo at the Circus.*

The expense of producing these combinations presents problems. Speaking from the standpoint of the possibilities for good entertainment and education through this approach, I should like to urge all of us in the field of education to encourage companies to do some more pioneering in this direction. It is a relatively unexplored field.

Participation Records

There are many degrees and many kinds of participation, depending upon the quality of attention that is brought to any experience. Some records have been specifically designed to encourage active responses from the listener. In this group are those for the preschool child in which the aim is physical activity, "teaching of skills" records, and records that give instruction in foreign language. Those designed to stimulate physical responses from the young child reflect a worthy enough aim. The trouble is, however, that when a writer aims at evoking activity, he usually comes out with a contrived story that has no real point and precious little literary quality. This does not mean that recordings cannot encourage children to respond actively. Children certainly should respond by physical movement if the story or music impels them to, but let us work harder on producing good material and less on pushing children around. The records that have been produced to teach subject-matter skills use a workbook

Finding out how it works

Discovering a two-toned bell

Listening and investigating

or how-to-teach approach. They are, for the most part, mechanical and dull and, in their concentration on rote memo-
rization, deny everything we know about how effective learning goes on.

At present a field that seems to offer promise is that of
foreign languages. One of the better albums is *Les Albums
de L'Oncle Max* (Folkways). Emphasis here is on the sound,
movement and rhythm of the language, and this is achieved
through narration of old French fables. A man and woman,
both natives of France, alternate in telling the stories. Illustrated books accompany the package, with the fables printed
in French.

Songs in Other Languages

Recordings of songs in foreign languages offer not only a
fine musical experience but also an opportunity to become
familiar with these languages. Short of living in a family or
in a country where a different language is spoken, I cannot
think of a more natural way to get acquainted with the tonal
qualities of its speech. The younger the child the more easily
he will pick up and repeat what he hears (see Chapter 4 on
singing).

Some of these records are made especially for children;
others are recordings of songs for general listening. In *Children of Paris* (Grand Award) French children sing their folk
songs. The material is well presented, accompanied by an
attractively illustrated book. In the *Obernkirchen Children's
Choir* (Angel) we hear children's voices as they sing their
native German folk songs—an exciting musical experience for
any listener. The infectious singing in *Songs in French for
Children* (Columbia), a group of lilting folk songs, and *Folk-
songs for Children of All Ages* (Cantemos), songs of Latin
America, evokes participation almost immediately. Even
after one hearing, or rather along with the first hearing, one
can join in the easy repetitive refrains in French and Spanish.

The printed words of the songs accompany both albums. Anyone who has been entertained in the concert hall by the delightful Marais and Miranda will welcome their albums *Songs of Many Lands* and *Songs of the South African Veld* (Decca).

Israel, Folk Songs and *Jewish Children's Songs and Games* (Folkways) are a recent addition to songs from other lands on records. Judson has initiated a series of songs in other languages for children with *Songs Children Sing in Italy*. Judging by this first release, the project holds much promise. What an opportunity familiarity with all of these songs offers toward a better understanding of people all over the world! What a rich, cultural experience in music is here for the interested listener!

Songs

Nursery, folk, ballad, religious, patriotic, camp, and popular songs of the present and past are all to be found on records. Children respond eagerly to folk music, and here we have a great deal of source material. The largest collection is to be found in the Library of Congress. This music has been recorded in the field and is authentic. It is not as acoustically smooth as commercial recordings, but older boys and girls who are especially interested in studying the folk culture of different sections of our country will find it rewarding.

The considerable number of folk singers that we have on records gives us an opportunity to bring a variety of singing voices to children. It is an interesting experience for boys and girls to hear the same song performed by different singers. A creative singer makes the song his very own, and there is no music that lends itself to this as do folk songs. Among the better known artists in this field are Burl Ives, Tom Scott, Tom Glazer, Alan Mills (the Canadian), Pete Seeger, and Richard Dyer-Bennett, whose singing is an esoteric experience and appeals to a sophisticated audience. The majority of young children, unfortunately, have too little opportunity to hear male voices at home and school. Television, radio, and records can bring these to all of us, and records, especially, give us an opportunity to be thoughtful and selective in our choices.

Children are unpredictable in their song choices. What appeals one week may be ignored the following. Nothing is more unrealistic than for us to make assumptions about what children will or will not enjoy over a period of time. Songs from musical plays, arias from light and grand opera, the great art songs—these and many more selections offer music to which all children should be exposed with the opportunity to be independent and self-selective in making their follow-up choices.

Instrumental Music

The "musical ocean" on records includes music from circuses, merry-go-rounds, old-fashioned music boxes, and player pianos; band music, popular songs, jazz, the light and serious classics, contemporary music, and music from other cultures.

There have been numerous approaches to the introduction of instruments to children via records; some are worthwhile, others are less successful. Stories in which instruments are personified have been recorded. The better examples of these are *Tubby the Tuba* (Decca) and *Pan the Piper* (Columbia), a fantasy story of the discovery of orchestral instruments. My experience with children supports my belief that they welcome direct information—that is, naming instruments and treating them as instruments without a coy and circuitous approach. Personification as a teaching method harks back to the days of a now discredited psychology of learning and, unless it is handled exceptionally well, it can be an ineffective experience. It not only may confuse the child but, more important, it indicates slight respect for his ability to react directly to the art of music.

In *Peter and the Wolf,* imaginative and skillful use of instruments offers an interesting approach in helping the listener to become familiar with certain instruments. Intended for older boys and girls, Benjamin Britten's *The Young Person's Guide to the Orchestra* is an exceptionally fine musical composition. Each of the four choirs of the orchestra plays Britten's arrangement of a theme from Purcell and as the finale the entire orchestra plays the theme again. This was composed as the musical score for the moving picture of the same name, but it is available on many records. Columbia has both of these compositions on a single long playing disc.

The Orchestra: Stokowski (Capitol), with its excellent accompanying booklet, is a fine "sound picture" of the orchestra.

Leonard Bernstein has recorded three musical treasures for Columbia: *What Is Jazz, Leonard Bernstein and Beethoven,* and *The Birth of a Symphony.* The focus here is on music content and its development. These records are of interest to older boys and girls and adults. Recommended also are some records of music produced by children's record companies such as Young People's Records' *Rondo for Bassoon* and *The Licorice Stick,* Mercury-Childcraft's *Great Music for Young Folks,* and others. The delightful *Major Classics for Minors* (Victor), dealing with composers from Bach to Prokofieff and with pertinent comments by the duo pianists, Whittemore and Lowe, brings to the listener the intimacy associated with chamber music. For older boys and girls (and adults) who are serious music students, Vox's Spotlight series on *Keyboard, Percussion, Brass, Strings,* and *Winds,* each with a beautifully illustrated and informative book, are a substantial and worthwhile investment.

We certainly want every child to know Haydn's *Toy Symphony* (Musical Sound Books) and today's musical counterpart, that amusing and charming *Concerto for Toys and Instruments* (Young People's). Musical Sound Books has a good catalog of 78 rpm records in which they have recorded many excerpts of classical music that have appeal for younger children. Different instruments play these selections, and thus the child gets acquainted with them in a natural way.

Then there are the "music appreciation" records in various forms. Representative are Columbia's Intoduction to Masterworks series, *Eine Kleine Nachtmusik* (45 rpm), without comments, and *Chopin* (45 rpm), story and music; *Diana and the Golden Apples* (Capitol), story and music; and *Child's Introduction to Great Composers, from Bach to Bartók* (Golden) music only.

Adult ears usually do not take to new and different sound experiences as quickly as children's do. The familiarity that accompanies repeated hearings of the new and the different may change our ears and our attitudes and extend our musical horizons in ways we did not think possible. Since we have too few opportunities to hear contemporary music and the music of different cultures in comparison with the familiar classics offered in concert repertories, we should welcome the increasing storehouse of the less familiar that is on records. Music in the modern idiom reflects the complex world in which we live today—its rhythms, its variations, its dynamics, its movement. For children and adults, a growing acquaintance with "music that is strange" can become a rewarding interest. A group of such records is listed at the end of the chapter.

Use of Records and Phonograph

Especially when younger children use records, the school and home must be prepared for certain replacements and minor repair jobs. But this is a small price to pay for the musical education that goes on when children are able to use records individually and independently. Besides, children develop a sense of responsibility for equipment to the extent to which we give them opportunity to use this equipment, and it is amazing how even the youngest respond to our trust in them. An occasional accident involving a record or phonograph is far less serious than having children live in an environment where they feel adults do not have faith in them.

What kind of record player should we buy? Should it have a single speed or three speeds? How much does one have to pay for a satisfactory phonograph? There are still a fairly large number of 78 rpm records, six-, seven-, and ten-inch size, for the very young child. A single-speed machine is simple for the preschooler to operate but, since there is an increasing number of records for children on 45 rpm and also on 33⅓ rpm, it is not an economical buy. With instruction and supervision, many children at four and five years of age can operate a three-speed player. A reasonably good phonograph can be bought for around thirty dollars. Keeping in mind that a phonograph is not a plaything, but rather a means to early music experiences, and that the quality of reproduction is dependent upon the quality of the machine, we should buy as good a portable as we can. The "permanent" needle needs to be replaced from time to time. When we notice a rattle or raspiness in the record, especially near the center, the chances are that it is the needle and not the record that is at fault.

The player should be placed where children can watch the disc go round and round. For the younger children a low table or the floor is suitable; older youngsters can make their own arrangements. It is hard to understand, but there seems to be something almost hypnotic in this desire to watch the turntable. Perhaps the rhythm of the movement relaxes children and helps them to listen. At any rate, accept the fact, and arrange for the children to be close to the record both in school and at home.

Sources of Records

In discussing records, we have indicated from time to time the names of the companies which produce them. Most of these records may be purchased through local record stores. A few of the companies that make a special effort to serve schools, such as Children's Record Guild, Folkways, Columbia, Enrichment Records, and Musical Sound Books, send catalogs on request. If records are not available through the local dealer, the two following sources are helpful: Children's Reading Service, 1078 St. John's Place, Brooklyn 13, New York, and Children's Music Center, 2858 West Pico Boulevard, Los Angeles 6, California.

An adequate record library, either in one's home or in school, is certainly desirable, but there are other ways to obtain records, too. In some communities local libraries have both a listening and a lending service. Family libraries should not be overlooked by the school. Naturally, the school must assume responsibility for careful handling. When schools have a certain amount of money in their budgets for records, it is hoped that teachers will not make all the decisions and purchases without consulting the children. A group of children together with their teacher can have an extremely valuable experience in listening to a variety of records and deciding which ones they should like to have permanently. Perhaps they will make a few unwise choices (in the teacher's estimation) from time to time, but that is part of learning.

Radio and Television

Radio and television provide both the stimulation for new musical experiences and the satisfactions that attend listening to what is familiar. In many sections of the country, radio stations have special music programs that are announced in advance. Television has brought us some truly outstanding music and dance programs, for example, Leonard Bernstein's clear and dignified presentations and explanations of great music; Yehudi Menuhin's introduction and interpretation of the music of India; programs of ballet, opera, and modern dance; and occasional appearances of great instrumental artists. Can we encourage boys and girls into more than a casual use of these resources, and what tie-up do we see between these and our music programs in school?

Closed-circuit television is being used in some school systems. What an opportunity this can offer for a music program! The quality of the program presented can inspire the listeners to search for more and more sound experiences; it can so deal with the heart of music that every youngster can find a beginning place and have respect for his own aural observations and explorations; or it can present the kind of lesson in which conformity of response—rabbits hopping to a piece of music or factual information about music—will be the measure of its effectiveness.

Is it a "how-to-do-it" program, or does it have the kind of momentum in what is done and, also, what is left undone to excite children's sound curiosities? And then, do they know their discoveries will be welcomed by the person responsible for the music program and by the classroom teacher?

Does closed-circuit television offer an opportunity to use the musical resources of the community—the nonprofessional singer of ballads, folk songs, spirituals; the nonprofessional instrumentalist; the bird caller, as well as those who are professionals? Do we think of television as bringing richness and variety of experience in music, or do we see it as teaching a "music lesson" to hundreds rather than to one class? Can we not use both approaches? Can we not judge our results on the degree to which youngsters follow up by propelling themselves musically, rather than by conforming to a response pattern?

Here are a few suggestions that may help in more effective use of records, radio and television. (These suggestions are directed to the adult as well as to the student.)

1. What is your favorite record?
2. What was your favorite a year ago?
3. How do you choose records?
4. Can we make a plan to bring selected records to school?
5. If you could make a record, what would you like to have on it?
6. What makes a recording appeal to you?
7. Examine the radio and television programs concerned with music for the week. Are there some in which the entire class would be interested? Are there others that appeal to individual interests?
8. What familiar or what new experiences do these programs offer?
9. Would you like to hear one or two of the works performed on records before the program, or would you prefer to wait until later?
10. Have you discovered unfamiliar music or instruments during the week on radio or television?
11. Have you heard a specially interesting program lately?
12. Scout for singing, instrumental, or dance programs.
13. Do you read the comments of critics on radio and television programs? Do you read reviewers' comments on new recordings?
14. Write a review of a recording or a radio or television music program.
15. Select a particular field of music such as folk, band, chamber, jazz, modern, or classical, and then follow through for several weeks in hearing as much as possible from it.
16. Are there records you prefer to listen to alone? Are there some you like to listen to with others?

Any classification of records must be used with great flexibility. This is specially true in the field of music where so much depends on individual interest, taste, and experience.

The records listed on the following pages are representative of a wide variety of interests. Many excellent ones will not be found here because of lack of space. See Schwann's *Long Playing Record Catalog* for the most complete record inventory available.

SUGGESTIONS FOR LISTENING

The criterion for selection is *variety* of musical experience. Although only a few classical selections are listed because of space limitations, they are very important and should be a part of every person's musical experience. For further suggestions and alternate performances consult record catalogs such as *The Long Player* or Schwann's. Unless otherwise specified, the records listed below are 33⅓ rpm.

General

Album for the Young, Schumann; *The Seasons,* Tchaikovsky. Ania Dorfman, piano (Victor).

Amaryllis, Ghys; *March Militaire,* Schubert. (Musical Sound Books, 78 rpm). Representative of a large catalog.

Appalachian Spring; Billy the Kid, Copland. Ormandy, Philadelphia Orchestra (Columbia).

The Birth of the Symphony. Leonard Bernstein (Columbia).

Bolero; Mother Goose Suite, Ravel. Koussevitzky, Boston Symphony Orchestra (Victor).

Bozo's Circus Band. (Capitol).

Bozo's Merry-go-round Music. (Capitol, 45 rpm).

Carnival of the Animals, Saint-Saëns. Kostelanetz, narrated by Noel Coward (Columbia).

Child's Introduction to Great Composers. (Golden). Music only.

Chopin. (Columbia, 45 rpm).

Christmas Eve Suite; *Flight of the Bumblebee; Sadko; Dubinushka,* Rimsky-Korsakov. Ansermet, Orchestre de la Suisse Romande (London).

Circus Time. Ringling Brothers and Barnum and Bailey circus band (Decca).

Country Dance, Pastoral Dance, Merrymakers' Dance, The *Nell Gwyn* Suite (Decca).

Diana and the Golden Apples. (Capitol).

Dress Parade. (Mercury-Childcraft, 78 rpm). Bugles, percussion, and fifes.

Eine Kleine Nachtmusik, Mozart. (Columbia, 45 rpm).

Great Jazz Pianists. Goldman Band (Camden).

Great Music for Young Folks. (Mercury-Childcraft, 78 rpm).

Hansel and Gretel, Humperdinck. Schwarzkopf, von Karajan, Philharmonic Orchestra (Angel). In German.

Hansel and Gretel, Humperdinck. Stevens, Conner, Brownlee, Rudolph, Metropolitan Opera Chorus and Orchestra (Columbia). In English.

International. Royal Australian Air Force Band (Epic). Songs and anthems of twenty-six countries.

Introduction to Masterworks. (Columbia).

Leonard Bernstein on Beethoven. (Columbia).

The Licorice Stick. (Young People's, 78 rpm).

Little Brass Band. (Young People's, 78 rpm).

Lollipops. Beecham, the Royal Philharmonic Orchestra (Angel).

Major Classics for Minors. Whittemore and Lowe, duo-piano (Victor).

Marches for Children. (Mercury-Childcraft, 78 rpm).

Marches for Twirling. Fennell, Eastman Symphonic Wind Ensemble (Mercury).

Music of Johann Strauss. Walter, Columbia Symphony Orchestra (Columbia).

The Orchestra: Stokowski. (Capitol).

Pan the Piper (Columbia).

Pipes and Drums. 48th Highlanders of Canada (Columbia).

Pizzicatto; Cortège de Bacchus; Sylvia Ballet Music, Delibes. (Musical Sound Books, 78 rpm).

Rondo for Bassoon. (Young People's, 78 rpm).

Square Dances. Lawrence (Columbia).

Semper Fideles–Sousa Marches. Goldman Band (Harmony).

Toy Symphony, Haydn. (Musical Sound Books, 78 rpm).

Tubby the Tuba. Danny Kaye (Decca).

What Is Jazz? Commentary by Bernstein (Columbia). Performances by many greats of the jazz world.

The Young Person's Guide to the Orchestra, Britten; The *Nutcracker* Suite, Tchaikovsky. Dorati, Minneapolis Symphony Orchestra; narrated by Deems Taylor (Mercury).

The Young Person's Guide to the Orchestra, Britten; *Peter and the Wolf,* Prokofieff. Ormandy, the Philadelphia Orchestra; narrated by Cyril Ritchard (Columbia).

Songs

Animal Fair. Dorothy Olsen (Victor). Folk songs.

Beasts, Birds, Bugs and Bigger Fishes. Pete Seeger (Folkways). Folk songs.

The Best of Burl's for Boys and Girls. Burl Ives (Decca). Folk songs.

Burl Ives Sings. (Columbia). Folk songs.

Captain Burl Ives's Ark. Burl Ives (Decca).

Calypso Songs for Children. (Columbia).

Campfire Songs. (Mercury-Childcraft, 78 rpm).

Children of Paris. (Grand Award). Folk songs sung by French children.

Children's Songs. Johnny Richardson (Folkways).

Child's Introduction to Gilbert and Sullivan. (Golden).

Clooney Tunes. Rosemary Clooney (Columbia). Junior "pops."

Cowboy Songs. (Mercury-Childcraft, 78 rpm).

Deep River and Other Spirituals. Robert McFerring (Riverside).

Fireside Treasury of Folk Songs. (Golden).

Folk Songs of Acadia. Alan Mills (Folkways). Songs of Acadia sung in French.

Folk Songs for Children of All Ages. (Cantemos). Songs of Latin America.

Folk Songs of Our Land. (Mercury-Childcraft, 78 rpm).

Great American Folk Heroes. Will Rodgers, Jr., and Tom Scott (Judson). Songs and stories.

Israel, Folk Songs. Hillel and Aviva (Folkways).

Jewish Songs and Games. (Folkways).

Little Pedro. (Children's Record, 78 rpm). Latin American game songs in Spanish and English.

Lullabies for Sleepyheads. Dorothy Olsen (Victor).

More Songs to Grow On. Alan Mills (Folkways). Especially for the young child.

Mother Goose. (Golden, 78 rpm).

Mother Goose. Cyril Ritchard, Celeste Holm, and Boris Karloff. (Caedmon).

Mother Goose Songs. Alec Templeton (Judson).

Oberkirchen Children's Choir. (Angel). Folk songs sung by German children.

Sleep Time Songs and Stories. Pete Seeger (Folkways).

Songs Children Sing in Italy. (Judson).

Songs in French for Children. (Columbia). Folk songs.
Songs of Many Lands. Marais and Miranda (Decca).
Songs of Our Patriots. (Mercury-Childcraft, 78 rpm).
Songs of the South African Veld. Marais and Miranda (Decca).
Train Songs. (Golden, 78 rpm).
The Weavers on Tour. Peter Seeger *et al.* (Vanguard).
Yankee Legend. Bill Bonyun (Heirloom). New England through
its ballads and songs.

Stories

Alice in Wonderland, Carroll. Jane Powell (Columbia). Words
and music.
Alice in Wonderland, Carroll. Narrated by Cyril Ritchard;
musical introductions by Alec Wilder and the New York
Woodwind Quartet (Riverside).
But Muffin Can Hear. (Young People's). 78 rpm.
Cinderella. Julie Andrews (Columbia). Words and music.
The Elephant's Child and others. Gary Moore (Columbia). From
the *Just So Stories.*
Favorite Stories for Children. Paul Wing (Camden).
Grimm's Fairy Tales. Schildkraut (Caedmon).
Just So Stories. Boris Karloff (Caedmon). No accompaniment.
Lady and the Tramp. (Capitol).
Lentil. (Young People's, 78 rpm).
The Little Engine That Could; Winnie the Pooh. (Victor).
Many Moons. (Columbia).
Mark Twain. Walter Brennan in *The Celebrated Jumping Frog
of Calaveras County* and Brandon de Wilde in selections from
Huckleberry Finn (Caedmon). No accompaniment.
The Nonsense Verse of Carroll and Lear. Beatrice Lillie, Cyril
Ritchard, and Stanley Holloway (Caedmon).
A Paul Bunyan Yarn. (American Library).
A Pecos Bill Tale. (American Library).
Perri. Jimmie Dodd (Disneyland).
Peter Pan. Basil Rathbone, Victor Jory, and Jean Arthur (Co-
lumbia).
Peter and the Wolf, Prokofieff. Fiedler, the Boston Symphony
Orchestra; narrated by Alec Guiness (Victor). Or Ormandy, the
Philadelphia Symphony Orchestra; narrated by Cyril Ritchard
(Columbia).
Pinocchio. (Disneyland).

Robin Hood; Treasure Island. Rathbone (Columbia).
The Saggy Baggy Elephant. (Golden, 78 rpm).
Sinbad the Sailor. (Columbia).
The Steamboat Round the Bend. Ben Lucien Burmen (Folkways). No accompaniment.
Three Musketeers. Errol Flynn (Columbia).
Treasure Island. Basil Rathbone (Columbia).
Uncle Bouqui. (Folkways). Haiti's well-known clown, unaccompanied.
Walk in the Forest. (Young People's, 78 rpm).
The Wheel on the School. (Newbery Award).

Documentary

The Living Constitution. (Kaydan).
Nueva York. Tony Schwartz (Folkways).
This Is the UN. Franchot Tone (Tribune).
The Union: The Sounds and Music of the Civil War. (Columbia).
The United States Air Force. Godfrey (Vox).
I Can Hear It Now. (Columbia).

Christmas Songs and Tales

Amahl and the Night Visitors. (Victor).
American Folk Songs for Christmas. (Folkways).
A Child's Christmas in Wales. Narrated by Dylan Thomas (Caedmon).
Christmas Carols. (Mercury). Organs and chimes.
Christmas Carols. (Mercury-Childcraft, 78 rpm).
Christmas Carols in Hi-Fi. Carlos Salzedo, harpist (Mercury).
Christmas Hymns and Carols. Robert Shaw Chorale (Victor).
Christmas Songs from Many Lands. Alan Mills (Folkways).
Christmas Tunes. (Bornand Music Box). Old-fashioned musicbox recordings.
A First Christmas Record for Children. (Columbia).
Oberkirchen Children's Choice: Christmas Songs. (Angel).
The Twelve Days of Christmas. (Young People's, 78 rpm).

Contemporary Music

Adventure in Time. Sauter-Finegan Orchestra (Victor). Percussion music.
Afternoon of a Faun, Debussy. Stokowski, Symphony Orchestra (Victor).

Appalachian Spring, Ballet Suite, Copland. Koussevitzky, Boston Symphony Orchestra (Victor).

Bell, Drum and Cymbal. Saul Goodman (Angel).

Classical Symphony, Prokofiev. Markevitch, Philharmonia Orchestra (Angel).

Concerto for Clarinet and Strings, Copland. Benny Goodman, the Columbia String Orchestra (Columbia).

Concerto for Toys and Instruments. (Young People's, 78 rpm).

Concerto Grosso for Strings and Piano Obbligato, Bloch. Kubelik, Chicago Symphony Orchestra (Mercury).

Evolution, Faberman; *Toccata for Percussion,* Chavez. Boston Percussion Group (Boston).

Fountains of Rome, Respighi. Quadri, Vienna State Opera Orchestra (Westminster).

Le Sacre du Printemps, Stravinsky. Stravinsky, New York Philharmonic Symphony Orchestra (Columbia).

The *London* Symphony, Vaughan Williams. Boult, the London Philharmonic Orchestra (London).

Music for Strings, Percussion and Celeste, Bartók. Solti, London Philharmonic Orchestra (London).

Pacific 231, Honegger. (Musical Sound Books, 78 rpm.)

Portsmouth Point Overture, Walton. Sargent, London Symphony Orchestra (London).

Quartet No. 6, Bartók. Juilliard String Quartet (Columbia).

Seven Popular Spanish Songs, de Falla. (London).

Skyscrapers, Carpenter. (American Recording Society).

Symphony No. 3, Harris. Hanson, Eastman-Rochester Symphony Orchestra (Mercury).

Symphony No. 3, Riegger. Hanson, Eastman-Rochester Symphony Orchestra (Columbia).

Three Places in New England, Ives. Hanson, Eastman-Rochester Symphony Orchestra (Mercury).

Verklärte Nacht, Schoenberg. Hollywood String Quartet (Capitol).

Music from Other Cultures

Africa. (Esoteric). Recorded in Africa.

Azuma Kabuki Musicians. (Columbia). Japanese music for dance accompaniment.

Exotic Dances. (Folkways). Recorded in India, Burma, Spain, the Crimea, and elsewhere.

Drums of Trinidad. (Cook).

Folk Music of Haiti. (Folkways).
Folk Songs and Dances of Puerto Rico. (Folkways).
Music of India. Shankar and Lal (Angel).
Sioux and Navajo. (Folkways).

RECORD COMPANIES

American Recording Society
100 Sixth Avenue
New York, N.Y.

Angel Records
319 West 44 St.
New York 36, N.Y.

Bornard Music Box Records
333 Fifth Ave.
Pelham 65, N.Y.

Boston Records
246 Huntington Ave.
Boston 16, Mass.

Caedmon Publishers
277 Fifth Ave.
New York 16, N.Y.

Camden, see Victor

Cantemos Records
Taos, New Mexico

Capitol Records
Sunset and Vine Sts.
Hollywood, Calif.

Children's Record Guild
27 Thompson St.
New York 13, N.Y.

Columbia Recording Co.
1473 Barnum Ave.
Bridgeport, Conn.

Cook Laboratories
Stamford, Conn.

Decca Records
50 West 57 St.
New York 19, N.Y.

Disneyland Records
c/o Walt Disney Productions
477 Madison Ave.
New York 20, N.Y.

Enrichment Records
246 Fifth Ave.
New York 1, N.Y.

Esoteric Records
238 East 26 St.
New York 10, N.Y.

Folkways Records
117 West 46 St.
New York 19, N.Y.

Golden Records
Simon and Schuster
650 Fifth Ave.
New York 22, N.Y.

Grand Award Records
Harrison, N.J.

Heirloom Records
Brookhaven, N.Y.

Judson Records
553 West 51 St.
New York 19, N.Y.

Kaydan Records
Studio City, Calif.

London Record Sales
16 West 22 St.
New York 11, N.Y.

Mercury (Mercury-Childcraft)
839 South Wabash Ave.
Chicago, Ill.

MGM Records
701 Seventh Ave.
New York 19, N.Y.

Musical Sound Books
Box 444
Scarsdale, N.Y.

Newbery Award Records
221 Fourth Ave.
New York, N.Y.

Riverside Records
553 West 51 St.
New York 19, N.Y.

Tribune Productions
261 Broadway
New York, N.Y.

Vanguard Records
256 West 55 St.
New York 19, N.Y.

Victor Records Division
Radio Corporation of America
Front and Cooper Sts.
Camden, N.J.

Vox Records
236 West 55 St.
New York 19, N.Y.

Young People's Records
27 Thompson St.
New York 13, N.Y.

Westminster Recording Co.
275 Seventh Ave.
New York 1, N.Y.

Chapter 10

CONCERTS

~~~~~~~~~~~~~~~~~~~~~~~~~~~~~~~~~~

Howmany of us are on direct speaking terms with a bass
fiddle, or have so much as touched the manual of a pipe
organ, let alone pulled out stops, stepped on pedals, or played
on two keyboards at the same time? How many of us are personally acquainted with a harp, or with a concert-size marimba?

Deep inside all of us there is, if we will admit it, the same
urge that a child has to feel and to handle, to touch and to try
the new and unfamiliar, but we have learned to control our
curiosity. It isn't only the youngster who is thrilled when he
"pulls out" an accordion; his father is just as eager to have
his turn playing it as he is to run his son's electric train! It
isn't only the little girl who likes to stroke the ballet dancer's
light, filmy skirt; her mother, too, surreptitiously wants to
"feel the goods."

The desire to be on speaking terms with an artistic experience is instinctive in young and old. A visit backstage, a
ringside seat at a night club, a coveted invitation to an afternoon of chamber music in a private home—all are occasions
that adults look forward to and do not forget. So we can easily
understand how much it means to a child to be close to the
performers at concerts.

236

In families which have musical friends or which are music-makers themselves, close contacts with players and instruments will occur as a matter of course in the children's lives. Two things are essential, however: first, there must be no sense of hurry in these contacts—they should be as leisurely as possible; and, second, the child should naturally have supervision, not in showing him how to play, but in seeing that he uses the musical instrument so that no harm may come to it. When a youngster discovers some ingenious and unconventional way of making sounds with an instrument, it is hard for the adult not to say: "But *this* is the way to do it!" Supervision must be largely a matter of adult self-control. On the whole, children live up to what is expected of them, and they are quick to appreciate and respect the desirability of using an instrument carefully.

People who make music are not always easy to find, but it has been our experience that, if one is sufficiently broad-minded about what constitutes a musical experience, interesting and unusual opportunities are sure to come.

What are some of the possible sources of music in an average community? Probably nothing delights a child more than to be able to sit on an organ bench and give himself over to making sounds. He may not find Sullivan's "lost chord," but for him there is magic in the way this majestic instrument responds to his touch. A sympathetic and understanding organist who is willing to give some time to children, making it possible for them to get close to the organ and try it, will be rewarded not only by their enthusiastic interest but also by their keen ears when it is his turn to play.

For the child, the success of these first contacts with an organ or with any other instrument will be in proportion to the player's willingness to let the child discover in his own way. The youngster does not want to be told—he wants to *find out for himself;* and enabling him to do this under the most favorable circumstances is a guarantee of the best kind of lesson. It goes without saying that no intelligent person would withhold pertinent information when the learner is ready to profit by it.

Another musical attraction the community offers is its church bells. Perhaps there is only a single bell, but what a thrill a tug on the rope can give a child! I well remember as a high spot of my childhood the time when I was allowed to play "Amen" on the church chimes by pulling down the old-fashioned levers. Bells had a new meaning after that! There is nothing more fascinating to anyone than a visit to a bell or carillon tower, even if it isn't possible to play the bells.

All over the country communities are becoming more and more music-conscious; many of them have organized bands, orchestras, or choral groups. Surely we should be able to tap some of these resources to bring children into closer contact with instruments and artists. Perhaps a member of an orchestra would be willing to come to a small group of children either at home or at school; or, if it is a question of some larger instruments like percussion, the children could go to the place where these are stored. If the group is small enough, each child can try out the instrument and then listen to it being played.

High school boys and girls are busy, we know, but we believe that those who play in the school orchestra would enjoy an occasional musical excursion either individually or in small groups to the rooms of the younger children in the school. If these music sessions are to be successful, it is important to work with a few children at a time, not with large groups, so as to give each child an opportunity to touch and to try.

Many music schools would probably be glad to cooperate in introducing children to musical instruments. This plan would have to be used wisely; obviously its purpose would not be to encourage the children to take lessons on any particular instrument, or to elicit admiring exclamations over the genius of some child prodigy. But in the long run any experience that gives music more meaning to children will eventually produce in them a heightened interest in learning music.

One of our most delightful music experiences in school occurred when a father brought his French horn and played for us. Here was an instrument that (for hygienic reasons) could not be "tried" in the usual sense of the word; but just to be able to hold it and admire its shine and its shape was a satisfaction to the children. We listened with both eyes and ears to its wonderful music; for many of the children it was the first time they heard Siegfried's horn call. Most of the time, however, was taken up by the playing of familiar songs on request.

There is nothing lovelier to hear than a well-played flute. With the exception, perhaps, of the violin, it does more to bring a lift in clearness and direction to a child's singing voice than any other instrument. In recent years, the "recorder" (fipple flute) has achieved considerable popularity among amateur musicians. It is fairly easy to learn to play, and its sweet, quiet tone provides a different type of musical experience for children.

Violin and cello are always enjoyable to hear. Both these instruments lend themselves particularly well to the performance of familiar songs, and the child not only enjoys singing along with the instruments but also likes to listen. He is interested, too, in using his ears to help in the tuning and in discovering what happens when the mute is used. Unexpected questions come up, too. We especially like to recall the four-year-old who, after watching intently and listening to a visiting cellist play Christmas carols, asked her if a mouse had ever crawled into the hole in the cello!

Probably one of the experiences that will live longest in the memories of our children was the time when a double bass came to live with us for several weeks. Here *was* a musical visit, the kind of visit that had real meaning. Day after day the children had ample opportunity to get acquainted with this old fellow, and from time to time parents, grandparents, sisters, and brothers were brought to school to see and to play on the great fiddle. The student teacher to whom the instrument belonged had a hard time keeping up with the children's requests. They were fascinated by it, for here was an instrument with an entirely different type and range of sound. Adding a violin played by a teacher, a piano, and the children's voices, we had some exciting times in putting sounds together. *Hickory Dickory Dock* lent itself well to our orchestration, some of the children "clucking" the tick-tock along with the plucked bass strings, and the violin and piano carrying the melody sung by another group of children. We had great fun, too, with *Old MacDonald Had a Farm,* the children deciding which instruments—voice, violin, bass, or piano—would best interpret the various animal sounds.

One day a Marine and his accordion came to school. He had the faculty of making himself at home immediately and, pulling a stool up near the fire, he was halfway through *The Marines Hymn* before most of the children realized he was there. The audience was so swept off its feet by his music that he had played several songs before requests came for favorites. Here was music full of the strength of a dynamic young man, music that in turn evoked from the children a quality of rapt listening too rarely aroused in an adult concert audience. The playing of *The Arkansas Traveler* inspired some of them to dance, but the majority were more interested in listening and especially in watching this Marine and his instrument, only occasionally joining in a song.

Possibilities for strikingly unusual musical experiences may be uncovered quite unexpectedly. A few years ago a trip on a Staten Island ferry boat was delightfully enlivened by an old man who played on a group of different-sized bowls of uncertain pitch, arranged according to his own "special scale" on a wobbly card table. This itinerant musician, carrying his table and his bag of bowls with him, gave his concerts on street corners and in various sections of the city. He was only too glad to come and play for our children, his calm dignity and self-respect convincingly corroborating his simple statement that he was "born a genius."

A Scotch bagpiper left his traveling automobile concert stage to come into our room one rainy day when it was too wet for us to stand outside and hear him play. Since bagpipes make a big sound, he suggested, after letting the children examine his instrument, that they stay at one end of the large room while he played to them from the other end. But after one number, he found it hard to stand still, and he marched around the room, playing martial airs, followed by the children. This was truly an inspiring experience for all of us.

A special treat for the last day of school one spring was provided by the visit of an organ grinder and his hand organ. As it was a cool day, he had left his monkey at home—at least, this was the explanation he gave to the children. But he had been engaged the day before, and he may have had other reasons for not exposing his monkey to a school group. In any case, the monkey's absence was undoubtedly a distinct advantage from the point of view of a musical experience! The organ grinder was a friendly and patient person. Opening the top of his music box, he let every child not only grind out music but also watch what happened inside the box as the metal records turned around.

These are only a few of a great variety of musical experiences that it was possible to bring to our children. Naturally some years produced a richer harvest than others, but we had few really lean ones. To the parents of our students goes a great deal of the credit for bringing in not only their own talents but those of their friends. Not long ago, a father, who is a dentist, persuaded a guitar-playing patient to play and sing for us. A mother brought in a friend who knows a vast number of American folk songs, and we not only heard some unfamiliar ones but discovered that we were already acquainted with many of her favorites.

Another parent beguiled a Russian dancer whom she had

met at a dinner party to come and entertain us. He rose to
the occasion by appearing in costume. His dancing plus his
infectious personality never will be forgotten. But our "amateur" experiences are not forgotten either. Some years ago a
friend who indulged in tap dancing purely for his own enjoyment visited us and danced for the children. Before he left,
he showed the children a little dance called *Sugar on the
Toe,* in which one foot brushed lightly over the toe of the
other foot. Five years later, two of our boys, passing this man
on the street, stopped to greet him; "*You* remember," one of
them reminded the other, "this is the man who danced *Sugar
on the Toe!*"

All over the country there is increasing awareness of the
need for bringing school and community into closer relationship with each other. For too long the emphasis has been
solely on acquainting the parents with the school. Though
this is important, the school should acquaint itself with the
parents and realize some of the valuable assets that are lying
dormant in every community. Cooperation is a two-way
process, and the more we can call upon parents to lend their
talents and abilities to the school, the richer are the experiences we can offer to the children, to say nothing of the
value of the relationship among parent, child, and teacher
that inevitably emerges. There will be no gap to bridge between school and community if these person-to-person contacts are established, taken advantage of, and respected.

The parents and friends who lent their talents for our
little concerts had a thoroughly enjoyable time, but we also
noticed that, if the children had any advance notice of a
musical visit, a surprising number of mothers dropped in at
"music time." These informal experiences were so enjoyed
that we had many requests to recommend "regular" concerts
to which parents could take their children. Mothers reported
that the children's concerts in New York City were primarily
designed for older children and were not suited to the
younger ones' stage of development; and that the audiences

were too large, the programs over long, and the seats uncomfortable for short legs. Yet these mothers believed that their children were ready for something of the kind, and did not know where to find it.

Neither did we, and so, together with a group of interested parents, we decided to give our own series of concerts for children on a professional basis, employing suitable talent and charging admission. There was no idea of substituting these concerts for our informal experiences, but rather we saw in them a way to supplement and enlarge the musical horizons of our children.

In planning these concerts, we thought back to our day-by-day experiences with children and music, trying to determine the reasons why children brought so much interest and enthusiasm to their listening. We knew we must retain these if the new venture was to be successful.

First of all we recognized the importance of nearness, which demanded reasonably small groups in a setting that offered an intimate chamber-music atmosphere. Fortunately, we had the use of a large room. The children's chairs were arranged in a wide semicircle, and the artists appeared, not on a distant stage, but on the same floor level and directly in front of the audience. Comfortable seats obviated the restlessness that results when short legs dangle; and ease in seeing and hearing did away with stirring and moving about. The parents sat on larger chairs directly behind the children.

A second important point was recognition of the fact that children cannot sit still for very long at a time; they simply aren't made that way. This meant planning a short program that would be well within their span of attention, rather than trying to hold their interest beyond its natural limits. Our experience had proved that a half-hour program, including a short intermission period, was about long enough for groups of young children. Not that there weren't always requests for more music; sometimes the children sat so tight to their chairs after the final number that, if we had not been careful, we might easily have been persuaded to let the programs grow longer. Naturally our plans were flexible, and an occasional encore took care of any unusual interest. But we kept watching for the subtle signs of a group's reaction, and held it safer to err on the short rather than on the long side. The audience ought to go home wanting more—that is good psychology whether applied to young or to old.

For the children, an intermission has value not only because it gives them an opportunity to get up and walk about and talk with their friends, but especially because they get a chance to meet the artists and see the instruments at close hand. They needed a little help from time to time in learning how to use this free time to best advantage, but achieving a good balance between freedom and self-control constitutes one of the most important aspects of the whole experience. Success here depended largely on the children's knowing that each one would have an opportunity to get close to what was going on, if not during the intermission, then after the concert was over. Occasionally it was possible to have the instrument on hand before the concert, as in the case of a harp that was rented by the school for several weeks and kept in the music studio; thus every child had unhurried time in which to try out the fascinating instrument. For one of our programs, the artist assembled her marimba during the morning while the children were in the room. She had a most attentive audience, which volunteered many suggestions for putting it together! After it was set up, each child had plenty of time to play on it; nor did the adults in the room miss out on their turns!

Perhaps the most thought-provoking part of a concert venture for young children is the planning of the program content. Here we proceeded on the assumption that children like music for its own sake, that its appeal comes to them directly through the medium of sound and rhythm, and that it is essentially a sensory and not an intellectual experience. We considered the "commentator" out of place at a children's concert, just as he is at a concert for adults. Why should we tell children what the music is going to sound like? Are we afraid that they are not going to react in our way or in the way the critics tell us to react? Let's give youngsters a chance to feel for themselves—or not feel, if that happens to be their disposition. So there was no *talking about music* at our concerts, for we believe, with the late Oscar Thompson, that "the highest degree of musical appreciation comes through the plain direct speech of music itself." [1] We showed no pictures; we told no stories; we did not ask children to listen for this or that; we did not talk about the composer. In other words, there was no build-up for the concert itself, though there *was* a build-up, a day-by-day one, a lasting one, that came from the children's continuous interest in sound and rhythm and from our seizing every opportunity to foster it.

It was not easy to know in advance what music would have the greatest appeal. Certain guiding principles, however, helped us to choose. Gay, spirited music was always enjoyed, and here we could draw from contemporary as well as the classical composers, for "modern" harmonies are much more likely to be accepted by youngsters than by older people. A very short group of pieces by Hindemith at a string-quartet concert and Salzedo's *Chanson dans la nuit* for the harp both received enthusiastic response.

Children are affected by the mass of tone produced as well as by the melody and rhythm of music. Mursell calls attention to this in his chapter on "The Psychology of Music Listening": "Not only children but many adults are affected by the sheer mass of the tone and this takes precedence over both rhythmic structure and melodic design. In this kind of listening we have the ultimate foundation of all music." [2]

Balance in each program was achieved through planning a succession of contrasting numbers, as well as through in-

---

[1] Oscar Thompson, *How to Understand Music*, New York: Dial.
[2] James L. Mursell, *The Psychology of Music*, New York: Norton.

cluding several that were already familiar to the children. When it was a singing concert, the children frequently joined in to sing their favorite songs, though this response was always spontaneous, not directed. A child may prefer just to listen to a favorite song sung by an artist, or he may be inspired to sing, too. At the instrumental and dance concerts the children were always given the opportunity to participate by singing one or two songs.

We were extremely fortunate in working closely with understanding artists who helped in arranging the programs. These musicians were unusually sensitive to the children's responses, and they had genuine respect for the children's musical intelligence. Our concerts were informal, yet at the same time dignified; no one played down to the audience and no one attempted to hold its attention by coy remarks. Our sincere desire was to encourage "good listening." If music had to compete with inattention and lack of interest, then something was wrong with our programs.

Just as we tried to offer a balanced diet within each program, so we planned for a variety of musical experiences in any given season. A series of three programs was given each year on alternate Friday afternoons in January and February, each one being repeated for the older children of the school on the same afternoon and in the same place, but at a different hour. The five-, six-, and seven-year-olds made up the younger group. The division into a younger and an older group, third grade through sixth, was made in order to keep the size of the audience relatively small.

Three types of concerts were given each year: singing, instrumental, and dance. The singing concerts offered a wide range of music: American and South American folk songs, accompanied by guitar, foreign folk songs and ballads, excerpts from Gilbert and Sullivan, short operatic arias, and Negro spirituals. Over a period of several years a large variety of instruments were presented: harp, flute, marimba, harmonica, violin, viola, cello, and piano—and one concert was

devoted exclusively to percussion. Our dance concerts included a Russian group accompanied by balalaika and
accordion, a program of contemporary dance, and a ballet
program in which the beautiful dancer had to be rescued
from her ardent admirers during intermission time and
placed on a table so as to be seen by all—one little boy offering to hold her up if she would stand on her toes!

What did we expect children to gain from these concerts?
First of all, we wanted to make sure that they did not come
to music too late, that they did not miss being at-home with
the best in music during their early plastic years. Children
are capable of seeing and hearing actively. They are not consciously storing away immediate experiences merely for the
purpose of adding to their repertories and becoming "cultured." Immediate results are not directly aimed at or even
thought about, but there was a sincere desire to live up to
children's musical potentialities. Children must be left free
to feel about music, each in his own particular way. We did
not ask questions about it, nor, on the other hand, did we
hesitate to talk with them about it or help to extend their
information and understanding if they seemed to want this.
We tried always to remember, however, that *verbal responses
are not necessarily indicative of music appreciation.*

The success of our concerts was in large measure due to
the enthusiastic support of the parents. From the very beginning we were able to count on their understanding and
their very practical help, not only in searching for artists and
in giving of their own talents, but also in such very important matters as the set-up and arrangement of the room
and the numerous details that accompany comfortably taking
care of large groups of children and adults.

After our first two seasons of concerts, the Parent-Teachers Association became so interested in the project that it
voted to give us financial support. Its generosity enabled us
to secure music talent at regular professional rates and gave
us access to a wider field than would otherwise have been

possible. We cannot think of a more valuable contribution for a Parent-Teachers Association to make than assistance in a school project of this nature.

The reactions of the artists who brought their talents to us are of interest. They declared that never did they have such enthusiastic and attentive audiences. They were likely at first to attribute the absence of behavior problems to training and discipline, but we pointed out quickly that this was not the case. Children respond with the best that is in them to that which is right for them. What is for them a full and satisfying experience is the result of our recognizing the limitations due to their stage of growth.

In Darien, Connecticut, a group of one hundred parents raise several thousand dollars each year to bring music into their six elementary schools. The artists visit each school separately and give a concert. This project, which the Board of Education cannot afford, is a highly rewarding one, not only for the children, but for the adults.

In addition to concerts for elementary-school children in which parents take responsibility, community-sponsored concerts for children are rapidly growing all over the country, as are such individual ventures as the concerts for young people in New York City directed by Thomas Scherman. We should like to suggest that the criteria for securing and maintaining children's musical interest, discussed earlier in this chapter, are equally valid in these more ambitious programs.

We do not want to give the impression that concert experiences for children depend upon the amount of money expended. Each community has its own resources (many of them unique), and discovering and utilizing these can very well be the most exciting and rewarding aspect of bringing more music to children.

PICTURE BOOKS OF INSTRUMENTS

Huntington, Harriet E., *Tune Up,* New York: Doubleday. Lovely photographs of the instruments of the orchestra and their players.

Lacey, Marion, *Picture Book of Musical Instruments,* New York: Lothrop, Lee and Shepard.

Chapter 11

THE CLASSROOM TEACHER AND THE MUSIC CONSULTANT

IF WE BELIEVE that the most important factor in children's musical development is the attitude toward music of the people with whom they live, then, whether they are specialists or not, the classroom teacher plays a major role in the teaching of music. Does this teacher hear music in children's sound-making? Does she feel dance in children's natural use of movement as they go about their daily work? Does she have a quick ear for a child's humming of a song as he browses, works, or plays? Is her understanding of what constitutes music constantly growing and expanding? Is she wide awake to her own musical possibilities, or does she shut off any use of her own resources by feeling inadequate because she cannot play an instrument or because she perhaps occasionally sings off key? Is she the kind of person who is willing to jump in and do the best she can with what she has? Is she at ease with children *and her coworkers* so that she can make

250

A folk-singing band in Brooklyn

Putting sound and rhythm together

mistakes—even enjoy them—and learn from them? Or is she a perfectionist who is ever on guard against making a mistake, thus stunting her growth, to say nothing of the unfortunate psychological aspects of an environment for children which result from being taught by this "all-complete" person? These characteristics naturally apply to all aspects of school life, but it is necessary to remember that, in providing a good musical life for children, we must be concerned with the child's total day and not just with music periods.

Skills of Classroom Teachers

Teachers need to be alert to and to have respect for their own ways of making music and to utilize their resources with children. The following incident illustrates my point: I was participating in a music workshop on the campus of a large southwestern university. One morning, in search of a respite from work, I found a quiet corner of the campus, and, while enjoying the wide green spaces and listening to the birds, I was suddenly aware of a "bird" behind me. Turning around, I saw one of the teachers who was studying at the workshop who also felt the need for relaxation. But she was enjoying herself by whistling bird calls.

"Fun, isn't it?" she asked.

"But where did you ever learn to do such whistling? You can match those calls perfectly," I replied in astonishment.

"Oh, I have always whistled, I guess. My mother used to whistle when she churned butter, usually to the tune of *When the Roll Is Called up Yonder,* and my sister and I learned from her. Only we always were much more elaborate in our whistling. We really improved on Mother!"

"Your third graders must think you are a pretty wonderful teacher, and I can well imagine the good whistling times you have together," I responded.

"But, but," she replied, "I have never whistled in school.

I have been teaching for twenty years, and part of that time I taught music, but I just never thought of whistling being 'school music.' It was never mentioned in the course of study. Do you really think it is all right?" she asked breathlessly, and, without waiting for my reply, she went on, "I can't wait for school to begin next fall."

Here was a truly musical person who had never called upon her own unique talent because of her concept of school music. It is inconceivable that any music supervisor would have objected to her using this talent, but, on the other hand, no one had ever taken the trouble to encourage her to exploit her own resources. Certainly, no course of study intends to set limits on the teacher, but no one has yet seemed to have found the answer to the problem of discovering what the teacher already has to offer or what she is especially fitted for musically. And this will never happen so long as we think of music in terms of a few categories! If we continue to use the commonly accepted musical measuring stick to discover the teacher's musicianship, we shall never take advantage of many of the talents which teachers have. Does this mean that this teacher will, for example, have only whistling music in her room? Certainly not, for to the extent that she is a person who finds satisfaction and joy in releasing her own talents, she will, in turn, be better able to appreciate the necessity for having equal respect for the musical talents of each child in her room. Together teacher and children will be eager to reach out for new experiences.

How can we live with children so that they know that we are honestly interested in their musical interests? Recently I observed a session where a group of eleven- and twelve-year-olds were running a guessing contest on television commercials. Each child would tap out on his desk the rhythm of a particular commercial, and the others would guess which one it was. In this contest the teacher came out at the bottom of the class! The children were quick, too, in identifying similarities in rhythm with well-known pieces of music. This same teacher happens to be particularly fond of Bach's *St. Matthew Passion* and one day, while writing some work on the chalk board, she was humming some of the more familiar passages to herself. One of the children said, "What is that, Miss F.?" "Oh, it's some music that I like," and she named it. "Sing it again," asked several children. She did, and then they asked her if she would bring the phonograph record of this music to school. She did, but doubted if it would really appeal to them. However, she was amazed at the interest they brought to it, and they have asked to hear certain parts of it again and again. This teacher does not play an instrument or even sing well, but her children have a rich musical environment because it is a place where each person lives at ease and feels that what he has to offer is of worth. "Lives at ease"—this is the secret. In a relaxed, tension-free atmosphere, children catch the intangibles that contribute so much to receptivity in learning.

Children are fortunate, too, if they live in a classroom where their immediate interests and emotional feelings are respected by the teacher, as the following incident in a third-grade room illustrates. The children had just returned from the playground and were lively, talkative, and exuberant. Suddenly one youngster started singing *Yippy Ti Yi Yo.* All joined in at once, and it was clearly evident that no football cheerleaders ever sang with more fervor. The teacher, however, waved her hand, and everyone stopped while she went to her desk and extracted a pitch pipe from the drawer. "We must be sure to sing in the right key," and then proceeded to give them the pitch of the song. By this time cold water had been thrown on the group's enthusiasm and feeling for singing, and the result was straggling and limpid. Now the fact that the group felt free enough to start singing on their own is a fine commentary on the friendly atmosphere that existed in this room. For this, the teacher is to be commended. Also, she was eager to follow the children's lead, and only sought to do a good job of guidance. But in this case she found herself dealing only with the perfection of the product *at an inopportune time,* neglecting the bouyant spirits that had motivated the singing. Should there be no guidance then? Most certainly there should be, but, in this instance, rather than promoting the quality of the music experience, the "guidance" terminated that experience.

In dealing with children's enthusiasms (and we are not talking about a case where a child is out to make trouble) we must have appreciation for children's ways of doing things. The chances are good that, from the repetition of this song, there would have come more control on the part of the children, especially if the teacher had joined in and had forgotten about the "right" way to sing the song. Let us examine this illustration further. Somewhere, as a part of her training, this teacher had been told that songs must always be sung in the key in which they were composed, and since she was not sure of herself, she felt it necessary to depend on a pitch pipe. The important thing about singing a song is to sing it in a key that is comfortable—a key that is within the range of the average group voices. It would be more than a little ridiculous if people always carried a pitch pipe with them when they sang on picnics, at games, or around camp fires. Occasionally a song gets started a bit too high or too low, but nobody minds, and they start over again. By trial and error they find the best singing place. Children are able to do this, too. In fact, this can be an excellent opportunity for them to learn in the same way. If it does not work the first time, try again. At certain times children are also interested in learning about different keys through the use of a piano or pitch pipe. The point here is that it is not a choice between no guidance or guidance, between no learning or learning, but rather a *sense of what comes first* and meeting the situation in such a way as not to dampen children's interest and thereby cut off any possibility for growth. In this particular case the teacher's goal for perfection ended rather than promoted a musical experience.

Classroom teachers have skills—skills which are unique to each one—skills which create an environment for children that respects the worth of each child *and* the teacher, that encourages each one to be his own best self, that recognizes and values the many ways in which music and dance are evidenced and enjoyed by individuals. In addition, many teachers have skills such as "whistling" that have been long buried in the classroom. And, then, some have music and dance skills which they do not use in school, thinking them inappropriate for young children. If we live at ease with these skills and with children, our skills cannot help but overflow into our day-by-day teaching. We are interested in children's interests. Can we assume that, at times at least, they are not interested in what is important to us? Children are quick to show us when we bore them and when learning has stopped going on. Let us take a few more chances in sharing our music interests with them.

We have been talking about the responsibility of each teacher in accepting and releasing her own skills and those of the children in her group. Nor are we unaware of or unsympathetic to the many pressures under which teachers work. They are very real but sometimes, because of tension and exhaustion, they become exaggerated, and we think there are more obstacles than there really are. A teacher in a large city system recently commented on this matter of restrictions: "All too often we accept limitations in our working situation rather than probe our working situation to the absolute reaches of its limitations, and then look again and again and again to be sure that we can't wangle just a little bit more." Someone has said that it isn't so much the system as man himself that needs to change. I wonder if we cannot work in both directions. Surely thoughtful teachers have a responsibility to work toward conditions for the entire school so that better education may go on, but they also have a responsibility for "moving freely within harness."

The Music Consultant

Teachers are human. They can struggle against odds just so long, especially if they do it alone. But given understanding and encouragement from administrators, they can do a valiant job. The principal of a school and the music consultant (if there is one) can release teachers' talents and help them discover and cultivate new ones, or they can shut them off.

In the educator's language of today, the music supervisor has become the music consultant. This is the result of the trend in many schools toward a different concept of the role of the specialist. Unfortunately, some serious misunderstandings have come about both on the part of the classroom teacher and the specialist. The specialist may feel her job is threatened, and the classroom teacher frequently feels inadequate in meeting children's needs in special areas such as music. Both teachers are necessary. What is at stake is a more economical way of working, a way more in keeping with the way in which children learn, so that the competencies and skills of the specialist can be used effectively.

What we call the music teacher may not be too important, although the term consultant has significant connotations in defining her function. It is her way of working with people and her respect for the many varied and different degrees of ability in teachers that makes for a good music program in her school. Can she spark the classroom teacher musically? Is she willing to put aside her carefully prepared plans for a particular situation in the light of deeper and more immediate interests of children? Is she a learner in the matter of taking cues from the classroom teacher about a special group of children? A few years ago, when the customary procedure in teaching music in a certain school included two visits a week to each classroom by the music teacher, there was a second grade in charge of an unusually creative sixty-year-old teacher.

This teacher liked music in a reserved sort of way, but her enjoyment had been that of a spectator rather than a participant, feeling a part of it. A new music teacher arrived, and in a few months this classroom came alive musically as never before and Miss B., the teacher, found herself humming songs while she worked, and she even tried to pick out melodies on the piano—things she had never dared try before. How did it happen?

The music teacher was so impressed with Miss B.'s understanding of children that she made a point of dropping in to this room whenever she could to learn more about children and about teaching. She was accepted as a member of the group and frequently was called on to help with everything from teaching reading to helping at the workbench. This person was no longer a "music teacher" but, first of all, a *person,* with a special skill, however, in music. It was an exciting year musically, and the children's musical growth was nothing short of spectacular.

This illustration shows the importance of the music teacher taking time to learn about children—this time in a classroom situation and with their regular teacher. In the following account we have the interesting story of a musically educated person who volunteered to work in a neighborhood after-school program and thus learned about youngsters in a very different way. To begin with, unless she offered something of interest, she had no children to work with, for they did not have to come to this group. These children lived in a crowded section of a large city. After a few weeks she found herself both musically and physically exhausted and with a dwindling group of children. So she tried a different plan. She collected a number of large drums, making most of them herself out of barrels, keys, and wooden pails, some wooden temple bells, gongs, and tambourines; and she decided to let this group find out for themselves about these instruments. Here is her story.[1]

[1] Used by permission of Louisa Harris.

A group of ten eleven-year-old boys and one girl came regularly twice a week for several months. Each day they started off drumming, each one as an individual at first, but soon they would become aware of each other and some group activity would develop. At first it was mostly Indian dancing. They danced around a large old scrap basket which represented the fire, and they also wandered all over the room. They thought up a play—some Indians drumming, some dancing, getting wilder and wilder, beating faster and faster, until at a sign from one of them they all collapsed around the "fire" and slept. At this point they sometimes asked me to play sleeping music on the piano. They lay with their eyes shut, completely relaxed, for several minutes, then they were up and at it again.

Exhausting this idea, they went on to play the army. They divided themselves into three groups, the United States, the enemy, and a drumming group for sound effects. They came from home loaded with props—helmets, guns, pistols, knapsacks, canteens, and ammunition belts. After a great deal of discussion and planning of the play, they ended up under the tables, except for the drum crew, and made sorties from time to time, crawling, then dashing, only to be hit by one of the constant volleys of machine-gun fire and exploding bombs. Their body movements when "hit" were magnificent—a sudden stiffening, then a struggle, and an abandoned fall—quite reminiscent of many of Martha Graham's movements. Then the snooping enemy, the United States troops discovering them—all done in a mixture of stylized dance and realism, primitive and full of vitality, but often surprisingly relaxed with an almost "floppy" quality to their movements. They often ended these afternoons with demands to sing *Caissons,* the Army Air Corps song, *Anchors Aweigh,* and *John Brown's Baby Had a Cold upon Its Chest.*

After several weeks of this play, they came in one afternoon and started jumping high in the air. They all seemed to have acquired springs in their shoes. During their usual preliminary session they decided to do tricks, such as jumping over as many as five chairs laid down on the floor next to each other. They lined up and, as they ran to the point of the take-off, the drummers played a roll; then there was silence as they went through the air followed by a good resounding bang as they landed. Then they asked for circus music from the piano. They stood on their heads, or on their hands; some lay on their backs and kicked their legs; some marched around. All the time there was a drum beat as well as the piano. When the drummer felt like joining the active group, he would lay down his sticks, which would be picked up by someone else who needed a rest.

Two weeks later, they suddenly thought of sending messages on their drums. They made up their own Morse code. One beat meant A, two beats B, and so on until they reached ten (J). This stumped them a bit, so I suggested that they beat once and then make a gesture with their hand for the zero. For K they decided on one loud beat followed by one soft. They followed through the alphabet this way and were soon busy with paper and pencil making copies of the code for everyone. Then they spent a fascinating afternoon beating out messages to each other. Suddenly Jimmy said, "Wait a minute, listen!" Code was forgotten for the moment. "Do you see how the sound goes on after it's hit?" They all listened while he showed them what he meant, and then they all experimented. David said, "Yes, and my drum reverberates when you hit yours." So they discovered sound waves, and we discussed them and likened them to ripples in a pool when you throw in stones. The rest of the period was spent in experimenting with sound, one drumming gently in the middle of the group, while the rest listened intently, both hearing and feeling with their hands if their drums would reverberate. They moved away from the drummer until they discovered the place farthest away where they could still pick up the vibration.

Are there some implications in this music teacher's interesting experience for those of us who work in schools? When she worked hard and conscientiously to "put across music," she found herself not only worn out but also without children. In order to hold these youngsters, she simply had to get on their side and first find out and then accept what was musically important for them. It took courage and faith to let them find their way. The first few sessions were noisy and to the observer at first seemed overstimulating (until she became an active participant). It soon became apparent, however, that the contrary was true. These children were having an opportunity to work out their tensions through the use of primitive instruments that required no lessons on "how to play." In addition to the musical values in working in sound and rhythm, have we given enough consideration to the opportunities children need for "sound therapy"? Schools put a great premium on being quiet. Even the use of instruments is highly controlled, and yet what youngster does not yearn for just one resounding whack at these sound-provoking instruments.

In spite of the explosiveness of the first few sessions with these groups, there was order, in that each child was working out his own feelings on his own instrument and in his own way and never interfering with another. It was not long, however, until they began to relate to each other and evolved their own organization, which included using the special skills of the teacher. We all want children to like music, to find release, satisfaction, and enjoyment in it. If we are honest in wanting them to meet these needs, we must accept their ways of doing it. We must, first of all, get on their track. Perhaps some of our goals may even be the same, but the routes in reaching these goals are different.

I have used this illustration as a way of getting at an idea —the importance of discovering and understanding the varied ways boys and girls may approach music, so that our efforts to teach music will have a reasonable chance of hitching on and having meaning. Is it necessary to point out that the above kind of "working out of feelings" could not take place in a regular classroom situation? A thoughtful teacher, however, could so invest her work with imagination that she and her group would find ways of encouraging the explorations that are close to children. The group described above were the "victims" of a "pouring in" school program that put a premium on quiet. These children had problems, plenty of them, but their solution was conceived of by their school as more and more discipline without an attempt to discover the roots of their problems. In a similar situation, could not a music consultant, working with a classroom teacher, find ways to open the doors in music and dance so that the vistas of these children could be extended?

The importance of increasing our sound perceptions has been discussed earlier in this book. Let us look at several other ways of becoming more ear-conscious. Do you ever listen to the sounds of children's voices in a group? Are you able to relax enough during a busy activity period in a class-room to listen to sounds—variations in pitch, different rhythms, the timbre of voices en masse, gradations and changes, almost rhythmical at times, from much sound to a lull? When you call a group of children together for a meeting or a story at the end of a busy work period, they come bubbling over with matters important to them which they must share immediately with their friends. Confronted with this buzzing, can you relax and listen to these buzz groups, feeling pretty certain that there will soon be enough of a lull for you to start the business of the hour? At the most, this waiting is usually only a matter of a few minutes, but it makes all the difference in the world in the kind of climate that exists in a group coming in a "natural way" to attention than is produced by a sharp "Attention, please." It is interest-ing, too, how some of the children become aware of this wait-ing and react in opposite extremes from not only sensing pauses and trying to "shush" their neighbors to playing a game of outtalking teacher, which a teacher with a good sense of humor can appreciate and also handle. (We are not talking here about emergency situations that demand im-mediate attention from children, for no teacher has a right to live long with a group without planning and developing with them a way of securing immediate response when neces-sary.) These few minutes of waiting pay dividends, not only in terms of relaxation for teacher, but also in cultivating her ear for sound. Sometimes the thoughtful and *listening* teacher may decide that *these buzz groups*—and not what she had planned—are the important business of the hour!

Let us listen to ourselves while we are waiting for a faculty or a parents' meeting to begin. The writer has become especially sensitive to college-class sounds and can almost predict by the high pitch of voices a test or examination coming up next period. Usually the register of voices is one or two tones higher than on an average day when it is likely to hover around A flat. Sometimes it is fun to catch the "key" of the group as its members are talking with each other and "easily" play into it a selection on the piano or sing a song in the same key. Try it, and see what happens!

Let us listen through the ears of a music teacher to the sharp staccato voices as children play.[2]

Children's own original songs, hums, chants, and piano pieces tend to be cast in rhythmic patterns and tonal patterns which are most sensible and interesting to the accomplished be-bop musician and to the successful composer who feels at home in the modern idiom. In order to foster musical growth, I believe it is important that the classroom teacher recognize and use contemporary music in the classroom, and I also suggest that contemporary music is much closer to where the child is than the many diatonic tunes our "methods" masters publish by the endless series. My thesis supports, rather than supplants, the use of folk-song material, insisting, however, that we use the raw, unedited form untouched by the diatonic ditty writers who squeeze good folk tunes into the major scale. Take, for example, that wonderful Scottish ballad *Henry Martin* as sung by Burl Ives and accurately notated in the Kolb *Treasury of Folk Songs*. The section, "and they did cast lots," falls into a pure Dorian mode in exactly the same way that Aaron Copland harmonizes the fiddle tune in the "Hoedown" from his ballet *Rodeo*.

Children's experimentation in the unusual or irregular cannot be treated as a phase which precedes the study of the elements of diatonic music. The children's experiments *must con-*

2 Used by permission of Arnold Caswell.

stitute the study. It is very easy for a teacher to smile approval only on the child's experiments which exactly fit the first-grade music book and so the child learns to reject his honest musical expressions and substitute those which might have been honest in the seventeenth century. Small wonder that so few show talent. The less talented ones are the ones that merely refuse to graft seventeenth-century ears on to a head that sees and imitates trains, airplanes, and fathers who play be-bop and Bartók. I certainly do not want to give the impression that I would force the child to fit my contemporary music mode instead of the classical mode, but I do strongly suggest that the experiences we bring to children should be of all kinds and should also contain contemporary material.

Group Experimentation in Sound

We hope by this time the reader will be ready for what we have been working up to all along—eagerness to jump in and make sounds herself. Sometimes all a group needs is a chance to open up and let go with long repressed sounds as a mature music professor did recently when he gave vent to a shattering machine gun which, he later confessed, he had been itching to do for years. Again it may be necessary to turn out the lights or pull down the shades, for it is truly amazing what people can do when they feel that no one can see them. If it is still hard to get started, suggest that members of the group recall and reproduce children's sounds that tend to irritate teachers. Here we are almost certain to get a minor third chant with such words as "He is a sissy!" and usually it is as compelling with adults as it is with children; everyone gets on the bandwagon with such momentum that one wonders if it will ever stop. Just for fun, try letting it go on until it wears down (perhaps after such an experience the chanters will have a little more sympathy with the youngsters who do the same). When it dies down, pick it up again and experiment with it in ways as the following.

Divide the group in half. Let the first half start the chant and get well established with the rhythm. Have the other half *listen* and then let each one as an individual *feel* his way into what is going on and relate to it. Some may fall into the same pattern but others are sure to complement or supplement it or even come against it as in counterpoint. Out of the variety of responses—*and not until they have had some satisfaction in enjoying what they are doing*—we may choose one response and ask the group to listen to it for a moment. Then pair this off with one individual who is using the original chant and have everyone listen. One might then build two groups, one around the original and one around the contrasting response. By this time all kinds of leads will present themselves as variations for use. It is hard to describe this kind of sound experimentation, for the outcome is always unpredictable— that's why it is such fun. Its success depends on the extent to which the leader of the group has a quick ear for the unusual and is *willing to take a chance* with it.

What the leader is really doing is looking to individuals in the group for leadership, her job being that of a chairman who is seeking to extend the group experiences through many individual contributions. Her reasons for choosing one leader rather than another are varied. A very quiet member of a college class was interested in one of these sessions but never "let go" in the way the others did. Without knowing it, however, she was tapping out the rhythm of the sound play on her notebook. "Let's take her lead," said the teacher. The group listened and then used this student's simple quiet rhythm as a "theme." From this small beginning the group experimentation developed to the place where not only sound but also movement were used, this particular student leaving her seat and her original tapping to move around the room in harmony with the group play.

Again the leader may recognize a significant musical lead in the sounds offered by the group and use this for a different purpose, such as helping the group be aware of the fact that they are having an experience in harmony or dynamics. This is really dealing directly with the raw materials of music without being handicapped by the lack of technical knowledge. In this way we are enriching our understanding of music through our inventions in pure sound. We started out with a minor third chant, but you see that we lost it along the way by utilizing the inevitable variations and inventions supplied by individuals. Is not this matter of recognition of individual contributions perhaps as important as learning about music? Need we point out the implications here for working with youngsters? Would it frequently be the better part of wisdom to accept that annoying little drumming in the back row, motivated probably by an unconscious need for release from tension or boredom, or probably a neat little plan to irritate teacher—accept it as a sign that the group would benefit by a few moments of relaxation? Wouldn't that class be surprised if teacher joined in the same rhythm and gave her sanction and even perhaps used her own initiative in helping everyone have a good time? When children realize that a teacher welcomes occasional sorties in the use of sound and rhythm, that teacher never will need worry that she will not know how to proceed, for children will have many suggestions of what to do. Perhaps the group may develop sounds and rhythm that call for additional experiences, such as songs or use of instruments or movement to be combined with the original.

Another interesting experiment for use in a class of adults was suggested by a music student. Choose three or four people who speak different languages. Ask them to stand together and each speak, all at the same time, in a different language. They can say anything they want, tell a short story, or relate an experience. Ask the listening group to close their eyes and listen to the sounds of voices—differences in pitch, inflection, quality, pace. In a short time even though there are many variations, one will sense a kind of "sound" relatedness. This can also be done by using people who speak the same language but whose voices vary, or by having a group count together or repeat the alphabet over and over, letting come what may (that is the trick here; you must not plan ahead).

Another experience that groups enjoy is a more highly organized one. Divide the group into four sections and give each one of the time value of a quarter note. Have the members of each section get together and decide how they will use this time and all agree to do the same thing. Then the leader claps out or plays a phrase of four measures in 4-4 time in order to get a group feeling for this rhythm. At a signal, group one takes the first count, group two the second, and so on, each using only the time of one count. Since no group knows what the other plans to do, this is full of surprises and fun. After a few rounds the groups become inventive and think up all kinds of sounds and rhythmic variations from absolute quiet to jumping up and shouting. There are many variations in the ways this can be handled, such as using different rhythms and giving a group an entire measure or a phrase. Older youngsters love this, too!

No group can experiment long with sound without becoming involved in some kind of movement, even if it is only the tapping of feet or an almost imperceptible movement of the body. The two just naturally go together. Nor does it matter where we start, but frequently grownups feel more comfortable in beginning with sound experimentation. Once the group gets warmed up and a few "adventurers" start using movement, the leader, rather than taking a "sound" lead, may choose a movement and ask the group to follow. Or he may suggest that everyone walk around the room (without music). No two people really walk alike. Some will swing their arms, some have a spirited quick walk, some are lackadaisical, some will walk in different directions, some give the appearance of walking with their whole body rather than with their feet. The leader then may take his cue from anyone (it is unfortunate to start out with a fancy stepper). Suppose we take, for example, a person who is walking in many different directions and ask everyone to experiment spatially (children do a specially skillful job in this). Then take another lead, and so on, working in the ways we described in sound. Sometimes youngsters call this playing "copy cat," and since this term has fallen into disrepute, we must point out that, in a very real sense, we all learn from others and to some extent copy them. If every member of a group is a potential "cat" to be copied and each has something unique to offer, then the teacher, in recognizing these contributions, is really capitalizing on the contributions of all. Does it matter what we call it?

Groups of teachers can experiment with sound and movement, using their own initiative and resourcefulness. They are fortunate if they have the support of a music consultant, a person whose guidance encourages them to hold on to their own ideas and who, out of her knowledge of music, will see relationships between the improvising of teachers and the structure of music; a person who is willing to improvise and experiment along with teachers and isn't afraid of the unpredictable. It is unfortunate when the music consultant deals only with the things she knows how to do well and shuts off any unknown musical excursions so that she will avoid being in the position of not seeming to know her job.

The music consultant can be invaluable in helping children and teachers to *discover music resources*. What may seem to be an almost barren environment musically speaking, as looked at through the limited concept of music existing in too many schools, may well turn out to be rich in possibilities. Here we have to think of such things as variety of music experiences, use of equipment already owned by the school, freedom from grade-level approach, possibilities of renting or borrowing suitable instruments, and enlisting the cooperation of parents and laymen in the community, as discussed in Chapter 10 on concerts.

A very interesting experience was related by a teacher of

second grade in a small midwestern community. Her father frequently told his family how much he enjoyed his visits to the town barber because he combined his trade with the singing of operatic arias! The fact that his voice was not equal to all of the operatic demands concerned neither him nor his customers. Here was the "natural" that teacher had been looking for, and, when she asked him if he would come and sing with her first and second grades, he was delighted. Most of the children knew him, but this special arrangement gave status not only to him as a person but also to music. He sang, of course, in Italian, and it was not long until he had help from the children in the easily singable parts of his arias. The enthusiasm for singing generated by this and later visits carried over into all of the children's musical activities. Perhaps, however, the most important overtones in this experience were in the field of human relationships!

A music consultant who can roam freely in the field of music can be of tremendous support in helping to free the teacher from a *grade-level* approach. She can help remove the arbitrary ceilings imposed on any grade by encouraging the teacher to take her cues from children as well as from the course of study. There is logic and continuity in the way children learn, but the logic and continuity are in terms of what goes on *inside* the individual and may have nothing to do with simple to difficult or content relationship apparent to the teacher. It really hinges on what makes sense to the child. Psychologists have been telling us this for some time [3] but nowhere has it been more clearly and convincingly pointed out for the classroom teacher than by Alice Miel.[4]

Continuity in learning has been confused with sequence of activities or experiences as arranged mechanically for the learner by someone else. The fact has been overlooked that continuity in

[3] Donald Snygg and Arthur W. Combs, *Individual Behavior*, New York: Harper. J. L. Mursell, *Education for Musical Growth*, Boston: Ginn.
[4] Alice Miel, *Continuous Learning*, Bulletin No. 87, Association for Childhood Education International, p. 5.

learning is an individual, internal affair; that the individual himself must see new relationships, new likenesses, and differences.
In fact, arrangements made by the school often have made it
more difficult for individuals to take the next steps in learning
for which they are most ready. . . . Some individuals have been
put under so much pressure to follow an externally imposed,
artificial continuity that their own best sequence has been inter-
rupted.

This understanding of the learning process has implications for the ways in which we use our music books and, indeed, all of our musical equipment.

Teachers within schools are learning more and more the
benefits of working cooperatively with each other in the use
of school equipment. This can be facilitated by the music
consultant. Rather than allotting musical instruments to
certain grades, with the idea that these are the instruments
to be used only by this grade because of the children's age,
both teachers and children should be able to turn to the total
resources of the school. This cannot be done by rotating
them mechanically. A principal of a ten-room school in
Wyoming relates a unique and profitable use of the school's
one piano. The spinet piano's home base is in the auditorium, but it spends most of its time visiting. Attached to
ball-bearing rollers, it is easily moved from classroom to classroom according to children's needs. The length of its stay in
one room depends upon its use and the needs of other groups.
The important thing in this situation is that the teachers are
willing to allow time in the school day for the children to
"play" the piano, especially those who have no piano at home
or who have taken no piano lessons.

Another school, for the past several years, has been able
to have an allowance in its budget for renting instruments.
A harp was rented for a month and arrangements made so
that each classroom had the loan of it for several days. This
gave both children and teacher an opportunity to get acquainted with it first hand and play it in the ways they could

play. At the end of this period, a harpist gave a concert, playing some music chosen by the children. At another time, a concert-size xylophone was rented and used in the same way, followed by a concert. A great many elementary schools are unable to employ a special music teacher and yet may be able to have a moderate sum set aside for music purposes. They could well supplement their program in the ways described. Children and teachers could plan together for a variety of informal music experiences and employ artists for a reasonable fee.

In more and more school systems the music consultant is able to use *radio* and, in some instances, *closed-circuit television* for music experiences. What an opportunity this presents for working with a committee of boys and girls representing the various grades in planning the programs. Their special interests in music, as well as those experiences which the consultant feels are appropriate, would be presented. Surely such programs, if the children have a stake in their planning, would evoke enthusiastic interest. There are many potential "talent scouts" in any school. Shall we give them a chance?

Music consultants usually do a major part of their work with *teachers in workshops*—preschool meetings, those held during the school year, "all-in-one" meetings, special interest groups, grade-level groups, and so on. One consultant has given me permission to include here some of the plans she made recently for her work with teachers.[5]

Fall Preschool Workshop

The aim will be to give teachers a feeling about the need to believe in themselves and in their own powers. The participation in some exploring of space—even in the small room in which the meetings are held—is the best way I know to demonstrate to each teacher the tremendous possibilities each of us has to express our ideas through movement and to convey the type of freedom we

5 Cecelia R. Nelson.

want for children. This is far better than to worry teachers with songs, with specifics to teach. Believe in yourself, what you already *have*.

On the tables I will have many instruments; some I already have, some I will make. As the teachers come into the room there will be some exploration but I will use part of the meeting for further experience with instruments. Even 15 minutes of such exploration can be very revealing to them and can do more than I have ever been able to do to "cancel out" the idea of rhythm band for primary children and the feeling that instruments in upper grades is "baby stuff."

Music Coordinators' Meetings (Once a month for an hour)

We shall explore together sound and movement. Since co-ordinators are from every grade level, we will include activities which can be used at any grade level as indeed any of them can be. Heretofore I have used this meeting for singing activities, for learning how to play instruments such as the autoharp, for adding rhythm instruments to singing, for listening, and for information about source materials of interest. Much of the information can be mimeographed and distributed without comment.

The main activity in each meeting will be participation in exploration of sound and movement. The attitudes and feelings teachers "pick up" through this will be carried back to their buildings. At the staff meeting which follows each of these all-in-one meetings other teachers in each building will hear about it and cannot but help become interested in having fun like that themselves.

Grade-level Meetings (Once a month for an hour and a half)

Grade-level groups often ask me to come to their meetings. Once teachers are aware of the possibilities along the line of movement and sound, chairmen of grade-level groups will be asking me to come and help them in this area. If possible I shall try to have them arrange to give 45 minutes of their meeting for actual participation. I would aim to clarify the fact that if children are free to explore they tend to organize themselves, they will not "go wild" but indeed if they are allowed freedom they will more readily accept the controls we *must* place upon them from time to time. They would discover this though from their own activity and not from my talking about it.

Interest Groups (Once a month for an hour)

I have requested the chairman of our In-Service Training Committee to add to the list of interest-group titles one called "Exploring Space and Sound."

In the activities of this group I would try especially hard to give recognition to the teachers we have who are doing excellent work in this area and who are free at this time and could help us. Also, Miss C., who teaches modern dance and who is very interested, would be free to come in the evening and would be glad to contribute to the experiences of the group.

The music teacher, then, may work in a number of ways: serving small groups of interested children, working with classroom teachers to make them more comfortable musically, and offering herself as a resource person to whom both children and teacher turn for help in materials, in instruments, and in skills. Plans for working in any particular school may include scheduled periods in the classroom by the music teacher or scheduled periods in the music room for the children or no regularly scheduled visits, music needs being met entirely through individual planning or working entirely with teachers. The music teacher may be called consultant or supervisor. She remembers that teachers are individuals, and that the way in which she works with one will not necessarily be effective with another. Above all, the quality of her working relationships with the classroom teachers will determine the quality of music teaching in that school. For a thoughtful and valuable study on this subject, the reader is referred to a recent study.[6]

To the extent that both music and classroom teachers keep their ears to the ground in the matter of discovering and

[6] Lorene Marvel, *The Working Relationship between the Music Consultant and the Classroom Teacher,* unpublished doctoral study, New York: Teachers College, Columbia University, 1958.

accepting children's *real* music interests, to the extent that they get on the same track with them, to the extent that they are accepted members of the group *who also bring ideas and suggestions,* they will find countless opportunities to extend and broaden children's musical horizons. Not all children in any one school will have identical experiences, but they will grow musically. Moreover, exposure to the same program is no guarantee that there is acceptance of this program. Do we not stand a better chance of educating children musically in a school where many kinds of music are accepted?

The classroom teacher is central to a good music program. She can work effectively in this field, even without a music consultant. But a music teacher is also important. She reaches out to the many children through and with their teachers, and she knows the field of music and the untold opportunities for enrichment which it offers. "Music has many faces," and the music consultant who is constantly extending her recognition of these faces stands an excellent chance of tuning in with all children and all teachers.

Chapter 12

THOUGHTS ON TEACHING MUSIC AND DANCE

To use the gift you do possess
And sway with reason more or less.
—To a Thinker, ROBERT FROST.

T HIS FINAL CHAPTER might be thought of as a way of thinking about teaching music and dance. What is said here has
been implied and frequently stated all through the discussions. I feel a strong inclination, however, to hold some of
these ideas together unrelated to their application. I venture
to hope that this chapter will be read somewhere along the
way. No sequence is implied in placing it at the end of the
book. I believe that a reader has a responsibility to examine
and entertain, even though briefly, the reasons underlying a
writer's philosophy so as to better understand his point of
view. Entertaining a way of thinking, however, most certainly does not imply acceptance of it. I have tried to present
ideas as clearly as possible. If, out of experience, I may offer
them with enthusiasm or conviction, and these tend to be
persuasive (I hope they are), I would wish that the reader
274

keep in mind the need to test these ideas, to modify, reject or accept, and evolve his own way of implementing them.

A century ago, in his famous Phi Beta Kappa address, "The American Scholar," Emerson sounded a warning about the danger that threatened American life of that time—the tendency of man as he takes on a trade or profession to become, for example, a farmer rather than a *man who farms*. Today this danger is even more threatening. Pressures from every direction tend to rob man of his own ability to think. One of the many voices sounding against these forces is that of Albert Schweitzer who says that we turn more and more to authority for answers and become skeptical about our power to develop our own thinking.[1] We are easily led into becoming tools rather than *people who use tools*. We in the teaching profession are fortunate, for nowhere is there more opportunity and encouragement to grow as a person. Thinking is respected. And yet some of the very practices that have been encouraged in helping teachers do a better job are *interpreted* by many as a closed frame within which to work or the setting of limits or ceilings.

I do not intend here to suggest that all parents and all teachers are or should be equally interested in music and dance. Many have interpreted the idea of the self-contained classroom to mean that each teacher should be equally proficient in all subjects to be taught. This is highly unrealistic and even denies the birthright of teaching itself—the joy and satisfaction that come to each one of us as we follow our special interests. As children's lives are touched year after year by individuals of diverse talents, they take on some of the spirit of adventure that accompanies the pursuit of a special interest.

It is true that one's own interest can make one intolerant of those of others. If, however, our experiences are truly deep and satisfying, I believe it is much more likely that we shall respect the interests of others. I also suggest that the encour-

[1] *Out of My Life and Thought,* New York: Holt.

agement of diversity is a potent method of evoking new interests, one from the other, and extending the awareness of each of us as we are touched by the special music and dance "affections" of others.

In a sense we can all be gifted in music and dance—in our *attitude* toward these arts, in being respectful and encouraging of them in others. As we probe to the heart of these, we shall find that we have more within us than we realize. We do not wait to get ready. We start where we are. We play with the cards we have and, as we play, we increase our knowledge and skill. Teaching is always a growing thing, and there is no better stimulation for our growth than children's desire to know. Our first job is to liberate our own thinking, to recognize and have respect for degrees of ability—to "use the gift we do possess." We can grow in our ability to look around and appropriate everything we can find that will nourish what we are trying to teach. If a system or method gives us help, we can use it as a crutch, gradually freeing ourselves and making a go of it, not alone, but with children. As one classroom teacher, whose special interest is science, puts it, "This matter of music and dance is new to me but again as in many other instances children come to my rescue and the burden is lessened." A system may be of help, for a time, as long as we do not keep our eyes so intent on following it as to fail to observe what actually happens in practice.

In our continuing emphasis on constantly reaching out to discover the roots of music and dance in children's behavior, to make these arts vital living forces in their lives, I am far from suggesting a laissez-faire program. It is not an easy road, for I am unwilling to settle for anything less than the best that is within each of us. The cultivation of music and dance with children and with ourselves demands all we can bring to it. It can even be hard at times but, when this hardness makes sense, it becomes an adventure in education. We need to be alive with knowledge about the subjects we teach. More than that, we need to be alive with thoughts and ideas about our knowledge. We can light up our day-by-day living with children with ideas and, in turn, illuminate our ideas with the realities as perceived in the day-by-day living with children. The chances are good that the longer we work with children in these arts, the more we will be turning up questions rather than answers. But we shall also learn to trust children more.

> A Child will grow fully if only we allow him to keep on the track of the law of his own growth.
> —*Letters of Rainer Maria Rilke,* Vol. I.

Children's instinctual sound and movement behavior offer us a way of knowing the music and dance track they are on. Does our way of living with boys and girls elicit their unique abilities in these arts? Can we find the track on which they are moving? Can we see possibilities for extending and enriching their interests and also the opportunities for hitching on new and fresh experiences, and encourage them to be self-seekers in these fields? Virginia Woolf has said that, if we can help a child get astride his saddle, his whole world will fall into shape. We can make it possible for him to discover, uncover, and use his talents—to develop them "out loud"—or, through lack of perception and imagination, we can successfully bury them for him or at least make them a clandestine affair.

The more we can work toward stimulating the internal growth of a child, the more effectively he will learn. Spontaneity and initiative are necessary in music and dance education. Training is also necessary. The challenge to teachers is to keep a delicate balance between the two. It cannot be done mechanically. There are times when a child or group of children is highly receptive to having knowledge "poured in," and seems to have an insatiable desire for more and more. There are other times when they need extended opportunities to put their newly found information to work. Most of the time there is a continued interplay between these two extremes. This threshold for learning is maintained through the adult's sensitive awareness and the kind of knowledge in his field that permits him to roam freely within it, thus recognizing many paths and directions. By reducing the disconnection that too frequently exists between the child's world of music and dance, and music and dance as conceived of by many adults, we can bring not less but more of what is lasting in these arts into the lives of boys and girls. We can concern ourselves too much with oversimplification in teaching rather than with that which makes learning vital. When one considers the kinds of skills a child learns from infancy on through his preschool years, how can we say that he is not interested in doing hard things—hard things that have meaning.

There is a rare freshness in children's discoveries and in their expectancies related to these discoveries in the limitless field of education. They are not so much aware of what they do as they are possessed by it, in the same way that a poet is possessed by an idea and allows himself to go along with its development. As we live with them, we can help them "name" their ideas and take them beyond the beginning stage and work consciously toward their development. This is a fascinating journey for the adult, too. For a provocative and enlightening discussion of the necessity of holding on to "discovery" in the educational program and the tragic consequences of passing on inert ideas, I refer the reader to Alfred North Whitehead.[2] Children blossom in a home and school where adults are explorers and discoverers. This way of living is contagious and in such surroundings there is little danger of passing on inert ideas. The track of children's own growth patterns is recognized and accepted. Education in music and dance moves forward with excitement and vitality.

2 *Aims of Education*, Mentor.

The poet . . . uses forms according to
the life, and not according to the form.
  —*The Poet*, RALPH WALDO EMERSON

All through this book I have consciously and consistently
tried to share with the reader where I am heading. I have
tried to track down the roots of music and dance—within the
limitations of my knowledge and experience—as these roots
are manifested in the work and play of boys and girls. There
is a hope that in so doing we may establish a fresh acquaintance with these arts and so do a better job as teachers
whether we are teacher-teachers or parent-teachers. My thinking has been directed to the satisfaction and the interest and
eagerness of children and also to the obstacles that teachers
may feel prevent them from pushing through to the heart of
music and dance. There is no denying the fact that dealing
in sound and movement with children, according to the
form that has meaning to them, is a bold adventure in most
of our classrooms. But it is amazing how one's courage increases the more adventurous one becomes. Perhaps teaching
best moves forward with a combination of "forms." Following our "forms" may give us security and may be accepted by
children, but being willing to reach toward form "according
to the life" is the path that leads to experiencing the profession of teaching as an art.

INDEX

280